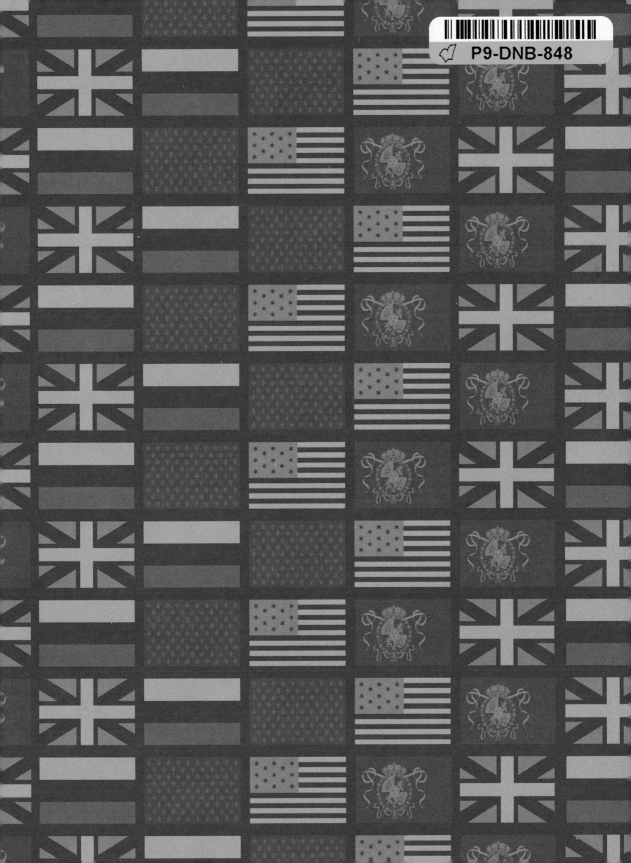

THE AMERICAN REVOLUTION

Edited by
David K. Allison
& Larrie D. Ferreiro

THE AMERICAN REVOLUTION
A WORLD WAR

Essays by

José María Blanco Núñez

Olivier Chaline

Kathleen DuVal

John D. Garrigus

John L. Gray

José M. Guerrero Acosta

Agustín Guimerá Ravina

David J. Hancock

Marion Huibrechts

Jean-Marie Kowalski

Andrew Lambert

Alan Lemmers

Richard Sambasivam

Robert A. Selig

Alan Taylor

Patrick Villiers

Smithsonian Books
Washington, DC

CONTENTS

FOREWORD

As director of the National Museum of American History, I have no greater privilege than that of sharing the incredible meaning and power of our nation's past through our research, collections, exhibitions, publications, and collaborations. Sometimes these efforts yield great insights into topics that we think we already know well, among them the story of the American Revolution.

Most of us were raised to think of the Revolution as the triumph of the American colonists, who—oppressed by the faraway British government—took on the mightiest army and navy in the world and miraculously defeated them. We see our nation's founders as people fired by lofty ideals, documented in their Declaration of Independence, who risked their lives and sacred honor to cast off aristocratic rule and embrace freedom. Over the years, this heroic view has been reinforced by popular art, books, museum exhibitions, and memorials. This conventional view is embodied by, for example, the iconic image dubbed *The Spirit of '76*. Painted by Archibald Willard, it was originally created for the 1876 Centennial of the Revolution and was reproduced widely once again to commemorate the Bicentennial in 1976. You likely have seen it many times—and in many parodies, too, which have only woven it deeper into our collective consciousness. Although panned by art critics from the very beginning, it has remained among the most popular illustrations of the Revolution. But what if it is not only simplistic but also misleading? What if the even more important "spirit of '76" was the colonists' willingness not to fight alone but to form strategic alliances with other nations?

Archibald Willard, *The Spirit of '76* (originally *Yankee Doodle*), ca. 1875. Oil. (Abbot Hall, Marblehead, Massachusetts; courtesy Town of Marblehead, Massachusetts)

Of course, we have always known that the story of the nation's founding is much more complicated than simple iconic imagery suggests. We know that the colonists first had wanted only to reform their relationship with England, not claim full independence. We know that they were bitterly divided among themselves, and that the Revolution became a civil war that pitted neighbors and regions against one another. We know that the "freedom" the Revolution's leaders sought was never something that the founders, despite their lofty words, planned to grant to everyone in their new society. We sadly reflect on the terrible realization that the founders were even willing to legitimize slavery in the basic documents of their new government. Finally, we know that the colonists did not fight entirely alone but had support from Europeans, including a dashing young French aristocrat, the marquis de Lafayette, whose name still appears on towns, schools, streets, and parks across the country, including Lafayette Square, across from the White House.

Recent years have brought us a vigorous expansion of new research, publications, exhibitions, and public history that are exploring the degree to which the "American Revolution" was not simply a colonial uprising but a world war. As the war progressed beyond the rebellion in its colonies, Britain faced attacks on its territories and naval power around the globe—including on its homeland. Not until we delve into these global dimensions of the conflict does the seeming "miracle" of the American triumph in its Revolution actually begin to make sense. We have come to realize that the portion of the Revolution fought on American soil was only one theater of the wider war and that it was not—perhaps astonishingly to most Americans—even the most critical to Britain. Ultimately, it was the global scope of the world war that determined the outcome in America. This realization leads us to ponder, "What does this truth mean for our national identity?"

This book includes a broad selection of new scholarship on the global dimensions of the war. Its chapters are written not only by American historians but also by historians from other nations that were part of that revolutionary world war, and thus these essays offer balance to the one-sided "spirit of '76" perspective.

This book accompanies a yearlong exhibition at the National Museum of American History, *The American Revolution: A World War*, which explores

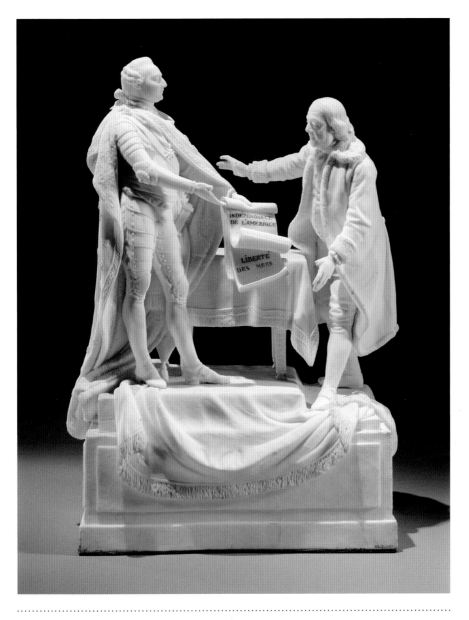

Charles-Gabriel Sauvage, called Lemire père, *Louis XVI and Benjamin Franklin*, *"Indépendence de l'Amérique"* and *"Liberté des Mers,"* manufactured 1780–85, Niderviller Factory, Lorraine, France. Porcelain. This figure commemorates the signing of the Treaty of Alliance in 1778, through which France recognized American independence. (Courtesy Metropolitan Museum of Art, Gift of William H. Huntington, 1883, 83.2.260)

similar themes. As you read the essays—and, I hope, visit the exhibition—you likely will find yourself saying, as I so often do, that you had no idea that "this, too," was part of the Revolution.

America's attention to its own founding is heightened during anniversary years. It is at these times that the nation as a whole refocuses on how it came to be and what its founding means for its future. During past anniversaries, we often have looked inward. My hope is that as we prepare for our 250th anniversary, in 2026, we will look outward to remind ourselves that the United States is the result of its close involvement with other nations as part of a seminal world war. Our future, like our past, requires that we pay close heed to our international relationships, and that we nurture them carefully.

JOHN L. GRAY
Elizabeth MacMillan Director
National Museum of American History
Smithsonian Institution

INTRODUCTION
The American Revolution and the Second Hundred Years' War

Larrie D. Ferreiro

The American Revolution, as John L. Gray notes in his foreword, was just one theater in a world war. Although the Revolution had begun in 1775 as a small series of skirmishes between British troops and American militia at Lexington and Concord, Massachusetts, by the time of the siege of Yorktown, in 1781, Britain was becoming overwhelmed by the effort of fighting five separate nation-states around the globe — France, Spain, the United States, the Dutch Republic, and the Kingdom of Mysore, in India. Ultimately, it was the events in that wider global war that led to America's independence.

While the global extent of the Revolutionary War may be astonishing to Americans today, it was not surprising to Americans living at the time. Since their creation in the 1600s, the American colonies had been intimately involved in wars between England and other European powers, and their engagement in those wars increased with every new conflict. The period between 1689 and 1815 was dubbed the Second Hundred Years' War by the British historian John Robert Seeley, and the name has stuck. The name alludes to the original Hundred Years' War, fought between England and France during the Middle Ages. Like that conflict, the Second Hundred Years' War was fought primarily between the two great European powers of the day, France and England (Britain after its 1707 union with Scotland), but it also pulled in allies on both sides from across Europe and even from Asia. It was a series of eight wars rather than one long conflict, during which one out of every two years saw major hostilities between nations. Americans fought in every one of those wars.

The Second Hundred Years' War differed from the first in that the belligerents were now colonial powers, and much of the conflict revolved around protecting and expanding their overseas empires. These European wars for dominance were increasingly fought on North American soil and with colonial

American troops. The first of these, the War of the Grand Alliance (1689–97), erupted as France attempted to extend its borders into neighboring monarchies, an effort opposed by a coalition led by England and the Dutch Republic. In America, this war was known as King William's War, and on American soil it primarily involved small companies of New England militia unsuccessfully attempting to invade French Canada and Acadia in response to cross-frontier raids.

Just four years later, after Spain's King Charles II had died without an heir, the War of the Spanish Succession (1701–14), called Queen Anne's War in America, pitted the Hapsburg powers of Britain and Austria against the French Bourbon crown for control of the vast Spanish colonial empire. Although this war was fought primarily in Europe, British colonists were now engaged on two fronts in America: against Spanish Florida in the south, and against French Canada, Acadia, and Newfoundland in the north. The colonists organized and deployed far larger, more aggressive, and more effective expeditions than they had previously done, and although they suffered many defeats, the efforts of the colonials ultimately won Britain important concessions that expanded its North American empire.

During the next three wars, American colonists were fully engaged in fighting. The combined War of Jenkins' Ear and War of the Austrian Succession (1739–48, the latter known in America as King George's War) saw American troops deployed overseas for the first time. In 1741, the four-thousand-strong American Regiment, under the overall command of British Admiral Edward Vernon, fought valiantly at the Battle of Cartagena de Indias (in modern-day Colombia) but lost to the defending Spanish troops. The American Regiment included a twenty-two-year-old infantry captain named Lawrence Washington, the older half-brother of George Washington, who would later name his estate Mount Vernon in honor of his admiral.

In 1745, the colonies of Massachusetts, Connecticut, and New Hampshire mounted an expeditionary force of four thousand troops that besieged and captured the French fortress at Louisbourg in Nova Scotia. The subsequent peace was short-lived: less than a decade later, George Washington—now a lieutenant colonel in the Virginia Militia—led an assault on a French scouting party at Jumonville Glen, in today's Fayette County, Pennsylvania, which triggered the massive, globe-spanning Seven Years' War (1754–63), known in

America as the French and Indian War. Tens of thousands of colonists fought on the front lines against France and Native American nations in Ohio, New York, Canada, and Acadia. By the end of that war, France had ceded all its North American territories to Britain, and colonial Americans celebrated the victories with as much fervor as their British kin across the ocean.

In short, by the time the Revolutionary War began in 1775, the colonials already had experienced almost a century of British-European warfare, and they fully understood America's role in wider wars around the world. For this reason, most colonials recognized that their own fight for independence against Britain would necessarily involve other European powers, notably France and Spain. As Arthur Lee, a colonial representative in London, told Benjamin Franklin in 1774, "America may yet owe her salvation [to European powers] should the contest be serious and lasting." His brother Richard Henry Lee furthered this sentiment when he wrote to Patrick Henry in April 1776 that "a timely alliance with proper and willing powers in Europe" was needed to win the upcoming war. But he also noted that "no state in Europe will either treat or trade with us so long as we consider ourselves subjects of Great Britain." For this reason, he argued, "It is not choice then, but necessity that calls for independence, as the only means by which foreign alliance can be obtained" (all quoted in Ferreiro 2016: xxi).

Several weeks later, on June 7, 1776, Richard Henry Lee introduced a measure before the Second Continental Congress that called for a declaration of independence. The resulting document, approved on July 4, 1776, was in reality an engraved invitation to France and Spain to go into battle alongside the Americans. The declaration succeeded beyond the Americans' wildest imaginings, for the Revolutionary War eventually drew hundreds of thousands of soldiers and sailors from nations across North America and around the globe to fight against their common enemy.

The American Revolution: A World War, the title of both this book and the accompanying exhibition at the Smithsonian National Museum of American History, captures the spirit of the age. As John Adams noted, "A compleat History of the American War . . . is nearly the History of Mankind for the whole Epocha of it. The History of France Spain Holland, England and the Neutral Powers, as well as America are at least comprized in it" (letter to Abbé

John Bower, *A View of the Bombardment of Fort McHenry . . . 13 September, 1814*, 1819. Etching. During the War of 1812, the British navy failed in its attempt to capture Fort McHenry in Baltimore. The flag raised at the fort after the attack inspired Francis Scott Key to write what became the national anthem of the United States. The fort's flag is now preserved at the National Museum of American History. (Library of Congress, Prints and Photographs Division, LC-DIG-ppmsca-35544)

Luis Fernández Gordillo, *Defensa de Cartagena de Indias*, 1741. Oil on canvas. The 1741 attack on this Spanish stronghold, in modern Colombia, by British Admiral Edward Vernon included four thousand British-American troops. (Ministerio de Defensa, Spain, Archivo del Museo Naval, MNM04144)

de Mably, Paris, January 15, 1783). In this book, we have attempted to "comprize" these histories from scholars around the globe into a more "compleat" and accurate picture of the American Revolution. A number of themes emerge from these wide-ranging studies.

The most important point, which is demonstrated time and again, is that each nation fighting against Britain had its own reasons for entering the war, which had little or nothing to do with aiding American independence. Alan Taylor points out that France and Spain, humiliated by their defeats in the Seven Years' War, "resolved to strike back and restore the balance of power at the next opportunity," which turned out to be the American Revolution. Richard Sambasivam notes that after the British began attacking French trading posts in India in 1778, the Kingdom of Mysore, which depended on its alliance with France for important trade, "resolved to expel the British from the region." Alan Lemmers highlights the fact that Dutch leaders felt that their country, as a neutral power, had an "indispensable duty to guard the trade interests . . . of the entire country," which included supplying Britain's adversaries. Their choice eventually provoked the wrath of the British navy and plunged the Dutch Republic into the war.

A second recurring theme is the vital importance of sea power in the Revolutionary War. Any nation or coalition fighting Britain in the eighteenth century knew that it must fight and win a naval war because, as Andrew Lambert notes, "British strategy was dominated by . . . maritime concerns. Everything depended on command of the sea, which would enable Britain to weaken the economies of hostile powers" and was far more important than territorial control in North America. France, too, saw maritime dominance as the crucial element in victory. As Olivier Chaline and Jean-Marie Kowalski point out, "The French navy acted everywhere in the world," carrying out almost all land battles as amphibious operations while also protecting its ocean commerce. The Spanish navy, as José María Blanco Núñez and Agustín Guimerá Ravina note, fought "to control the seas and to protect trade routes" and was key to dispersing and diluting British naval strength. It was sea power that brought Spain both its greatest victory, at the battle of Pensacola, and its greatest defeat, at the siege of Gibraltar.

J. Stevens, *View of the Landing the New England Forces . . . against Cape Breton, 1745*, eighteenth century. Engraving. In the spring of 1745, British-American colonial forces from New England captured the French fortress at Louisbourg, capital of the French province of Île-Royale, today's Cape Breton Island, Canada. (Courtesy Yale University Art Gallery, 1991.1.44)

Although the war was fought for larger political and imperial goals, its history is constructed from thousands of individual stories. This theme is examined by Patrick Villiers, who explores the nuanced participation in the war of Gilbert du Motier, marquis de Lafayette, which was much more complex than the heroic narrative the marquis himself spun in his memoirs. Marion Huibrechts describes how Dutch merchants and Liège arms makers supplied guns and munitions to the American insurgents during the early days of the war, while José M. Guerrero Acosta reveals that Spain provided critical supplies, such as uniforms and silver coin, to the United States as the war expanded. John D. Garrigus sheds light on the role of free black soldiers, the Chasseurs Volontaires from Saint-Domingue, at the Battle of Savannah in 1779.

Another powerful theme that emerges in several of the essays is that the European powers all agreed to the peace treaties that ended the war because each nation was able to get what it really wanted. David J. Hancock shows that Britain retained its maritime empire, which would grow even larger as it brought India into its sphere of influence. France regained its dominant position in the balance of European power; Spain ensured the survival of its American possessions and trade routes; and the Dutch Republic affirmed its right to free navigation.

As the war drew to a close, a new American identity was being forged. Kathleen DuVal explores this theme by noting that the Gulf Coast and the Mississippi Valley were home to large numbers of American Indian nations, as well as free and enslaved Africans, who had little in common with British colonists yet participated equally in the war and afterward had to find their own places in the new nation. Robert A. Selig highlights the fact that the Revolutionary War was the only time in American history when foreign troops were stationed on American soil, but he also points out that Americans' close contact with French and German soldiers encouraged some of the latter to remain in America and help to shape their adopted home.

The peace treaties of 1783 did not signal the end of American involvement in the Second Hundred Years' War. The French Revolutionary Wars (1792–1802), which pitted France against a coalition of European powers and was fought in part over American war debt repayment, drew the United States into a state of undeclared war with its former ally France. The final phase of the Second Hundred Years' War, the Napoleonic Wars (1803–15), saw the United States fight Britain to a tactical draw in the War of 1812.

For the next century, America largely stayed out of European wars, though it remained intimately connected to the rest of the world through trade and immigration. Only in the twentieth century did the United States, as an emerging world power, resume the kind of global warfare that had brought the nation into being.

The editors of this book—David K. Allison and myself—have used its final chapters to explore how the visual imagery and the historical narrative of the American Revolution have evolved over the past two and a half centuries according to the popular and political imaginations of different eras, as well as to demonstrate the importance of understanding the American Revolution as a global conflict. We hope that a broad audience of readers will learn from these essays that the American Revolution is really the story of how the United States was born as the centerpiece of a broad coalition of nations and peoples, both here and overseas, who worked together to defeat a common adversary, and that the newborn American nation built on this legacy to create a dynamic, ever-changing culture that is still inexorably intertwined with the wider world.

Timeline of the American Revolution

Key Events Involving Each Major National Player

YEAR	UNITED STATES	GREAT BRITAIN	FRANCE
1775	Battle of Lexington and Concord (April)	King George III declares to Parliament that Americans are trying to "establish an independent empire"	France sends agents to offer aid to America
	Battle of Bunker Hill (June)		
1776	Declaration of Independence signed (July)		French merchants form companies to supply arms to Americans
	Battle of Long Island (August)		First French volunteers arrive in United States
	British occupy New York City		
1777	British occupy Philadelphia	British occupy Philadelphia	France sends major shipments of arms and munitions to United States
	Defeat of General John Burgoyne at Saratoga (October)	Defeat of General John Burgoyne at Saratoga (October)	French volunteers fight at Battle of Brandywine (September)
	Encampment at Valley Forge		
1778	French-American alliance formed		French-American alliance formed
	Battle of Monmouth (June)	British forces leave Philadelphia	France goes to war with Britain
	French-American forces fail to remove British from Newport, Rhode Island		French-American forces fail to remove British from Newport, Rhode Island
1779	Battle of Stony Point, New York (July)		French navy captures Grenada
	French-American forces fail to remove British from Savannah		French-American forces fail to remove British from Savannah
	U.S. privateer John Paul Jones captures HMS *Serapis* off Britain		Joint French-Spanish expedition fails to invade Britain

SPAIN	DUTCH REPUBLIC	INDIA (MYSORE)
Spanish merchants begin sending arms to Americans		
Spain sends gunpowder up Mississippi to Fort Pitt, Pennsylvania	Dutch merchants send muskets and gunpowder to Americans	
Major shipments of Spanish supplies for American use arrive in New Orleans		
Spanish observers scout Mobile for attack		
Americans defeat British along Mississippi with Spanish munitions and aid		British East India Company captures Pondicherry
Spanish observers scout Pensacola for attack		
Spain joins France in war against Britain		British East India Company captures Mahé
Spanish capture Mobile and Baton Rouge		
Joint French-Spanish expedition fails to invade Britain		

YEAR	UNITED STATES	GREAT BRITAIN	FRANCE
1780	Continental Army surrenders Charleston to British	Caribbean hurricanes destroy British fleet	Caribbean hurricanes leave French and Spanish fleets largely intact
	Patriot and Loyalist Americans in South begin fighting each other, resorting to guerrilla warfare tactics	Britain gains control of much of Georgia and South Carolina	France sends army to United States under General Jean-Baptiste Donatien de Vimeur, comte de Rochambeau
1781	Articles of Confederation ratified (March)	British leave West Florida	Battle of the Chesapeake (September)
	Battle of Yorktown (September–October)	Battle of Yorktown	Battle of Yorktown
1782	United States begins separate peace negotiations with Britain	Britain agrees to give United States favorable peace terms	British defeat French naval forces at Battle of the Saintes in Caribbean (April)
			British capture Admiral François-Joseph-Paul de Grasse in Caribbean
1783	United States signs separate peace treaty with Britain	Britain signs separate peace treaty with United States	France signs separate peace treaty with Britain

SPAIN	DUTCH REPUBLIC	INDIA (MYSORE)
Spanish navy captures major British convoy in Atlantic	Britain declares war on Dutch Republic (December)	
Spanish capture Pensacola	Britain captures Sint Eustatius in Caribbean	French support of Mysore collapses
	Dutch and British navies battle to a draw at Dogger Bank in North Sea (August)	British victory at Porto Novo (modern Parangapetti)
Spanish and French capture Minorca from British	Dutch Republic recognizes United States	French Admiral Pierre André de Suffren arrives in India to support alliance with Mysore
Spanish and French forces fail to defeat Britain at Gibraltar		Joint French-Mysore campaign captures Cuddalore
		Tipu Sultan succeeds his father, Hyder Ali
Spain signs separate peace treaty with Britain	Dutch Republic signs separate truce with Britain	British victory at Cuddalore marks last battle of American Revolution

PART I
·····································
MAJOR POWERS

···
Artist unknown, *The Battle of Minden in Westphalia, 1st August, 1759* (detail), 1801. Engraving. Charles Cornwallis, the first Marquess Cornwallis, and Marshal Jean-Baptiste Donatien de Vimeur, comte de Rochambeau, were both involved in this particular battle during the Seven Years' War, as was the marquis de Lafayette's father, Michel du Motier, who died in the conflict. (From *Alphabetical Digestion of the Principal Naval and Military Engagements in Europe, Asia, Africa, and America, Particularly of Great Britain and Her Allies from the Ninth Century to the Peace of 1801* [Bibliothèque Nationale, Paris, France, Archives Charmet / Bridgeman Images])

GLOBAL REVOLUTIONS

Alan Taylor

> The American Revolution was but one part of an ongoing contest among
> major European powers for global power. Its origins lie principally in the Seven
> Years' War, and winning independence required Americans to develop effective
> alliances with Britain's rivals. — *Editors*

The American Revolution was a world war begotten from a preceding global
conflict known as the Seven Years' War (although it began in 1754 and lasted
until 1763). The British triumph in the earlier war generated an internal conflict
as imperial officials pursued centralizing policies meant to rationalize a larger
but more expensive empire. Needing funds to sustain about ten thousand men
in the conquered North American territory, the British also sought to tighten
control over colonists deemed insufficiently cooperative during the recent war.
To demonstrate Parliament's sovereignty over the entire empire and collect
additional revenue, the empire levied provocative new taxes on the colonists,
who balked at the new arrangement and its higher costs to them.

Less well known is the disruption wrought in the global balance of
power by the Seven Years' War. That imbalance drove the French and Spanish
to reform their militaries and empires in preparation for the next chance to
even scores with the British. Those initiatives in turn alarmed British leaders,
who worried that growth rendered their empire more vulnerable to its enemies,
both within and without. Everyone—colonists, Britons, French, Spanish, and
even Russians—reacted to exaggerated fears of the others, breeding a new
global conflict from the disruptions caused by its predecessor.

In the Seven Years' War, the British overwhelmed their French and
Spanish rivals by projecting power across the oceans of the world. Never before
had a European empire dispatched so many warships, sailors, and troops to so
many corners of the globe. In 1758, the Royal Navy won control of the Atlantic

Richard Paton, *British Burning of the Warship* Prudent *and Capturing of the Warship* Bienfaisant *during the Siege of Louisbourg, 1758, 1771.* Engraving. Britain's victory in this siege was a crucial step in its defeat of French forces in Canada and its ultimate victory in the Seven Years' War. (Courtesy Maritime Museum of the Atlantic, Halifax, Nova Scotia, a part of the Nova Scotia Museum, M55.7.1)

and devastated French shipping, reducing the transport of reinforcements and munitions to French Canada and Louisiana. The same year, a massive British fleet and thirteen thousand regular soldiers captured the great fortress at Louisbourg on Cape Breton Island in Nova Scotia, near the mouth of the St. Lawrence River. A year later, the invaders swept up the river to attack and capture Quebec. In 1760, British forces from Quebec and New York converged on Montreal and compelled the capitulation of Canada, including the forts around the Great Lakes to the west (Anderson 2000: 257–58, 267–85, 340–409).

In 1762, the Spanish belatedly entered the war as French allies and suffered massive losses for their pains. In the Caribbean, the British captured the great Spanish colonial port of Havana, Cuba. In the western Pacific, another British fleet seized Manila, the capital of the Philippines. For the Manila attack,

Pistol given by British General Edward Braddock to George Washington during the Seven Years' War, ca. 1752. Wood. Washington would carry this pistol in several campaigns during the American Revolution. (National Museum of American History, AF.245168.126)

the British relied on troops recruited in India, attesting to the increasingly global and multiracial composition of their empire. In India and West Africa as well, the British routed the French and their local allies. In the West Indies, Britain captured the French islands of Guadeloupe, Martinique, St. Lucia, Grenada, and St. Vincent (Anderson 2000: 490, 497–502, 515–17).

The British prevailed thanks to their greater capacity to project power overseas, overwhelming French and Spanish colonies with superior numbers of soldiers, sailors, warships, and cannon. Behind that logistical supremacy lay Britain's advanced financial institutions and abundant investment capital, which jointly enabled the government to borrow and spend more money than the French and Spanish could (Gould 2005: 22).

In February 1763, the British diplomatically secured most of their military gains in the Treaty of Paris with the French and Spanish. The French conceded all their claims to North America east of the Mississippi River. This cession included Canada, the Great Lakes shores, and the eastern half of the Mississippi watershed. The British also retained Senegal, a valuable West African base for the slave trade, and the lesser islands of their Caribbean conquests: Dominica, Grenada, St. Vincent, and Tobago. To mollify the French, the British returned the larger islands: Guadeloupe, Martinique, and St. Lucia. The French also recovered their fishing stations at Saint Pierre and Miquelon, near the rich cod fishery off Newfoundland. The French readily sacrificed Canada, which had run a great annual deficit, preferring to regain their profitable sugar islands and access to the northern fisheries (Calloway 2006: 7–10).

To appease their Spanish allies, the French gave them New Orleans and most of Louisiana: the portion west of the Mississippi River. Although Louisiana was a money loser, the Spanish hoped to enhance the security of Mexico by deepening the frontier buffer zone meant to repulse the British. To regain Havana and Manila, the Spanish ceded Florida to the British. The

Mississippi became the new boundary between the British and Spanish empires. After the Treaty of Paris, British America stretched from the Arctic to the Caribbean (Calloway 2006: 9–10).

On both sides of the Atlantic, Britons and colonists celebrated the great British victories and the triumphant peace. The subjects of George III danced around bonfires, fired volleys of cannon, rang church bells, lit up the sky with fireworks, and toasted the king, the Royal Navy, the army, and colonial volunteers. Far from seeking independence, colonists cherished the liberties, military security, and profitable trade provided by a triumphant empire. Benjamin Franklin rejoiced "not merely as I am a colonist, but as I am a Briton" (Franklin 1760: 005A). The city of New York raised an equestrian statue of the king. In Boston, a minister preached that British America would "become in another century or two, a mighty empire," but he quickly added, "I do not mean an independent one" (quoted in Conway 2006: 240–41).

Within a dozen years of the peace of 1763, however, another global conflict would disrupt and divide the triumphant empire, as thirteen British colonies along the Atlantic seaboard of North America rejected the authority of Parliament and, in 1776, declared independence. A Briton later recognized that his empire's triumph in the Seven Years' War had borne bitter fruit: "What did Britain gain by the most glorious and successful war on which she ever engaged? A height of Glory which excited the Envy of the surrounding nations and . . . an extent of empire we were equally unable to maintain, defend or govern" (quoted in Anderson and Cayton 2005: 135–39). Because of that triumph, the empire would reap a revolution in British America.

By conquering French Canada, Britons and colonists unwittingly created a crisis within their shared empire. After their victories, the British felt emboldened to rearrange the empire, and colonial leaders felt freer to defy those changes. In 1775, a London newspaper blamed the conquest of Canada for spoiling the colonists: "The moment their fears . . . were removed by the cession of all Canada to Great Britain, [at] that moment the dutiful colonies began to change their tone; America was no longer *ours*, but *theirs*" (quoted in Draper 1996: 5–29; emphasis in original).

Victory had not come cheap: the conflict nearly doubled the British national debt, from £74 million to a postwar £133 million. The government also needed £360,000 annually to sustain ten thousand troops to garrison the conquests in North America. Already paying higher taxes than the French and Spanish, Britons demanded that Parliament find new sources of revenue in the colonies. After making such a major investment of soldiers and money to fight in North America, Britain's rulers would not let the colonists remain the most lightly taxed people in the empire. Moreover, during the war, British officials had discovered just how prosperous the free people in the colonies had become. Britons insisted that colonists, as the chief beneficiaries of an expensive war, could and should pay more to the empire (Brewer 1989: 114).

Imperial officials also complained that the colonists had performed poorly and selfishly during the war. Sticklers for discipline, British officers derided colonial troops as laxly trained, insubordinate, and ineffective in combat. Britons also denounced as profiteers the colonial merchants who had traded with the enemy in the West Indies. Frustrated with colonial legislators, troops, and merchants, British officials decided to tighten their control over the colonies through stricter commercial regulations, tougher enforcement by the Royal Navy, and new taxes (Anderson 2000: 167, 286–88, 519–20).

Rejecting colonial pretensions to a privileged place in the empire, imperial officials wanted to govern colonists as subordinates and tax them to fund the enhanced garrisons needed to defend an enlarged empire. The colonists, however, resented the new garrisons as an unnecessary expense and a potential threat to their liberty. Britons took colonial opposition lightly because they credited victory in the recent war almost entirely to the regular army and Royal Navy, which allegedly had rescued inept, conniving, and bickering colonists from French and Indian aggression. British leaders doubted that colonists could defy the empire. By underestimating colonial capacity and alienation, the British presented the French and Spanish with a chance to recoup their lost global power (Conway 2006: 236–37, 240–43).

Humiliated by their defeats, the French and Spanish resolved to strike back and restore the balance of power at the next opportunity. In that subsequent conflict, the British could not count on assistance from other European allies, for all concluded that Great Britain was growing too rich and too powerful. The British had supplanted the French as the expansionist power considered most dangerous to the peace of Europe (Dull 1985: 14–16, 19).

The war had left the French and Spanish with leaner and more effective empires, while Britain had taken on vast and expensive new responsibilities. With good cause, the leading French negotiator at the Treaty of Paris, Étienne François, duc de Choiseul, boasted that he had burdened the British with future woes. The British victory also inspired the French and Spanish to adopt reforms that bolstered their colonial and military resources. In the next war, the French would have a modernized army and a bigger navy of better-designed warships. During the 1760s and 1770s, the Spanish adopted new colonial policies meant to enhance their empire's revenues and defenses. Named for Spain's ruling dynasty, the "Bourbon reforms" promoted economic development and strengthened fortifications and garrisons. Thanks to new and increased taxes, Crown revenues from Mexico soared from 12 million to 50 million pesos annually (Weber 1992: 215–20).

Spanish officials also pushed their colonial frontier northwestward from Mexico into California in response to alarming rumors of Russian advances eastward, from Siberia via Alaska to the northwest coast of North America. Other reports suggested that British fur traders were approaching the Pacific coast via Hudson Bay. Vague in their knowledge of the vast Pacific Northwest region, the Spanish prematurely concluded that Russians and Britons were closing in on California and would soon attack Mexico. In fact, the imperial rivals were fewer and farther away than the Spanish imagined. In Alaska, a few dozen Russian traders were harvesting sea otter pelts, while the reach of the Hudson's Bay Company had not yet extended beyond the Rocky Mountains to the Pacific. Among imperial officials, however, fearful misunderstanding was more motivating than reassuring truth. Beginning in 1768, the Spanish occupied the California coast, developing a string of missions and small presidios that by 1774 stretched as far north as Monterey. Lacking colonists, Spanish officials attempted to turn Native Americans into Hispanics at the new missions (Weber 1992: 240–65).

A more substantial threat to Spain came from the Pacific voyages of exploration led by Captain James Cook of the Royal Navy. Seeking new trade routes and perhaps colonies, Cook's expeditions documented and mapped the islands, shores, currents, and peoples of the Pacific. These incursions especially imperiled Spanish interests. From Peru and Mexico, the Spanish shipped silver across the Pacific to the Philippines and China, a lucrative commerce that would be at risk if the Royal Navy were to dominate the Pacific. The British were acting on their own exaggerated fear that the French would somehow seize control of the Pacific islands and shores to rebuild their global power. As with the Spanish occupation of California, the British acted to preempt their greatest dread. In doing so, they provoked another round of alarm and response in Madrid (Weber 1992: 266).

Newly fearful of their position in the Pacific, the Spanish sought to control access to it from the Atlantic by renewing their claim to the Falkland Islands near the strategic Strait of Magellan. Although unpopulated, cold, and relatively barren, the Falklands offered coveted harbors as a way station for sailing ships. In 1766, British marines constructed a fort on West Falkland Island. In 1770, the Spanish governor of Buenos Aires ousted the intruders with military force. While the Royal Navy mobilized for war, Spain looked to France for support. But France's financial and naval recovery from the last war remained painfully incomplete. Denied French support, the Spanish grudgingly conceded the Falklands to Britain. That new lesson in British aggression compounded French and Spanish zeal to narrow the gap in naval power and prepare for the next big war (Dull 1985: 29–30, 36).

Despite prevailing in the Falklands crisis, British officials were of two minds about their power. While confident that they could overawe their own colonists, British leaders continued to worry that their empire was dangerously vulnerable to challenge by the French and Spanish. Fear, rather than tyranny, induced British leaders to take a hard line against American dissidents in early 1774. Persuaded that the malcontents were a noisy few who served French interests, British leaders felt compelled to restore colonial order with armed force or else risk the loss of their North American colonies. Without those colonies, officials feared, the rest of the empire would collapse, exposing Britain to domination by the resurgent French and Spanish. In June 1774, William Legge, Lord Dartmouth, the secretary of state, assured General Thomas Gage, the British commander in North America, of the following:

> The constitutional authority of this kingdom over its colonies must be vindicated, and its laws obeyed throughout the whole empire. . . . Not

only its dignity and its reputation but its power, nay its very existence depends upon the present moment; for should those ideas of independence . . . once take root, that relation between the kingdom and its colonies which is the bond of peace and power will soon cease to exist and destruction must follow disunion. (Quoted in Marshall 2003: 14)

The American Patriots (as pro-independence advocates were known) regarded the British as powerful aggressors imposing their domination, but Britain acted out of fear for the security of its vulnerable empire. The competing colonial and British fears became intertwined in an escalating crisis that culminated in revolutionary war in the spring of 1775 (Thomas 1991: 40–41, 81, 86–87).

To win independence, the new United States had to cultivate military and economic ties with European allies. Lacking industries, the Patriots needed to import arms, ammunition, and uniforms to sustain their forces. For want of money to purchase these supplies, they sought credit from European governments and bankers. Congress also coveted military advisers with expertise in artillery and engineering. Ultimately, the Patriots wanted the support of the French and Spanish fleets to compete with the formidable Royal Navy and to protect merchant ships carrying the European supplies needed to sustain the war effort (Gould 2012: 1–13).

But many Patriots distrusted the French and Spanish and worried that any foreign alliance would lead to a new dependence. As British colonists, they had long dreaded the absolutist regimes and Catholic faith of France and Spain. Many in the Continental Congress, which coordinated the Patriot resistance to Britain, also cherished independence as a precious chance to escape involvement in European imperial wars. They expected their new nation to prosper by freely trading with all nations rather than to accept economic domination by another European power (Stinchcombe 1969: 10).

The Patriots also wanted a free hand to build their own empire in North America at the expense of the Native peoples who still dominated the continental interior. In September 1776, Congress approved the Model Treaty of Amity and Commerce and planned to propose it to France and Spain. Drafted by John Adams, the document reveals both the Patriots' imperial ambitions and their wariness of European allies. The proposed treaty required European allies to forgo taking any North American colonies from the British. Instead, those allies would have to recognize the United States as entitled to all of British America, including Canada, Nova Scotia, Newfoundland, and Florida. While claiming all potential conquests in North America, Congress expected France and Spain to fight the British without binding Americans in any way. Members of Congress liked to believe that American trade alone would suffice to entice European nations to assist them. In 1776, however, after the Patriots' forces had suffered severe defeats, they decided that beggars could not be choosers. Desperate for French and Spanish help, Congress urged its diplomats to seek a more conventional alliance (Gould 2012: 104).

The French foreign minister, Charles Gravier, comte de Vergennes, was diligent, resourceful, experienced, and patient in his drive to restore France's military might and diplomatic clout. To enrich France and impoverish Britain, Vergennes sought to wrest away the profits of North American trade, but he had to proceed carefully in assessing whether the Patriot revolt provided the right moment to challenge the mighty British Empire. Betting on a lost cause would expose the French to dangerous risks and enormous costs. The finance minister, Anne-Robert-Jacques Turgot, astutely warned that a new war would prove fiscally ruinous (Dull 1985: 38–39, 48–51, 60).

In the spring of 1776, Vergennes decided to covertly help the Patriots sustain their revolt, but he balked at alliance and open war. Deeming the French fleet not yet prepared to take on the Royal Navy, he feared that war would expose French colonies in the West Indies and French fishermen in the Atlantic to devastating British attacks. Vergennes also wanted to line up the Spanish as allies: this would take time, because they were wary of both British power and American expansionism. Both the French and Spanish agreed, however, to ship munitions to the Patriots. Merchant ships carrying these cargoes slipped through the inefficient and porous British blockade of the long Atlantic coastline of the rebellious colonies. Unwilling to add to their open enemies in 1776, the British could only protest and seethe about the aid, which the French and Spanish officially denied providing. Britain hoped to crush the rebellion before France and Spain fully entered the war (Sadosky 2009: 93–95).

Antoine-François Callet, *Charles Gravier, Comte de Vergennes, Ministre d'État des Affaires Etrangères (1719–87)*, ca. 1774–87. Oil on canvas. As King Louis XVI's powerful foreign minister, Vergennes directed France's involvement in the American Revolution. (© RMN–Grand Palais / Art Resource, NY)

J. Barrow, "The British Lion Engaging Four Powers," June 14, 1782. Color etching. The cartoon depicts France as a rooster and Spain and Holland as dogs. All three are ranged against the British lion as they attempt to use their alliance with the American revolutionaries (here represented by a snake) as an opening to attack the British Empire. Each country is depicted as having a distinct objective in the war. The fox in the lower right corner urges Britain to punish France first. (© National Maritime Museum, Greenwich, London, PW3918)

In early 1778, Vergennes concluded that the French navy was ready for war. He also took heart from the Patriots' improved military performance in 1777, particularly their success at Saratoga in compelling the surrender of a British army that had invaded New York from Canada. The Patriots' pluck reassured Vergennes and King Louis XVI that a French-American alliance could beat the British. On February 6, 1778, French and American commissioners signed treaties for trade and alliance. The parties agreed to make no separate peace and accept no British terms short of American independence. France renounced any intention of retaking Canada but could seize British colonies in the West Indies. Retreating from the naïve principles of the Model Treaty of 1776, Congress accepted an entangling alliance in 1778 (Dull 1985: 192–96).

The Patriots and the French hoped to draw the Spanish into their alliance, but the latter balked at encouraging an expansive republican empire peopled by Protestants. Although tempted to exploit the rebellion to weaken the British, Spanish leaders were wary of helping any independence movement lest its success set a bad example for their own colonists. Spanish leaders also worried that the rapidly growing and westward-expanding American population threatened the thinly settled Spanish frontier colony of Louisiana (Chavez 2002: 47).

In April 1779, Spain entered the war in alliance with France—but not with the United States. Spanish leaders did continue to advance modest loans and arms shipments to the Patriots, who also indirectly benefited from Spanish attacks on British positions at Minorca and Gibraltar, in the Caribbean, and around the Gulf of Mexico. The resourceful Spanish governor of Louisiana, Bernardo de Gálvez, invaded and captured the British posts and settlements in Illinois and the western half of Florida. In his culminating victory, Spanish troops seized the fortified seaport of Pensacola in May 1781. By restoring Spanish dominance in the Gulf of Mexico, Gálvez reduced British pressure on the American South (DuVal 2015: 35–42, 116–27, 146–52).

The British could find no allies in Europe to counterbalance the French and Spanish. The British success in the Seven Years' War had upset the balance of power, arousing fear and jealousy in other European capitals. The Russians organized the League of Armed Neutrality with Denmark, Austria, Sweden, and Prussia to defy British efforts to blockade their trade with France and Spain. In late 1780, the British even added the Dutch Republic to their enemies by attempting to suppress its profitable neutral trade with the French and Americans (Dull 1985: 13–25, 43–44, 121–36).

The entry of the French and Spanish (and later the Dutch) escalated the American conflict into a world war. As the world's second- and third-largest naval powers, the French and Spanish navies combined could outnumber the Royal Navy's warships. Facing attacks on colonies and shipping around the globe, the British could no longer concentrate troops and warships in North America to suppress the rebellion. Instead, they had to divert military resources to defend Gibraltar and Minorca, the West Indian sugar colonies, the slaving entrepôt at Senegal, and their holdings in India. Dreading a French and Spanish invasion across the English Channel, Britain kept half the Royal Navy in home waters. In America, the British had to deploy their reduced military resources more cautiously and efficiently. "Everything is now at stake," the lord of the Admiralty worried. George III agreed that Britain confronted "the most serious crisis this nation ever knew" (quoted in Chavez 2002: 138–39).

In April 1778, Congress unanimously ratified the treaty with France. "I believe no event was ever received with a more heart felt joy," George Washington exulted. "America is at last saved by almost a Miracle," declared another Patriot. To celebrate the alliance, Washington staged a pageant in which his republican troops chanted, "Long live the king of France!" (quoted in Stinchcombe 1969: 14–24). After three years of hard struggle against long odds, Patriots anticipated easier victories with French help.

By rushing a fleet to American waters, the French government sought to demonstrate the benefits of alliance. But the naval commander, Jean-Baptiste Charles Henri Hector, comte d'Estaing, and Patriot forces failed to cooperate in their joint assault on a British garrison at Newport, Rhode Island. In November 1778, the French admiral sailed away under orders for the West Indies. His withdrawal restored British naval supremacy along the Atlantic seaboard, leaving the allies with little to show for their first campaign together. Coordinating their interests and forces proved more difficult than either had expected during the initial euphoria. Giving priority to protecting the West Indies and their highly profitable sugar production, the French could spare their fleet for North American operations only during the late summer and early fall, when hurricanes menaced ships in the Caribbean. In the West Indies, Estaing won his first victories by capturing the islands of St. Vincent and Grenada during the summer of 1779. But later that year, he botched another coordinated attack with the Patriots, this time on the British garrison of Savannah, Georgia (O'Shaughnessy 2000: 169–70, 209–10).

In 1776, John Adams had opposed a French military alliance for fear that the Patriots would relax their own efforts and count on their allies to bear the brunt of the fighting. That fear proved apt after 1778, as the public grew weary of the financial and human costs of the long struggle and sought to shunt the hazards and burdens of war onto someone else. Meanwhile, Congress lost credibility as it failed to supply soldiers or control rampant inflation (Shy 1990: 243, 254–55).

Starved for funds and men, Washington's ragged little army remained on the defensive, of necessity playing the long game of attrition. Growing impatient, Vergennes urged the Americans to make greater sacrifices and take decisive measures, for he longed for a quick victory before French finances collapsed under the strain. French officials suspected that the Patriots expected their allies to fight their battles for them. "I confess," Vergennes wrote to a friend, "I have only a feeble confidence in the energy of the United States" (quoted in Higginbotham 1983: 248–51). But he had to compound the French investment in the American cause, lest its collapse further expose France to British might. Vergennes offered additional loans to Congress and sent five thousand troops under Jean-Baptiste Donatien de Vimeur, comte de Rochambeau, to bolster Washington's dwindling army in 1780.

Despite the French reinforcements, the Patriot cause verged on collapse in early 1781. Americans were sick of war and hyperinflation. Mutinies had rippled through the Continental Army, and new enlistments dwindled while desertions soared. Washington's main army shrank to just 3,500 troops in the spring. Meanwhile, Congress ran out of money as the states dodged making their payments, while citizens evaded paying taxes to their states. Respect for Congress dissolved into mockery, suspicion, and contempt. "Our affairs are in a most wretched situation," a Maryland congressman noted. "Congress is at its wits End . . . and unless the French fleet and Army arrive very soon we shall in all probability be in the most deplorable situation." Alexander Hamilton concluded, "If we are [to be] saved, France and Spain must save us" (quoted in Dull 1985: 119–20, 139–40).

And France and Spain would indeed help Washington to save the Patriot cause. In June 1781, the French admiral François-Joseph-Paul, comte de Grasse, received an alarming dispatch from Anne-César de La Luzerne, the French ambassador to the United States. La Luzerne worried that the British invasion of Virginia, under Lord Charles Cornwallis, would complete the accelerating collapse of Patriot resolve and unity. La Luzerne warned de Grasse, "It is you alone who can deliver the invaded states from that crisis which is so alarming that . . . for their existence it is necessary to do all you can" (quoted in O'Shaughnessy 2000: 230–31). The French admiral resolved to sail north with his fleet to trap Cornwallis in Virginia.

To procure supplies and pay his crews, de Grasse got financial support from Cuba's colonial government. The Spanish also assumed responsibility for defending the allies' islands and shipping in de Grasse's absence. This financial and naval assistance became Spain's most important assistance to the Patriots during the war. In the summer of 1781, key French and Spanish officers

....

French artillery piece used at the siege of Yorktown in October 1781. (Courtesy Christopher Bryant)

acted decisively to advance a larger strategic vision that would benefit the United States more than their own empires. In early August, de Grasse's fleet, with three thousand troops on board, sailed north from Cuba for Chesapeake Bay (Chavez 2002: 200–03).

Repulsing a British fleet sent to retrieve Cornwallis, de Grasse enabled Washington and Rochambeau to besiege the British army, holed up at Yorktown. On land, Washington commanded sixteen thousand troops, nearly half of them French. With the nineteen thousand sailors of de Grasse's fleet, the siege involved more than twice as many French as American combatants. On October 19, 1781, Cornwallis surrendered his army, a quarter of the redcoats in America. Too hard-pressed elsewhere in the world to replace those losses, British rulers entered negotiations for peace with the Americans in the spring of 1782 (O'Shaughnessy 2013: 4–5, 360–61).

Despite paying an immense price in lives and money, France and Spain gained precious little from the war, in part because of British victories late in the war at Gibraltar and in India and the Caribbean. The French and Spanish exertions primarily helped the United States, which obtained independence on generous terms, thanks to Britain's indulgent diplomacy. The Spanish recovered Florida and Minorca but not their primary target, Gibraltar, which they had lost to the British at the beginning of the eighteenth century. Thanks to a crushing British naval victory over de Grasse's fleet in the Caribbean in 1782, the French could add only Tobago—a small island in the West Indies—to their empire. The war also doubled France's national debt, adding to a fiscal crisis that compelled the king to summon the long-suspended Estates General, the French parliament. In 1789, that parliament initiated a revolution that destroyed the French monarchy and sucked Europe into a massive new war during the 1790s (Dull 1985: 161–62).

Next to the Americans, the British fared best from the peace settlement. Although they had lost in America, they won in the rest of the world. British leaders began the war dreading that losing America would set off a collapse of their entire empire and elevate France to global supremacy. In fact, the British quickly recovered the primary benefit of America: her market for imported goods. Moreover, the British not only saved the rest of their empire but also added to it in India. In the nineteenth century, India would become the primary base of renewed imperial expansion. Meanwhile, the United States would expand westward to the Pacific, becoming the dominant power in North America. Both the British and American developments got their start in the rearrangement of power wrought by the Seven Years' War in the middle of the eighteenth century (O'Shaughnessy 2013: 4–5, 360–61).

In CONGRESS.

The DELEGATES of the UNITED STATES of *New-Hampshire, Massachusetts-Bay, Rhode-Island, Connecticut, New-York, New-Jersey, Pennsylvania, Delaware, Maryland, Virginia, North-Carolina, South-Carolina,* and *Georgia,* TO *Anthonie Felix Wuibert Esquire*

WE, reposing especial Trust and Confidence in your Patriotism, Valour, Conduct and Fidelity, DO, by these Presents, constitute and appoint you to be *An Engineer with the Rank of Lieutenant Colonel*

in the Army of the United States, raised for the Defence of American Liberty, and for repelling every hostile Invasion thereof. You are therefore carefully and diligently to discharge the Duty of *Engineer* by doing and performing all manner of Things thereunto belonging. And we do strictly charge and require all Officers and Soldiers under your Command, to be obedient to your Orders as *Engineer* And you are to observe and follow such Orders and Directions from Time to Time, as you shall receive from this or a future Congress of the United States, or Committee of Congress, for that Purpose appointed, or Commander in Chief for the Time being of the Army of the United States, or any other your superior Officer, according to the Rules and Discipline of War, in Pursuance of the Trust reposed in you. This Commission to continue in Force until revoked by this or a future Congress. DATED at *Philadelphia June 24th 1776*

By Order of the CONGRESS,

ATTEST *Cha Thomson Secy*   *John Hancock*   PRESIDENT.

. . . .

"Continental Congress to Antoine F. Wuibert, June 24, 1776, Printed Commission." (Library of Congress, George Washington Papers, ser. 4, General Correspondence, 1697–1799, MSS 44693, reel 036; © 1976–79 by the Rector and Visitors of University of Virginia; used by permission of the publisher)

ANTOINE-FÉLIX WUIBERT

This printed commission of Antoine-Félix Wuibert as a lieutenant colonel of engineers was apparently the first official document issued by the Continental Congress to bear the words "United States." It was written ten days before the Declaration of Independence formally announced that the United States of America was an independent nation.

Wuibert (written as Wiebert in this document) was one of the earliest French volunteers to join the American cause. He arrived in Philadelphia from Saint-Domingue just as the Congress was debating independence, and he led a storied career that took him to many theaters of the Revolution. Wuibert was assigned to build fortifications in New York, where he was captured by the British after they overran the city in November 1776. He was paroled from Forton Prison in Gosport, Britain, in 1779, after which Benjamin Franklin recommended him for naval service under John Paul Jones. Wuibert was assigned as captain of the marines aboard Jones's *Bonhomme Richard* and was instrumental in helping Jones seize HMS *Serapis* on September 23, 1779. Attempting to return to the United States to resume fighting, he was twice more captured by the British, but at last he was paroled in 1781. He served the rest of the war in the western theater at Fort Pitt, Pennsylvania. After the war, he settled permanently in that state, where he became a staunch abolitionist.

THE BRITISH GRAND STRATEGY

Andrew Lambert

Britain viewed its opposition to the American Revolution as only one element of a broad strategy for securing global maritime and economic power. Far from losing the war, Britain used its involvement to foster a second empire that ultimately exceeded the size of the first, which had been centered on the Americas. — *Editors*

From the perspective of Great Britain, America's War of Independence was not a continental conflict but the beginning of a global one. When France and Spain, the allied Bourbon monarchies, joined the conflict, they threatened the British Isles, British shipping, Britain's Caribbean and Indian imperial possessions, and its strategic bases in the Mediterranean. For Britain, these concerns took priority over recovering the American colonies. Ultimately Britain lost the American colonies, but it turned back the far greater threat to its maritime and imperial power posed by France and Spain and began building a second British Empire in Asia, Africa, and Australasia, one that would be far larger than the first, American-centered empire.

The development of an extensive territorial empire of settlers in America had been a by-product of British maritime expansion. America was part of Britain's expanding Atlantic empire of trade, dominated by ports, linked by shipping, and directed from London. In the Seven Years' War (or French and Indian War) of 1754–63, Britain's acquisition of Canada, Florida, and key Caribbean islands secured its dominance of the region. For the British, America was a collection of trading centers, and thus it was Atlantic port cities such as Boston, Philadelphia, Charleston, and New York that mattered, not the backcountry or the frontier. After 1763, the marginal role of territory in British ideas of empire prompted ministers to side with Native Americans to restrict the expansion of the thirteen colonies beyond the Appalachian Mountains. These restrictions were deeply unpopular with land-hungry colonists. Elsewhere, British territorial possessions were limited to small islands and coastal enclaves.

Throughout the war, British strategy was dominated more by maritime concerns than by attempts to control distant continental territory. These concerns included the defense of ocean shipping, including vital food imports, access to the rich islands of the West Indies, and, above all, protection of the British Isles themselves against invasion. Everything depended on command of the sea, which would enable Britain to weaken the economies of hostile powers as well as to attack the American rebels. Britain used economic warfare, sustained by a contentious legal regime, to stop and search neutral merchant ships on the high seas and seize them or their cargoes on the charge of trying to break a legally declared blockade. This strategy, which had to be used with care to avoid annoying powerful neutrals, was critical to British strategy against the rebels and other powers.

Having blundered into a war that proved impossible to win quickly, Britain came under pressure from European rivals, who saw the conflict as an opportunity to weaken the dominant maritime power. France and Spain wanted to recover possessions, prosperity, and prestige lost a decade earlier; reduce Britain's naval dominance; and stop the spread of Britain's progressive, inclusive political ideology—the same ideology that had inspired the American rebels. Royal resentment and revenge, not republican solidarity, underpinned their decision to support the Americans. They sought global, maritime, and economic domination as eagerly as the British did. France threatened to destroy British trade and invade the British Isles, while Spain was anxious to recover the two strategic naval bases that controlled the western Mediterranean: Gibraltar and the island of Minorca (Richmond 1931: 74–93).

Yet France, Spain, and the Dutch Republic had no wish to destroy Britain: they sought only to reduce British power and curb British arrogance. France needed Britain's support to counter the growing power of Russia in Eastern Europe and protect the Ottoman Empire. Thus French invasion plans were designed to shake commercial confidence, not overthrow the British state. France hoped to spark a panic on the stock exchange that would force Britain to restore French possessions in the Caribbean and India. Spain aimed to recover Gibraltar and Minorca to remove the British from the Mediterranean.

Until 1778, Britain's uncontested command of the seas had enabled the Royal Navy to conduct offensive operations against the American rebels while blockading the coast to stop the import of money, supplies, and weapons. This dominance had allowed Britain to focus on mobilizing troops. However, since the end of the Seven Years' War in 1763, France and Spain had been rebuilding their navies. By 1778, they had more battleships than Britain. When France declared war in the summer of 1778, naval weakness made it difficult for Britain to defend all its strategic and economic interests, which extended around the world from northwestern Europe to the Caribbean and China, by way of Africa and India. After 1778, Britain ceased to focus on recovering the American colonies and concentrated on defending its shores and shipping interests.

British trade stretched around the globe. Although the tea that sparked the Boston Tea Party was sent from London, it had originated in China and was owned by the East India Company, the greatest trading company on earth. The Royal Navy's primary role was to protect British trade and maintain commercial confidence: trading profits enabled the great financial houses of the City of London to lend the British government the money it needed to wage war. The defense of trade depended on a chain of global naval bases stretching from the Channel Islands, close to the French coast, through Gibraltar and Minorca, Halifax, Antigua, Barbados, and Port Royal in Jamaica, to Bombay and Calcutta in India. Britain could have secured peace with Spain by surrendering Gibraltar and Minorca, but doing so would have been a national disgrace and annihilated British trade in the Mediterranean.

British ministers demonstrated less interest in the American colonies than in trade. Trade paid taxes, it had a powerful voice in Parliament, and it could be defended by the Royal Navy, considerations that did not apply to colonial farmers and manufacturers. Furthermore, while the American colonies were the largest in the empire, they were not the most important. The West Indies and India generated more wealth, and both were under threat from France and Spain.

After France joined the conflict, British strategy was influenced by the need to deploy battleships and infantry regiments to meet threats outside America. Meanwhile, political opposition in Parliament urged concessions to the Americans' demands, while those representing merchants, West Indian planters,

W. N. Currier, *Destruction of Tea at Boston Harbor*, 1846. Colonists' anger over the tax system that sustained British global trade and funded American defense erupted in this memorable event in 1773. (Library of Congress, Prints and Photographs Division, LC-DIG-pga-08593)

investors, and insurers—almost all of whom were focused on issues outside continental America—demanded that the government protect their property.

Although French intervention alongside the rebel colonists had seemed inevitable in early 1778, Britain was still adjusting to the new threat when France declared war in July. France posed a far more serious threat than the colonial rebels: it could invade Britain, disrupt British trade, and attack British possessions in the Mediterranean, the Caribbean, and India. In short, France had the naval and military power to defeat Britain. Responding to these threats took priority over subduing the rebel colonists. The ministers hoped that running down the American campaign, notably by evacuating Philadelphia, would release enough troops to land a knockout blow in the French West Indies. John Montagu, Lord Sandwich, the first lord of the Admiralty, knew that everything depended on maintaining a powerful fleet in the English Channel. In previous wars, the Channel fleet had secured the country against invasion, protected the focal points of British trade (the English Channel and the Thames estuary), crushed the French maritime economy, and supported naval operations in distant theaters. With no distractions in Europe, France could focus on offensive operations and ignore shipping losses in the short term.

Although British statesmen worried about an invasion, experienced British naval officers focused on the real threat—to trade. The tension between these concerns, one local and the other global, disrupted naval deployments throughout the war. When invasion fears prevented the dispatch of a Mediterranean fleet, not only was British trade left unprotected, but the French Mediterranean fleet sailed to America, with disastrous results for Britain, while Spain, observing that Gibraltar and Minorca had been left exposed, was encouraged to attack. These dangers could have been averted by stationing a powerful British fleet in the Mediterranean. However, Britain did not have enough naval power to deal with every threat. The priorities it set would determine the outcome of the conflict.

In 1778, Britain had fifty-eight battleships in service, thirty-three of which made up the Channel fleet. After escorting huge merchant convoys through the Western Approaches (the area of the Atlantic southwest of Britain and Ireland), the fleet met the French Atlantic fleet off Ushant on July 27. Despite having thirty battleships under his command, to twenty-seven French battleships, Admiral Augustus Keppel failed to take a single enemy ship. The French fought to a draw, keeping their distance and firing high to disable the British ships' masts and sails. The Battle of Ushant shattered British expectations that an early victory would crush the French navy, prompting acrimonious political exchanges and the resignation of several prominent naval officers. With such a large French fleet concentrated close to the Channel, Britain had no spare battleships to defend the West Indian islands, prompting complaints from politically powerful Caribbean planters and merchants. They were placated by the retention of troops in the Caribbean who were needed in America. Furthermore, the outcome of the Battle of Ushant encouraged Spain to join the war.

Once Spain declared war in 1779, the insignificance of America to the conflict became clear. Parliament voted to abandon America in order to fight France and Spain. King George rejected this option, fearing that the loss of America would be followed by the loss of the West Indies, which would reduce Britain to a minor power. George prepared for an invasion and placed his third son, Prince William, in the navy.

In 1779, the Bourbon allies planned to destroy the naval base at Portsmouth to shake the confidence of Britain's commercial and political elite. This threat pinned the bulk of the Royal Navy in the Channel. As British frigate squadrons scoured the French coast for intelligence, the Franco-Spanish armada assembled off Corunna, in northwestern Spain. Rather than risk battle, the British fleet, outnumbered two to one, opted to secure trade and protect the Irish coast. By avoiding a battle it could not win, the fleet prevented an invasion.

The combined French-Spanish fleet was weakened by disease, supply failure, and mutual recrimination. The Spanish ships arrived late and sailed badly: the French ships were dirty and their sailors disease prone. Neither navy could catch the faster British ships, whose hulls were sheathed with copper. This covering prevented fouling by weed and shellfish, and clean-hulled ships sail faster. To preserve this advantage, Britain used every means possible to prevent France from obtaining copper sheathing from Dutch suppliers.

Many historians see 1779 as a period of great danger to Britain, when an invasion loomed, ignoring the overriding importance of British trade and the capacity of a fast, well-handled fleet to destroy transport shipping. Losing an army in the English Channel would be a catastrophe for France: even Napoleon did not dare take that risk.

To expand its offensive naval capacity while most of its battleships were pinned in the Channel, Britain mobilized a massive fleet of some 2,600 privateering ships and craft. These licensed predators swarmed across the key sea lanes in the Atlantic theater, eviscerating French, Spanish, and Dutch commerce, capturing hostile privateers, securing intelligence, and cutting off the Bourbon dockyards' access to naval supplies shipped from the Baltic Sea. In this conflict, privateers were both the cutting edge of British economic warfare and a vital strategic tool (Starkey 1990: 192–241).

After the 1779 invasion crisis, the British navy was determined to break the Spanish siege of Gibraltar. Ships from the Channel fleet, commanded by Vice Admiral Sir George Rodney, escorted the necessary troops and supplies. As he rounded Cape St. Vincent on the Portuguese coast, Rodney seized a Spanish military convoy and then captured six Spanish battleships in the Moonlight Battle of January 16–17, 1780. In contrast to the constrained tactics used at Ushant, Rodney ordered an aggressive "general chase" (in essence a full-speed pursuit, without pausing to first form a line of battle), releasing his ships to hunt down the enemy. This victory made it possible to break the siege. Rodney carried his prizes to Gibraltar, raising garrison morale and landing supplies for the next year. The captured battleships were added to the Royal Navy. This double success bolstered British spirits after a discouraging year, and Rodney proceeded to take command in the West Indies.

Late in 1779, France and Spain had abandoned plans to invade Britain, shifting their primary effort to the Caribbean, while small forces deployed to America and India to divert British resources away from the primary target. The Bourbon allies planned for a combined Caribbean force of thirty-five battleships and ten thousand troops to conquer Jamaica, the key to the British Caribbean. Once again, the British response to this threat emphasized the relative unimportance of the American colonies. After 1778, more British troops were sent to the West Indies than to America; moreover, regiments were sent there from America itself. Defending the British West Indies was far more important than subduing America.

While the British government desperately tried to counter each new threat, the king urged the nation to recover the initiative by attacking the French and Spanish. While this was sound strategy, without sufficient resources it

Richard Paton, *The Moonlight Battle off Cape St Vincent, 16 January 1780*, ca. 1780–82. Oil on canvas. Vice Admiral Sir George Rodney's victory in this battle lifted British morale and led to the first relief of the besieged bastion of Gibraltar. (© National Maritime Museum, Greenwich, London, BHC0429)

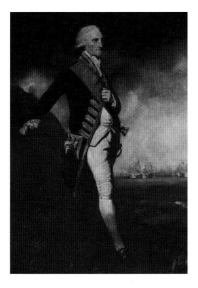

Joshua Reynolds, *George Brydges, Lord Rodney*, 1788–89. Oil on canvas. Rodney was Britain's most successful admiral during the time of the Revolution, winning important engagements both in the Caribbean and off Gibraltar. His victories saved the British maritime empire and redefined the meaning of naval power. (Royal Collection Trust / © Her Majesty Queen Elizabeth II 2018, RCIN 405899)

proved impossible. As the war spread around the world, Britain was weakened everywhere: it had little hope of success unless the enemy could be divided.

The first opportunity to do so came in the West Indies, but Rodney failed to defeat the French in 1780. His tactics were confounded by his unimaginative subordinates, while the French avoided decisive action at close range. The campaign season did at least end without any major losses. Although a Spanish fleet of ten battleships arrived at Havana, complete with ten thousand sickly soldiers, it did nothing. The threat to Jamaica, however, remained.

The British Channel fleet of 1780, with twenty-eight copper-sheathed battleships, was immediately sent south into the Bay of Biscay to escort vital East India and West Indies convoys. The loss of another convoy off Cape St. Vincent in August, shortly after the fleet had returned to the Channel, prompted fresh orders to head south to placate anxious merchants. The safety of floating trade remained the key concern. Although the Bourbons did not send a fleet into the Channel in 1780, even as a distraction, Britain was unable to regain the initiative. Its warships and regiments were wearing out: the mobilization of ships, sailors, and soldiers was not keeping pace with the wastage of war, disease, and desertion.

Spain, with its vast Latin and South American empire, had no enthusiasm for colonial rebellions. As noted earlier, it entered the war to recover Gibraltar and Minorca, and in late 1779 the British could have secured peace with Spain simply by handing over the two fortresses. But no one in Britain dared to suggest the surrender of Gibraltar, the fortress that had come to define British resolve, and the war continued. British attempts to attack the Spanish Empire failed; in 1780, Horatio Nelson had his first taste of independent command when he led the doomed San Juan Expedition toward the Pacific from the Caribbean coast of Nicaragua, traveling along a disease-ridden river in a failed attempt to seize the Spanish-held towns of Granada and León. He was lucky to survive.

The war had become a global defensive, and Britain desperately needed a major victory. The government was well aware that it was unlikely to come in America. This understanding prompted a dramatic redistribution of British forces between February 1778 and September 1780. Troops in America dropped from 65 percent of the national total to 29 percent; those in Britain went up from 26 percent to 55 percent; the West Indies took an extra 6 percent, and India another 1 percent. The 65/35 offensive effort of early 1778 had been replaced by a defensive balance of 71/29. The battleship balance moved in the same direction, with an even greater decline in America and increases in the West Indies and India (Conway 1995: 157–58). Britain was fighting for survival, and it lacked the resources to win. Finally the decision-makers in London accepted reality and opted to focus on the most important areas of the empire.

Throughout the war, Britain and France captured and recaptured West Indian sugar islands in campaigns dominated by the shifting balance of naval power, and it was here that Britain's war was ultimately decided. The British conquest of St. Lucia in December 1778 proved critical, providing the Royal Navy with a vantage on the main French naval base at Port Royal, Martinique. The other islands could be used as pawns in a diplomatic endgame.

The British position was further complicated in April 1780. British warships and privateers had driven American shipping off the oceans in the first months of the war, and Britain was aggressively searching neutral merchant ships, using force when necessary, to check whether they were carrying contraband—goods with military purposes—to the rebels. Neutral powers had long resented British methods but lacked the power to act. Britain had hoped to recruit Russia as an ally and hire Russian troops, but Russia declared an armed neutrality in March 1780. Denmark and Sweden joined Russia to form the League of Armed Neutrality in August of that year, and other minor powers followed suit. By demanding concessions from Britain, Russia hoped to earn diplomatic credit and prevent Britain from using these tools against Russia in the future.

This was a complex calculation for Britain. Russia controlled the supply of naval stores on which the Royal Navy depended, but conceding to Russian demands would destroy Britain's key strategic tool, maritime economic warfare. The British government opted decisively to uphold the economic blockade. Denying naval stores to the Bourbon fleets justified taking on an extra enemy and the cancellation of offensive plans against Spain. Citing Dutch smuggling of naval stores to France and Dutch support for the American privateer John Paul Jones, the British ended a treaty that allowed Dutch merchant ships to pass without being searched and declared war on the Dutch Republic in December 1780.

Within a few weeks, Britain had crushed Dutch trade. Within eighteen months, the Bourbon fleets had been soundly beaten, with poor maintenance and inferior stores a significant factor in their defeat. Acting decisively against the Dutch impressed both neutral powers and Britain's enemies. On August 5, 1781, British and Dutch fleets, both escorting Baltic convoys, fought in the North Sea. The battle was drawn, but the Dutch convoy turned back, while the British carried on. The North Sea and the Baltic thus were secured for the rest of the war. Dutch overseas territories were seized, helping to compensate Britain for losses in America. In February 1781, Admiral Rodney seized the Dutch island of Sint Eustatius in the West Indies, the center of a network that was smuggling munitions to the American rebels. Although the economic situation of the rebels was damaged, Rodney took his eye off the French fleet.

The crisis of the war came later that year, when the necessity for a second relief of Gibraltar prevented the British Channel fleet from blockading the French fleet at Brest, in Brittany. Once again Britain had sacrificed the initiative to conduct a vital defensive mission. Blockading Brest would have secured the West Indies and prevented the defeat at Yorktown by keeping Admiral François-Joseph-Paul de Grasse's French fleet in Europe. However, blockading Brest, a very dangerous coast, also would have required a fleet one-third larger than that of the French, which the British could not raise (Mackesy 1965: 384).

British decision-making in 1781 was dominated by a global vision. The American theater had been fading in importance since the summer of 1778. British economic warfare was working: if the British could avoid any serious defeats, poverty would force France to negotiate a settlement, and Spain would have to follow. Then it would be possible to deal with the rebels. In May 1780, France, already bankrupt, proposed making peace as the war then stood. The French were ready to abandon both the Americans and Spain to preserve the financial credit of the monarchy and France's ability to function as a European great power. France, a major colonial power, had no reason to encourage rebellious American colonists, let alone people demanding political representation. Aware that French credit had collapsed, George III urged his ministers to carry on. He still expected to win.

On March 22, 1781, de Grasse sailed from Brest with twenty battleships and two regiments accompanied by a squadron, heading for India. He passed without hindrance because the British Channel fleet was then sailing for Gibraltar past Cádiz, where the Spanish fleet was taking on stores. Gibraltar was relieved without a battle, but while the Channel fleet was away, British merchant shipping losses in the Channel rose. With the value of Asian trade about to overtake that of the West Indies, the defense of India was a priority for anxious investors. Four British battleships and ten battalions of troops were sent to India. British armies seized Dutch and French settlements there and checked the threat from the native Kingdom of Mysore. The naval war was fought to a standstill in five furious but inconclusive fleet actions, in which the tactical skill and unparalleled aggression of comte Pierre André de Suffren de Saint-Tropez were thwarted by Sir Edward Hughes's resolute line of battle. (Hughes later commissioned paintings of all five of these battles from Dominic Serres; Russett 2001: 163–70.) The war would be won elsewhere.

After Gibraltar had been relieved, the combined Spanish and French Mediterranean fleets landed an army on Minorca and sailed north, entering the English Channel with fifty battleships. The British, with only twenty-five, wisely refused action, focusing on trade defense. Once again the enemy was paralyzed by the presence of a faster force, unable to attempt an invasion until the British had been decisively defeated and rendered incapable of forcing a battle. Attention shifted to the Caribbean.

De Grasse secured the initiative in the West Indies by canceling the annual homebound convoys and using the escorting battleships to reinforce his fleet. The British, under pressure from the commercial community, could not follow suit. De Grasse's extra ships were critical to his strategic victory in the Battle of the Chesapeake, in September 1781, which prevented the smaller British fleet from relieving Lord Charles Cornwallis's army at Yorktown. King George lamented: "I nearly think this Empire ruined" (Mackesy 1965: 434). Lord Sandwich recognized that Cornwallis was doomed and that the American war could not be won without annihilating the nation's credit. The British belief in the nation's invincibility at sea had been shattered; news of Cornwallis's surrender brought down the government. High taxes, commercial losses, and unending strain made many favor peace on any terms. To reinforce the point, a massive enemy fleet was cruising in the Channel, preventing the relief of Minorca. It fell in February 1782, the garrison crippled by scurvy.

Yet the British defeat at Yorktown did not end the war. Just as Britain was facing defeat on all fronts, the balance of power reversed. The strategy of economic warfare had worked: without money, the Bourbon war effort faltered, exacerbating divisions between Paris and Madrid. Desperate for an early end to the war, the French placed all their hopes for success on a heavy blow in India and the seizure of Jamaica. After Yorktown, they abandoned the American campaign, sending their ships and troops to the West Indies. Having accepted the loss of their American colonies, the British were now able to respond.

The British campaign began with an early success. In December 1781, a battle squadron from the Channel fleet broke up a large French West Indian convoy, and the remaining French ships were scattered by midwinter gales. To achieve a decisive superiority in the Caribbean, additional British battleships were detached, leaving the defense of Britain itself to the army and twenty fast battleships. Sir George Rodney resumed command in the West Indies with fresh ships, while Admiral Robert Digby added battleships from the American station. In Rodney's absence, Admiral Sir Samuel Hood's outstanding seamanship and tactical genius distracted and delayed the superior French fleet. Rodney arrived just as the Bourbon allies began the attack on Jamaica.

By the spring of 1782, many of de Grasse's ships needed refitting, but British economic warfare meant naval stores were in short supply. This may explain a spate of collisions after the French sailed for Jamaica, which reduced the French fleet to thirty battleships. De Grasse encountered Rodney, who had thirty-six battleships, in the Saintes Passage between Guadeloupe and Dominica on April 12, 1782. As the fleets exchanged fire on opposite courses, a sudden shift in the wind disordered the French line of battle. British ships broke through, doubling on the enemy and capturing four ships, including de Grasse's flagship, the *Ville de Paris*. They captured two more French ships later. Naval battles of the time were decided at close quarters, and victory went to the fleet with superior morale. As the ships drew within pistol range — only seventy-five feet — British officers saw French gunners running below decks to escape the overwhelming fire. Rather than fight to defend their commander in chief, the French ships broke and ran. Aggressive tactics, close-range fire from new carronades, coppered hulls, and superior personnel had turned a small advantage in numbers into a decisive victory. The Royal Navy had restored its dominance

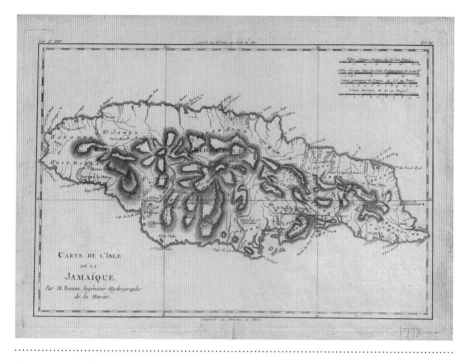

M. Bonne, *Map of the Isle of Jamaica*, 1778. Despite having excellent plans of its target, the combined French and Spanish Caribbean fleet failed in its effort to capture Jamaica in 1782. (University of the West Indies Historical Collection [Mona], X G4960.1778.B4)

by the sound strategy of massing resources in the decisive theater. Capturing the French admiral and his flagship made this Britain's greatest naval victory to date. France's defeat at the Saintes, added to bankruptcy, brought it to terms.

Lord Frederick North's government, which had waged the war since 1776, had fallen three weeks before Rodney's great battle, and the new ministers had immediately sacked Rodney, replacing him with a political nonentity. When they learned of his victory at the Saintes, they tried to reverse the decision, but it was too late. Rodney became a national hero, and the new government looked foolish. Their other decisions proved more profitable.

Admiral Lord Richard Howe took command in the Channel, where the destruction of a French convoy heading for India crippled Suffren's fleet. Howe's masterly third relief of Gibraltar in October 1782 broke Spanish morale, already depressed by the failure of a great naval attack a month before. While

Lemuel Francis Abbott, *Samuel Hood, 1st Viscount Hood*, 1795. Oil on canvas (replica of 1794 original). Admiral Hood, the outstanding naval tactician of the war, helped defeat de Grasse at the Battle of the Saintes in the Caribbean in 1782 and inspired the next generation of British naval heroes, including Horatio Nelson. (© National Portrait Gallery, London, NPG 628)

Britain anxiously shifted troops from America to the West Indies, where a Franco-Spanish threat persisted, Spain accepted that Gibraltar would remain British. Peace was quickly settled. Britain had defeated France, Spain, and the Dutch Republic by abandoning an American campaign that could not be settled from the sea. Neither France nor Spain had any interest in fighting for the Americans, and both lacked the money to carry on.

Largely overlooked amid debates about losing America, swapping sugar islands, holding on to India, and retaining Gibraltar was Britain's success in securing the one most important point at issue. When they made peace, the ministers refused to discuss with the Dutch or anyone else the claim that neutral ships had a right to trade with the enemy (the basis of the armed neutrality). The Peace of Paris of 1783 preserved Britain's primary strategic weapon, the legal basis for economic warfare. Despite military disasters in America, Britain's core concerns—trade, naval bases, the European balance of power, and above all control of the oceans—had been secured. In the wars of the French Revolution and empire, men who had learned their business with Rodney, Hood, and Howe blockaded France and won battles of unparalleled ferocity. After the loss of America, Britain put its trust in naval heroes.

Rather than lamenting their losses, the British celebrated success. It was no small irony that the leading artist of British victory was an American: John Singleton Copley's dramatic pictures of the defense of Gibraltar summed up the national mood, defiant and resolute. In 1780, George III hired Dominic Serres, "the artist of British Naval glory," as his official marine painter (Russett 2001: 180). The favorite of Hood, Rodney, and Hughes, Serres produced powerful images that became the defining popular motifs of the British sea-power state. Suitably inspired, Britain rebuilt its economy and its navy. A new oceanic empire in Asia and the Pacific developed after the voyages of Captain James Cook, which had been sponsored by George III and Joseph Banks, the president of the Royal Society. This "Second" British Empire, built on maritime commercial connectivity rather than continental American territory, once again privileged ports and trade routes over territory, capital over land, and industry over agriculture. This very different kind of empire, consciously echoing the Venetian sea empire, not Rome's terrestrial dominion, would endure far longer than the first.

John Singleton Copley, *The Defeat of the Floating Batteries at Gibraltar*, 1783–91. Oil on canvas. The defeat of the Spanish floating batteries in 1782 was the key to Britain's success in retaining Gibraltar, a victory that emphasized British resilience. (Guildhall Art Gallery, London, record no. 10045)

Dominic Serres, *Gibraltar Relieved by Sir George Rodney*, 1780. Oil on canvas. (© Royal Academy of Arts, London; photograph Prudence Cuming Associates Limited, 03/460)

FRENCH NAVAL OPERATIONS

Olivier Chaline and Jean-Marie Kowalski

> Most histories of the American Revolution discuss the French navy's involvement only near the end of the war, at the Battle of the Chesapeake in September 1781. In fact, from the moment France entered the war in 1778, its navy was fighting the British in many parts of the world, and this proved to be the most decisive factor in bringing the opposing parties to the peace table. — *Editors*

The American Revolutionary War was a truly exceptional event in French history. Only during these five years did the French navy matter more than the French army: naval expenditures (including colonial ones) were much greater than those for the army as a whole, and the navy sustained more casualties and engaged in more fighting than the army did. Most land operations were actually amphibious operations. To ally France with the American colonists was an exceptional decision by King Louis XVI and his powerful foreign minister, Charles Gravier, comte de Vergennes. The former enemies turned into comrades in arms and, after a difficult period of adjustment, were victorious in their common war against Britain.

In the Revolutionary War, the fighting took place beyond Europe, except for conflicts over the British-held and besieged Gibraltar and Minorca. For the first time, the most important military operations were overseas, while the European mainland became the support base of a global conflict. The French navy intervened almost everywhere in the world and for the duration of the conflict, maintaining long lines of communication, protecting French commerce, and challenging the British navy in several theaters at once, even at the entrance to the Channel. But Louis XVI's navy could not sustain the fight against Britain alone and needed allies. In 1779, the Spanish navy entered the war. After initial badly coordinated operations, cooperation between France and Spain

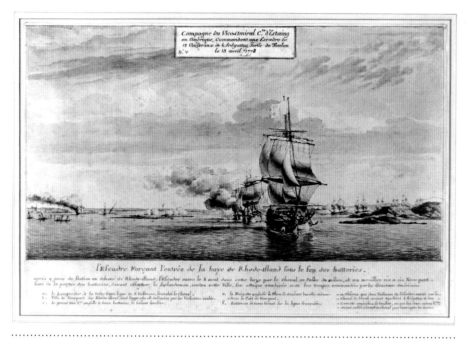

improved, and together they disrupted the British war effort. In 1780, Britain's declaration of war against the Dutch Republic enabled France to use Dutch naval bases and take advantage of Dutch finance and trade. France and Spain, the two Bourbon monarchies, ultimately prevailed over their enemy through an indirect strategy of attacking Britain's colonial possessions and commerce.

Globalization and the War at Sea

French naval activity in the Revolutionary War focused on the sea lanes crossing the Atlantic to America and the route around Africa to the Indian Ocean. France and Britain also had interests in West Africa, the center of the slave trade. In the Atlantic, the trade winds led directly to the Caribbean Sea, first to the French and British West Indies and then to the Spanish islands. Both sides considered conquering the enemy's sugar islands to be the best way to disrupt the other side's trade and force a bid for peace. Despite its lack of a real naval base in the Caribbean, France focused its war effort there.

France also deployed its navy in North American waters. The fleet of Jean-Baptiste Charles Henri Hector, comte d'Estaing, was sent to the American coast shortly before France entered the war. French squadrons had no naval base in North America, although Charles-Henri-Louis d'Arsac, chevalier de Ternay, and his followers used Newport. They had to learn how to cooperate with their new allies, and this took time, as was demonstrated by the unsuccessful attempt against Savannah in 1779. But the war was ultimately won when, in September 1781, the Newport squadron, led by Jacques-Melchior Saint-Laurent, comte de Barras, joined forces with the fleet of François-Joseph-Paul de Grasse sailing from the West Indies. Later the French navy destroyed British settlements in Hudson Bay and, after the Battle of the Saintes in the Caribbean in April 1782, sailed to New England for needed repairs before turning back to the Caribbean.

In the Indian Ocean, France's main objective was to disrupt British East India trade. In March 1781, two French fleets left the naval base at Brest, in Brittany, at the same time. One, led by Pierre André de Suffren de Saint-Tropez, sailed to the Indian Ocean, while the other, commanded by de Grasse, headed to the West Indies. Both of them were prepared for long missions with no support in the operations area.

The Western Approaches, the region of the Atlantic immediately southwest of France and Britain, was a critical theater. If the Brest fleet had been defeated by the Royal Navy at the beginning of the war, sailing to America would have been impossible. On the other hand, if the French and their Spanish allies could sail into the English Channel, land on the British coast, and blockade or burn Portsmouth (the main British naval base), they could win the war in one bold stroke. The waters surrounding the famous British naval base of Gibraltar were another focus of the war in Europe. Recapturing Gibraltar, which had been seized by the British from Spain at the beginning of the eighteenth century, was a major objective of the Franco-Spanish alliance and occupied a large part—perhaps too large—of French naval strength.

The Balance of Naval Forces

The British Royal Navy enjoyed numerical superiority over the French navy throughout the American War, though in 1778 the two navies were more closely matched than at any other time during the eighteenth century. The Royal Navy always enjoyed an advantage of thirty or forty vessels, at least on paper, over the French, and had more three-deckers (the most powerful class of battleship) than its adversaries. France's foreign minister, the comte de Vergennes, believed France needed to ally with Spain to counterbalance British sea power. With more than fifty Spanish vessels added to the power of the French navy, the Bourbon allies would have numerical superiority.

Achieving efficient use of that naval power, however, was difficult. Outnumbering British battleships was important, but smaller vessels were also needed: frigates, cutters, and schooners were indispensable for convoy escorts, for amphibious operations in the Caribbean, and for repeating signals and towing disabled battleships in combat. In addition, the quality and performance of the ships mattered: only at the end of the war were all French ships copperbottomed and able to match the speed of the British fleet. Coordinating the differently trained French and Spanish forces was a challenge, too, as became clear during their first Channel campaign in 1779. Two years at least were needed to make joint operations more efficient. But in the end, French and Spanish

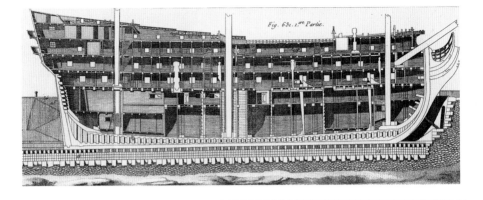

Artist unknown, *Section of the Three-Decker French Warship* Bretagne. Drawing. Following the Seven Years' War, France ordered seventeen new three-deckers; the *Bretagne* was completed in 1766. (Courtesy Smithsonian Libraries, Washington, D.C., Dibner Library, cat. no. [OCoLC]ocm33930010)

squadrons were able to act in concert, capturing Pensacola (1781) as well as Minorca (1782). By cruising in the Western Approaches (1781–82), French and Spanish fleets obliged the British Admiralty to keep many vessels in the Channel to protect British shores, although they were badly needed elsewhere.

By the beginning of the Revolutionary War, French naval power had grown considerably from its low point in 1759. This expansion was the result of efforts by Étienne François, duc de Choiseul, and his relative César Gabriel, duc de Praslin, both naval ministers under Louis XV. Their program of naval construction and rearmament was continued during Louis XVI's reign, thanks to Antoine Raymond Jean Gualbert Gabriel de Sartine, comte d'Alby, and later to Charles Eugène Gabriel de La Croix, marquis de Castries. Under their guidance, the number of French vessels reached a peak in 1782, and France lost fewer vessels than in previous naval wars. The number of effective, operational vessels — those in commission — was of course always smaller than the theoretical total.

When war broke out in 1778, the French were better prepared than the British, who had not been able to get their fleet on a war footing. British numerical superiority was obvious — sixty-six warships compared to France's fifty-two — but the geographic dispersion of the British fleet tangibly reduced its advantage at the beginning of the conflict. This explains why France chose this moment to intervene. It explains, too, why seeking an alliance with Spain was, for France, unavoidable. By the summer of 1779, France and Spain together could muster more warships than the Royal Navy: 123 compared to 117 on paper, and 121 compared to 90 in commission.

Financial Costs and Scattered Operations

The Revolutionary War was the most costly of all the wars of the ancien régime. In France, as in Britain, war expenditures surged to unbelievable heights: 183 million *livres tournois* (French pounds) were expended on the navy in 1782 alone. Immediately before the war, the state's income amounted to 370 million livres and its expenditure to 410 million livres. Soon afterward, its debt amounted to 3.3 billion livres, and debt service alone consumed 165 million livres each year. Altogether, France spent more than 1 billion livres on the Revolutionary War— perhaps as much as 1.73 billion livres, the equivalent of almost a trillion dollars today. The nation had never before spent so much money on waging war and supporting an ally. Britain, according to the historian Robert Harris, spent the equivalent of 2.27 billion livres and accumulated interest on this debt at a rate of 313 million livres per year. The whole British war debt amounted to the equivalent of approximately 5.3 billion livres. For Britain, as for France, the Revolutionary War was more expensive than the Seven Years' War. Yet the French war effort—financed primarily by borrowing and secondly by taxes—never failed during the period of hostilities.

Despite its numerical superiority, the British Royal Navy had to cope with a set of problems unique to this war. It had to keep the American shore-line under close watch and establish a difficult blockade a long way from Britain; to ship weapons, supplies, and troops to distant naval bases; to escort convoys; and, increasingly, to fight American privateers, even in European waters. At the same time, the Royal Navy had to protect Britain from a possible French invasion. Because of these multiple demands, the navy was unable to meet all of its commitments in North America while preparing to fight an unwelcome war with France and perhaps Spain as well.

Britain's war effort was also struggling under a heavy financial burden. Indeed, revolution started in America because Britain tried to oblige its colonies to help pay the costs of the Seven Years' War, which had left the nation heavily indebted. In part because of these financial difficulties, the Admiralty did not put the Royal Navy on a war footing before the spring of 1778: many of its ships were kept out of commission and unprepared for war. Meanwhile, the French were actively preparing for war, opening their ports in both France and the West Indies to American privateers and smugglers. Britain's restraint, due partly to its financial burdens and partly to a desire to avoid provoking Versailles, gave the initiative to France to choose the best time to go to war.

Britain's lack of preparation made it impossible for the Royal Navy to blockade the French naval bases: Rochefort, Toulon, and particularly Brest, the nearest to the British Isles. Even after France's formal declaration of war, the Admiralty did not have enough ships at its disposal to prevent French squadrons and convoys from sailing wherever they wanted to go. The Royal Navy was never able to deny France access to the oceans as it had during the Seven Years' War. The consequences were fateful to British sea power.

A War on Trade: The New Face of French Naval Tactics
In earlier wars, British blockades and the interdiction of French commerce by the Royal Navy had severely compromised the French economy. In the Revolutionary War, by contrast, French commerce was spared, due largely to the effectiveness of French naval operations.

Beginning in 1777, British warships and privateers intercepted French merchantmen suspected—sometimes correctly—of carrying contraband merchandise to the American insurgents. Once war was declared, the French navy assumed responsibility for protecting French merchant shipping along the European shoreline as well shipping between France and colonial ports in the West Indies and Indian Ocean.

At first, frigates were assigned to patrol the French coasts, but there were never enough of them for the job, and they were needed for other missions. At the end of 1778, the French naval minister, Sartine, required merchant ships to sail in convoys, and convoys became one of the main features of the Revolutionary War at sea. Each convoy was assigned a navy escort, and providing such escorts became one of the navy's main missions. When a squadron left for the French West Indies, it too often had to sail with a convoy. Convoy duty has been of less interest to naval historians than the famous and spectacular battles of this period, but its role in protecting French commerce was critical to victory.

From 1779 onward, the French system of convoys proved highly effective. Ever-growing numbers of merchant ships used it, with convoys sometimes numbering one hundred or more ships. For the outward journey across the Atlantic, convoys gathered in the Brest roadstead or near the island of Aix at the mouth of the river Charente, near the naval base of Rochefort. Some convoys sailed directly for Saint-Domingue (modern Haiti); others called at Martinique. For the return voyage, convoys gathered at Saint-Domingue before crossing the Atlantic, with some warships returning to France.

The system was not infallible, but it served to transport troops and supplies to the West Indies and the United States as well as to protect commercial traffic. It made it possible to land the troops of Jean-Baptiste Donatien de Vimeur, comte de Rochambeau, in Newport, Rhode Island, and reinforcements in the West Indies. Of course, a lot of convoys were attacked and some ships seized. Unfortunately for de Grasse's fleet, the highly awaited convoy escorted by Admiral Luc Urbain de Bouëxic, comte de Guichen, carrying much-needed naval supplies and stores, was intercepted by Admiral Richard Kempenfelt soon after its departure from Brest in December 1781 and scattered by a storm.

France was equally successful at intercepting British shipping. For example, in May 1781, French Admiral Toussaint-Guillaume Picquet de la Motte succeeded in capturing the convoy carrying British Admiral George Rodney's booty, taken as spoils of the war over the Dutch island of Sint Eustatius.

Through coastal patrols and the convoy system, maritime trading losses were kept low. Wartime losses after 1780 amounted to 10 percent or less of the value of French cargoes. As a consequence, maritime insurance rates remained relatively stable. French merchants, in France as well in the West Indies, continued to make profits. In turn, they subscribed to the loans necessary to sustain the French war effort.

French naval operations in the Caribbean were also vital to the American economy. The French navy made it possible to maintain trade between the West Indies, especially Saint-Domingue, and the American ports held by the insurgents. If British naval activity had interrupted this trade, the economy of

Thomas Maynard, *The Battle of St Kitts, 26 January 1782*, 1783. Oil. After victory in the Chesapeake in September 1781, de Grasse returned to the Caribbean. He defeated the British at St. Kitts but then lost the Battle of the Saintes in April 1782. (© National Maritime Museum, Greenwich, London, BHC0437)

the American states certainly would have collapsed, enabling George III to reestablish his authority over his rebellious colonies by force of arms. The French navy won this eighteenth-century battle of the Atlantic by protecting commerce.

Direct and Indirect Strategy at Sea

In each war with Britain during the second half of the eighteenth century, the French government wavered between a direct strategy (striking Britain by landing somewhere in the British Isles) and an indirect one (waging war at sea and overseas against British trade and colonial territories). During the Revolutionary War, France first pursued an indirect approach, then a direct one, finally achieving victory with an indirect strategy relying heavily on naval power.

At the beginning of the war, France had to choose between two options: it could launch a surprise attack on Britain, without waiting for Spain, in order to benefit from the British lack of naval preparation; or it could wait for Spain to enter the war, an alternative that involved forgoing the element of surprise but assured France of numerical superiority at sea. Four strategic plans were presented and discussed at Versailles. Charles-François de Broglie, marquis de Ruffec, and Charles-Pierre Claret, comte de Fleurieu, proposed an invasion

Jean-François Hue, *Naval Battle of Grenada*, 1779. Oil. (© RMN–Grand Palais / Art Resource, NY)

of Britain; Gilbert du Motier, marquis de Lafayette, proposed supporting the American insurgents by means of Atlantic convoys while attacking British trade; and Ternay and the famous explorer Jean-François de Galaup, comte de Lapérouse, recommended waging war in Indian waters. All these strategies depended heavily on naval power, although nobody knew how the navy would perform after fifteen years of peace and partial rebuilding.

In the end, Vergennes chose to negotiate with Spain while supporting the American insurgents. It was clear to him that France could not win alone. The Spanish, as expected, were reluctant to engage Britain and preferred to see what the French would do by themselves. Compelled to wait for Spain, Vergennes feared that the delay would give the British navy time to mobilize. He decided to develop a two-part French war effort, and secret instructions were given directly to admirals. On April 13, 1778 — before the declaration of war — the comte d'Estaing sailed from Toulon with twelve warships bound for North America to assist the insurgents. On July 18, Louis Guillouet, comte d'Orvilliers, sailed from Brest with a larger fleet of thirty-two ships of the line (large warships), under orders to keep the British Channel fleet in check. He met the British fleet in the Battle of Ushant and fought in the Western Approaches on July 27, 1778. This was the first great encounter between the two navies since 1759, the year of British victories. Tactically, the fighting was indecisive, but d'Orvilliers held fast against the Royal Navy, restoring French naval pride and enabling d'Estaing to sail on unimpeded to North America.

The first year of war proved disappointing, although d'Estaing defeated the British at Grenada, in the West Indies, and seized several British islands as guarantees for the future peace settlement. Along the North American shoreline, he failed to regain Savannah, but he obliged the British to evacuate Philadelphia and later Newport.

As France negotiated an alliance with Spain, its strategy shifted toward a direct approach. Spain's price for the alliance was high: it demanded French support for operations to recover Gibraltar, Minorca, and Florida, and above all support for a direct attack against Britain. The initial objective was a French landing on the Isle of Wight, near the main British naval base at Portsmouth. The plan called for a combined French and Spanish fleet of thirty vessels to move into the Channel, establish naval supremacy, and protect a cross-Channel landing. But that great design failed: the Spaniards were late and lacked naval experience, and joint operations in the Channel proved difficult to coordinate. Politicians and diplomats further complicated the plan by changing the objective to a landing near Plymouth in Cornwall. Precious time was lost, and disease laid waste to French crews, leaving the Brest fleet unable to take the offensive.

The indirect strategy was revived in 1780. The Spanish needed the French navy to escort a massive Spanish convoy to Puerto Rico. Admiral Guichen led this effort in the spring. A second convoy, with far-reaching consequences, succeeded, too: in May 1780, the chevalier de Ternay escorted a fleet of transports to North America, carrying five thousand French troops under the comte de Rochambeau, an experienced officer.

Nevertheless, 1780 was a difficult year for France. With no victory in sight, some people argued in favor of compromise with Britain. In October, financial difficulties provoked the fall of Sartine as naval minister. He was replaced by the marquis de Castries, a protégé of Queen Marie Antoinette. Not a naval officer but a general in the army with a strong service record during the Seven Years' War, Castries proved to be an energetic and determined leader.

V. Zveg (Vladimir Zvegintzov), *Second Battle of the Virginia Capes* (also known as *The Battle of the Chesapeake*), 1962. Oil on canvas. (Naval History and Heritage Command, NH 73927-KN)

He understood that victory was possible only if local commanders were allowed to act on their own initiative, without waiting for instructions from Versailles.

This victory was also the result of the political orders given to de Grasse before his departure, compelling him to cooperate with the Spanish in the Caribbean. When the Spanish allowed him to sail to North America, far away from hurricanes, he headed to the Virginia coast, with his vessels carrying troops from the West Indies, to surprise his enemies. He succeeded in mooring inside Chesapeake Bay, where he had to blockade Yorktown and land troops as well as some of his ships' guns and crews. Thus he had to fight Admirals Samuel Graves and Samuel Hood under unfavorable conditions when they tried to enter the bay on September 5, 1781. A fateful defeat seemed likely. But thanks to the ebbing tide and the ability of his captains, who got under way rapidly, without regard to any previous order of battle, de Grasse surprised the British. Twice he anticipated shifts of the afternoon winds more accurately than Graves did and was thus able to use his guns more efficiently than the British forces could. Despite some confusion, this was the finest hour for the French captains.

Tactically rather indecisive, the battle ended before nightfall and, surprisingly, never resumed; rather than reengage, the British headed back to New York. Meanwhile Barras's squadron arrived from Newport with all that was necessary to besiege Yorktown. The battle of the Virginia Capes left George Washington, Lafayette, and Rochambeau free to besiege the English stronghold and compel its garrison to surrender on October 19. The Royal Navy returned to the Capes too late to relieve the garrison, and British hopes of victory in America vanished. Very few battles at sea have had such far-reaching and lasting results: de Grasse's victory led to American independence.

Too Long, Too Far?

The French navy acted everywhere in the world, scattering British naval forces with relatively poor political guidance but highly capable sailors and ships. Nevertheless, the effort stretched the navy to its limits. The defeat of de Grasse and his fleet at the Battle of the Saintes on April 12, 1782, when five ships of the line were lost and de Grasse himself taken prisoner, reminds us that the French fleet consisted of ships that had been at sea for years and were badly in need of repair and short of supplies and naval stores, which had to be shipped from France. The lack of a real naval base in the French West Indies forced France to depend on its Spanish and Dutch allies for supplies. Yet the French fleet remained in the Caribbean; the British victory at the Saintes saved Jamaica from invasion but did not reverse the French and American victories at Virginia and Yorktown. Admiral Louis-Philippe de Rigaud, marquis de Vaudreuil, de Grasse's former deputy, assumed command of the French fleet and sailed to New England to repair the worst-damaged ships before returning to the West Indies, where a new attack against Jamaica was planned, although it was canceled with the end of the war. He went back to Brest only in June 1783.

At that time, the French commander of the East India squadron, Admiral de Suffren, was still waging a fierce war against the Royal Navy, at the end of the sea lanes and without supplies. Fortunately he could rely on Dutch support from Ceylon (modern Sri Lanka), and he could winter near Aceh, in Indonesia. Although he did not succeed in routing the British from the coast of India, he gave them a very hard time and gained his enemies' esteem.

A worldwide naval deployment remained an exhausting feat, especially with a lack of support bases overseas, which made it vital for the French to secure the maritime routes between France and America. Yet it succeeded, reviving the prestige of France and its navy and securing the independence of the United States. Naval debts rose to an unprecedented level, almost 200 million livres by the end of the war. After the Treaty of Paris in 1783, the question was open: should France continue to prepare for a decisive war against Britain or end the arms race through a compromise with the former enemy? Indecisiveness over this question was one of the main political and financial reasons for the French monarchy's insolvency, which in turn opened the door for the French Revolution.

PIERRE-AUGUSTIN CARON DE BEAUMARCHAIS

Pierre-Augustin Caron de Beaumarchais (1732–99), a French watchmaker and playwright, met Richard Penn, then lieutenant-governor of Pennsylvania, in London in 1775. Beaumarchais—who had a third career as an agent of the Secret du Roi, France's royal secret service—was in the British capital to conclude a clandestine arrangement intended to prevent a serious diplomatic embarrassment for the king of France. Penn was in London to offer the Olive Branch Petition, from the colonies' Second Continental Congress, to King George III, which asked him to avoid further conflict with his American subjects.

Penn's petition was unsuccessful, but in it Beaumarchais saw the opportunity to secretly provide munitions to the American insurgents while also making himself a handsome profit. Beaumarchais's idea won the support of the French and Spanish crowns, and in the summer of 1776, he embarked on yet a fourth career, that of arms merchant. With startup funds from the two monarchies equivalent to a billion dollars in today's money, Beaumarchais created a shell corporation, giving it the Spanish-sounding name of Roderigue Hortalez et Compagnie to hide from the British the fact that it was, in fact, buying surplus weapons from French armories and selling them to the Americans in exchange for valuable tobacco.

In October 1776, Beaumarchais signed a contract with Silas Deane, the American representative in France, for 1,600 tons of surplus muskets, cannon, and other military supplies to be shipped to the United States. The first ships carrying these goods, *Amphitrite*, *Mercure*, and *Seine*, brought their cargoes to New England in the spring of 1777, just in time to supply underarmed American troops fighting a desperate rearguard action against General John Burgoyne. The two armies clashed at the Battle of Saratoga in September and October 1777, and the Americans won in large part because they finally could outgun the British. Caleb Stark, one of the militia at Saratoga, stated, "Unless these [Beaumarchais] arms had been thus timely furnished to the Americans, Burgoyne would have made an easy march to Albany" (quoted in Ferreiro 2016: 73). The Battle of Saratoga proved to be a turning point in the war: it forced the British to revise their strategy, and it provided the French the pretext they needed to enter the war on the side of the Americans.

Beaumarchais sent not only supplies but also vital personnel to help the American cause. French artillery officers, infantry officers, and engineers accompanied these arms shipments, among them Louis Duportail, Johann de Kalb, and Baron Friedrich Wilhelm von Steuben, all of whom proved crucial in creating a professional Continental army that could stand toe to toe against the British. Beaumarchais even fronted some money for the marquis de Lafayette to come to America. In all, the watchmaker, playwright, spy, and arms merchant provided the Americans with hundreds of shiploads of supplies, with a modern value of over three billion dollars. He was never paid back, dying almost bankrupt in 1799. In 1837, his heirs were finally repaid by the U.S. government, but they received only half of what was owed.

....

Pierre-Augustin Caron de Beaumarchais, ca. 1755,
after Jean-Marc Nattier. Oil on canvas.
(© P. Lorette, coll. Comédie-Française)

SPANISH NAVAL OPERATIONS

Agustín Guimerá Ravina and José María Blanco Núñez

Although Spain never officially allied with the United States, its entry into the Revolutionary War alongside France turned a regional North American conflict into a global war and forced Britain to divert its vaunted Royal Navy to defend its other interests around the world. — *Editors*

When the thirteen American colonies rebelled against Great Britain, the Spanish monarchy saw an opportunity to diminish Britain's presence in the Caribbean as well as in the Gulf of Mexico, Florida, and the Bahamas. In Europe, Spain sought to recover the stronghold of Gibraltar and also Mahón, on the Mediterranean island of Minorca, which had been controlled by the British since the beginning of the eighteenth century.

The European Theater of Operations

We address here three lesser-known strategic campaigns that were carried out by combined French-Spanish fleets beleaguering the English Channel in support of an invasion of Britain, similar to the attack that King Philip II of Spain had attempted in the sixteenth century. These campaigns succeeded in diverting many of the British naval forces dispatched to America. We also cover Spain's successes and failures in the fight to control the seas and to protect trade routes, and briefly describe the siege of Gibraltar and the capture of Mahón, in which amphibious operations by the combined fleet played an important role.

Spain and France together planned an invasion of England for the summer of 1779. In accordance with the strategic principle of concentrating forces, the plan stipulated how the command of the combined fleet was to be

Translated by Mary Deirdre Casey

organized, the rendezvous point for the allied squadrons that would make up the fleet, and their order of battle. The French landing force—forty thousand strong—would be transported in four hundred merchant vessels and would disembark on the Isle of Wight in order to take the nearby town of Portsmouth, on the southern British coast, and its dockyard, Britain's most important naval base.

First Campaign of the English Channel, 1779

Once coordination with the Spanish fleet was assured, the French admiral, Louis Guillouet, comte d'Orvilliers, set sail from Brest, on the northwest tip of France, on June 3 with twenty-eight ships of the line (large warships), two frigates, ten smaller craft, and a large military force. Spain officially declared war against Great Britain on June 22. The following day, Vice Admiral Luis de Córdova set sail from Cádiz with a fleet of thirty-two ships of the line, nine frigates, one corvette, and 21,754 troops. Córdova was able to put to sea quickly, despite the common French criticism that the Spanish navy was slow. Vice Admiral Antonio de Arce's fleet, based in Ferrol, Galicia, had already set out. The French fleet was soon struck by dysentery, spread by conscripted sailors from the French mainland, which would soon affect the entire naval operation. On June 23, the three fleets made their rendezvous, creating one of the largest combined fleets in history: sixty-six ships of the line (along with many minor vessels), arranged into five groups.

Composition of the Combined Fleet

First Campaign of the English Channel, 1779

FLEET	COMMANDER	NUMBER OF SHIPS
Reconnaissance	Louis-René Madelaine Le Vassor, comte de LaTouche-Tréville (France)	5
Vanguard	Luc Urbain de Bouëxic, comte de Guichen (France)	15
Center	Louis Guillouet, comte d'Orvilliers (France)	15
Rearguard	Miguel Gastón (Spain)	15
Observation	Luis de Córdova (Spain)	16
Total number of ships		66

On August 14, the combined fleet reached Plymouth, in Cornwall. In Plymouth Sound were seventeen British ships of the line, which did not come out into the English Channel. Things started auspiciously for the combined fleet: panic spread on land, and the City of London closed its doors, but strong thunderstorms obliged the allied ships to modify their rigging, and most of the fleet's crews suffered considerable illness. Cherbourg's military governor and the commander of the port, Charles-François Dumouriez, grew impatient. He had proposed taking the Isle of Wight in order to deprive English shipyards of lumber and to gain an advantageous position for attacking England and taking the Portsmouth dockyard, with its ample stores. But on August 22, the French minister of the navy, Antoine Raymond Jean Gualbert Gabriel de Sartine, ordered the expedition to be redirected toward the Cornwall coast to land at Falmouth, where the expedition would winter and march on London the following year. Strategically and tactically, this decision was sheer lunacy, and it was harshly criticized by Dumouriez.

Following Sartine's new orders, d'Orvilliers held a council of war for the combined fleet, which decided to make for the Scilly Isles in search of the British home fleet. This was a wise strategic decision, but d'Orvilliers would undercut it by launching on a secondary objective. The British home fleet—commanded by Admiral Sir Charles Hardy and composed of thirty-six ships of the line, eight frigates, and some smaller boats—was sighted sailing rapidly through the English Channel, and the order was issued to give chase. The pursuit was maintained for twenty-four hours. The vanguard of the combined fleet managed to open fire, but then from the rearguard came word of a convoy sighted to leeward, and d'Orvilliers made a fatal mistake: he failed to properly identify the convoy and assumed that it was made up of merchant ships from the Indies expected by British traders. D'Orvilliers ordered his fleet to come about and attack the convoy, abandoning its first target, the home fleet. The convoy turned out to be Dutch, a neutral power, and while the combined fleet was occupied with this convoy, the British fleet was allowed to proceed undisturbed.

A demoralized d'Orvilliers made for Brest, entering the port on September 13 with only a captured sixty-four-gun British ship of the line to show for his efforts. At the end of the campaign, there were fifteen thousand sick among the French, compared with only three thousand on the Spanish ships. Under fire from the king of France for having abandoned Plymouth, d'Orvilliers resigned and was replaced by Louis Charles de Besné, comte du Chaffault. The latter decided to leave Spanish Vice Admiral Gastón in Brest with twenty Spanish ships.

This campaign succeeded only in immobilizing the home fleet. Nevertheless, this achievement gave some respite to the French squadrons in the American theater and to the American rebels, allowing their trade to recover. It also gave the Spanish forces besieging Gibraltar some breathing space while deepening the distress of the beleagured British garrison there.

Loss of the Caracas Guipuzcoana Company Convoy and the Battle of Cape Santa María, 1780

Once the combined fleet had disbanded, the Spanish implemented their plan to block British reinforcements from reaching Gibraltar. Rear Admiral Juan de Lángara was given command of ten ships of the line and the mission of maintaining a close blockade of Gibraltar by cruising between Spartel on the Moroccan coast and the cape of Trafalgar on the Spanish. Córdova set sail from Brest at the beginning of November 1779, just as troubling news began to arrive about Britain preparing a large convoy to deliver supplies to Gibraltar. He was obliged to leave four ships of the line in the Ferrol dockyard for repairs, and instead of quickly entering the Cádiz shipyard, he waited in the Gulf of Cádiz for Lángara's fleet, which had been blown into the Mediterranean by a storm. Córdova remained at sea until Christmas, but exceedingly bad weather forced him to take shelter in Cádiz, leaving three ships of the line at sea to keep watch over the access to the Mediterranean.

Lángara had his ships repaired in Cartagena and passed through the Strait of Gibraltar again on January 2, 1780, where Córdova's three ships of the line joined him. However, in the darkness accompanying a gathering storm, Lángara was unable to determine the position of his squadron. Guessing himself to be south of Cádiz, on January 16 he came across the fleet of British Admiral George B. Rodney, whose twenty-two ships of the line and ten frigates were providing safe conduct to a convoy of two hundred merchant vessels that were to supply Gibraltar and then go on to India. This fleet had set sail from Great Britain on December 27, 1779, and while in Portuguese waters had by chance encountered a Spanish convoy made up of fifteen merchant ships belonging to the Caracas Guipuzcoana Company, escorted by a sixty-four-gun ship of the line. Rodney captured the entire convoy, completely upending trade in San Sebastián in northern Spain, the headquarters of the company.

When Lángara encountered Rodney off Cape Santa María, south of Faro, Portugal, he ordered a hasty retreat to Cádiz. Lángara remained heroically in the rear guard in order to save the faster ships by distracting the English with his old flagship and the slower vessels. Though he was injured and his crews sustained many casualties, he kept up the defense until ten o'clock that night, when he finally struck his colors. In addition to his own ship, six others were captured. Taking advantage of the storm that moved in early the following morning, two captured ships managed to escape and reach Cádiz. In the end, Lángara lost five ships.

Rodney reached Gibraltar on January 18, delivering copious supplies as well as the prize ships, which kept the British garrison provisioned for another year. On February 13, upon the return of the convoy he had sent to Mahón, he set out into the Atlantic once again, this time heading toward the Antilles. Strategically, Rodney had successfully engaged eleven of the sixty-six operational ships of the line belonging to France and Spain, which highlights the organizational difficulties the combined fleet had to deal with in the Atlantic theater.

Tactically, Lángara's performance left much to be desired. He did not undertake the necessary reconnaissance, despite having two frigates at his disposal. He was still signaling to his commanders to decide what to do after the action had already begun, causing more confusion. Because of a hastily ordered retreat, several of his ships entered the Cádiz harbor without having fired a single cannon. And he made no attempt to maneuver his squadron into a formation that would have made Rodney pay more dearly for his victory.

The Continuation of the 1780 Campaign

This loss made the Spanish government still more intent on conquering Gibraltar, which was probably a secondary objective originally. If the British fleet had remained the principal target and been partly destroyed, the defeat at Cape Santa María would not have been repeated. The campaigns of the following two summers in the English Channel could have been totally offensive, and a decisive battle could have been sought.

France was in favor of organizing a second combined fleet and returning to the English Channel, but Spain rejected this proposal. While the Spanish were willing to coordinate to some extent with France, in large part they acted independently and kept their focus mainly on Gibraltar. The Spanish government ordered Gastón to return to Cádiz. He set sail from Brest on January 12, escorted by four French ships of the line under Lieutenant General Antoine Hilarion de Beausset; later five more French ships of the line would join his fleet.

The allies prepared for a strategic dispersal. In Brest, a fleet under Admiral Luc Urban de Bouëxic, the comte de Guichen, was being readied to sail for America, while in Cádiz, Vice Admiral José de Solano y Bote was organizing his expedition to support Spain's possessions in the Caribbean. After Gastón and Beausset reached Cádiz at the beginning of February, Córdova had fifty-one ships with which to engage Rodney's fleet, but the Spanish government decided to give twelve ships to Solano's expedition, ordering Córdova to maintain the close blockade of Gibraltar with the remaining thirty-nine ships.

Back in September 1779, the British had sought to open secret peace negotiations with Spain, offering to return Gibraltar in exchange for the artillery installed in the stronghold and a guarantee of Spanish neutrality in the American Revolution. In addition, if Spain joined the British in their fight against the thirteen colonies, Britain promised to cede Florida and to restore Spain's fishing rights off Newfoundland. Britain also attempted to trade Gibraltar for Puerto Rico, but the Spanish king rejected the proposal. These British overtures induced France to cooperate more closely with Spain in its push to recapture strongholds and possessions in Europe and America.

The Capture of the British Convoy by Córdova's Fleet, 1780

Córdova now made the shrewd decision to appoint Vice Admiral José de Mazarredo Salazar as his fleet's major general—that is, as his chief of staff—to replace Gastón. Mazarredo began by training the crews and continually dispatched squadrons of ships of the line and smaller craft to patrol the Gulf of Cádiz and the Strait of Gibraltar, a duty that occasionally included shelling Gibraltar.

In 1780, Córdova left Cádiz with his fleet three times. The second time, on July 31, he set sail with thirty ships of the line (twenty-four Spanish and six French) to cruise the waters off Cape St. Vincent, at the southwest tip of the Iberian Peninsula, and block Sir Francis Geary's British fleet, comprising twenty-two ships of the line. Córdova's orders prevented him from passing south of the latitude of Cape St. Vincent, but while he was at sea, he received a message that two rich British convoys had set forth together, one bound for the Caribbean and the other for India, which would separate after reaching the Azores (a case in which Spanish espionage worked perfectly). Consequently, Córdova prolonged his cruising mission in order to be positioned east of Madeira on August 8. From this position, on the advice of Mazarredo, Córdova maneuvered to cut off the usual routes to America. On August 9, the British convoy en route to India, escorted by a ship of the line and two frigates, appeared with fifty-six merchant vessels. Fifty-five of them fell to the Spaniards, who conducted them to Cádiz. The British ship of the line and the two frigates escaped because of the speed advantage offered by their copper-sheathed hulls, a recent technical innovation. The Spaniards had won a booty of 2,943 prisoners, eighty thousand muskets, uniforms for twelve British regiments, and all kinds of supplies and provisions. Its value was estimated at one million pesos, or £1.6 million sterling.

Artist unknown, *Portrait of Luis de Córdova y Córdova, Lieutenant General of the Spanish Royal Navy*, eighteenth century. Oil. (Courtesy Ministerio de Defensa, Spain, Archivo del Museo Naval, MNM0434)

Jean-François-Marie Bellier, *Portrait of José de Mazarredo Salazar*, 1800. Oil on canvas. Mazarredo was lieutenant general of the Spanish Royal Navy and Luis de Córdova's chief of staff, assisting him in the capture of the British convoy in 1780. (Courtesy Ministerio de Defensa, Spain, Archivo del Museo Naval, MNM00351)

Artist unknown, *View and Perspective of Fort San Felipe, Mahón, Minorca*, 1782. Engraving. Prior to their futile attempt to recapture Gibraltar from the British, the Spanish succeeded in capturing Minorca in 1782. (Courtesy Ministerio de Defensa, Spain, Archivo del Museo Naval, MNM08804)

The Second Campaign of the English Channel, 1781

In the summer of 1781, the Spanish government secretly sent a convoy from Cádiz to Minorca with eight thousand Spanish troops under the command of Louis des Balbes de Berton de Crillon, duc de Mahón. It was guarded by two ships of the line, five frigates, six *xebecs* (minor vessels navigating with sails and oars), and seven smaller craft under Rear Admiral Buenaventura Moreno. They made a successful landing and undertook a long but eventually victorious siege (from August 1781 to February 1782) of St. Philip, the main fort of Mahón, where the British garrison had taken refuge. More than four thousand French soldiers participated in the operation.

In the meantime, after concealing the Minorca expedition's departure from Cádiz, the new combined fleet sailed north to the English Channel. Its objective was to afford the forces landing at Minorca some breathing room. Mazarredo's instructions for this maneuver were sensible and not overconfident, and he looked the Spanish forces' strengths and weaknesses straight in the face: "In attempting this we have our fundamental seafaring inferiority to contend with . . . but on the other hand our superior numbers render an attack imperative, even if it is irregular" (Mazarredo 1781). The fleet made no engagement with the enemy in this campaign, but the allies did endure harsh conditions at sea: while cruising off the Scilly Isles, the combined fleet was caught by a storm but was saved by Mazarredo's excellent judgment.

The Third Campaign of the English Channel and the Battle of Cape Spartel, 1782
On February 2, Rear Admiral Francisco de Borja's fleet set sail from Cádiz, escorting a convoy carrying troops for an attack on Jamaica. In order to conceal the fleet's departure, and perhaps in imitation of the successful concealment of the Minorca expedition the year before, Córdova also set sail from Cádiz, with thirty-six ships of the line and five frigates. Once Borja's convoy had reached the open sea, Córdova's fleet remained cruising at the latitude of Cape St. Vincent. Again thanks to Mazarredo's good judgment, the fleet returned to Cádiz on February 10, just before a fierce storm blew in. On June 25, the combined fleet reassembled, and on that very day it captured eighteen vessels from a British convoy of twenty-seven merchant vessels en route to Newfoundland and Quebec.

On October 20, the combined fleet engaged the British at the Battle of Cape Spartel. A British convoy of 135 merchant ships had set sail from England on September 11, escorted by Admiral Richard Howe's fleet, which was made up of thirty-four ships of the line along with some minor vessels. Thirty-one of the ships, carrying munitions and 1,400 soldiers, were meant to supply Gibraltar. Howe took advantage of a fierce storm that kept the combined fleet (then made up of forty-six ships of the line) harbored at Cádiz. He left part of the convoy at Gibraltar and passed through the strait and into the Mediterranean on October 11. On his return, he was again favored by the wind, which had swept the combined fleet northeast, toward Vélez-Málaga, and Howe was able to get the rest of the convoy into the besieged stronghold and take his fleet into the Atlantic. On October 20, Córdova caught up with Howe off Cape Spartel: the battle lasted only five hours and was fought by only part of each fleet. The British managed to retreat, relying on their superior maneuvering capabilities and their faster copper-hulled ships.

The Disaster at Gibraltar, 1782
In 1782, Gibraltar seemed to Spain to be low-hanging fruit that it could easily pluck from Britain. Surrounded by Spanish territory on one side and ocean on three sides, the British inhabitants of Gibraltar were enduring hunger, epidemics, and fear of shelling. However, launching a decisive attack on Gibraltar proved more difficult than the Spaniards expected. The relationship between

the combined command in the theater of operations and in the adjacent Bay of Algeciras was not exactly harmonious. New kinds of weapons had entered the picture, too, such as the gunboats invented by Vice Admiral Antonio Barceló, which played an important role in the siege and were consequently used in the defense of Spanish and French ports during the wars of 1793 to 1814.

Another innovation was the ten floating batteries designed by the French general Jean Le Michaud d'Arçon. Meant to be "unsinkable and fire-proof," in his words, they were used in the attack on Gibraltar starting on September 13, 1782, following intense artillery strikes launched from the Campo de Gibraltar (on Spanish territory) and from the sea by the gunboats. But the British, using incendiary bombs—known as red cannonballs—managed to destroy d'Arçon's poorly constructed and ineffectively positioned batteries. Córdova's ships did not support the action, and the frigates were employed in retrieving survivors. The attack was a complete debacle that put an end to Spain's ambitions to recover Gibraltar.

Strategically speaking, the combined fleet did prove to be successful in the European theater of operations when it concentrated on its first objective: destroying the British fleet and British trade. However, the pursuit of secondary objectives such as Gibraltar proved damaging. By threatening the English Channel and feigning an invasion of England, the combined fleet tried to relieve its forces in other theaters of operation and to improve maritime trade and communications. Spain's defeat at Cape Santa María was made up for by the capture of two British convoys and the taking of Mahón, but its most painful defeat was the failure to take Gibraltar.

The American Theater of Operations

Even before it entered the war in 1779, the government of Spain had begun sending substantial sums of money to the rebels in North America through intermediaries. For his part, the governor of Spanish Louisiana, Field Marshal Bernardo de Gálvez, blockaded the lower Mississippi, allowing only American traffic to pass through. During that period of professed neutrality, Gálvez sent the rebels weapons, ammunition, blankets, and medicine.

When Spain declared war on Great Britain on June 22, 1779, it was pursuing the same strategic objectives in America as in Europe. The reconquest of Florida, which Spain had lost to Britain in 1763, was a top priority. British control of Florida, as well as the Bahamas, posed a direct threat to Spanish shipping and trade in the Gulf of Mexico, Havana, and the strait of Florida, which is both the natural gateway from the Caribbean to Europe and a strategic bottleneck. The Spanish monarchy also sought to revoke from the British the privilege of logwood exploitation in Central America and to expel the British from their commercial establishments in Campeche (modern Belize, Honduras, and Nicaragua). Last, if Spain managed to capture Jamaica, it would put an end to British naval and commercial interference in the Spanish Caribbean, which dated back to 1655.

By 1779, the strategic center of the war between the European powers already had moved from North America to the Caribbean and the Gulf of Mexico. The wide-ranging confrontation in the Americas, taking place far from the home countries, depended entirely on supplies delivered by sea and on amphibious operations to capture islands and strongholds.

Now Spain and France were threatening British possessions in the region, and the Spanish monarchy had committed itself to forcing the British into a defensive position. Taking those possessions and the resulting booty would provide compensation for the costs of the war and could also boost the prestige of the Spanish monarchy and provide a bargaining chip in future peace negotiations. Ultimately, Britain's shift from offense against the Americans to defense of its territories in North America against the Spanish and French was a major factor in the American victory.

The Guichen and Solano Convoys, 1780

In 1780, Spain decided to start joint preparations with France for the conquest of Jamaica, while their respective navies collaborated in other military operations in the Gulf of Mexico. Two allied convoys sailed from Europe for the Caribbean that year. A convoy of sixteen ships of the line and transport vessels, under the command of the French admiral Guichen, set sail from Brest and arrived in Martinique on March 23. A Spanish convoy under the command of José de Solano, comprising twelve ships of the line, 154 merchant vessels, and 12,500 troops, departed Cádiz on April 28. The allies scored a successful strategic victory in this episode: George Rodney's British fleet, with seventeen ships of the line, was lying in wait for Solano between Barbados and Martinique, but Solano changed course during the night and headed for a rendezvous with Guichen—whom he had sighted previously—between the islands of Dominica and Marie-Galante. The two allies met in the agreed-upon place and anchored together in Fort Royal, Martinique, on June 9. Given their superior numbers, Rodney did not challenge them. A part of Solano's convoy had arrived without incident in Havana before Solano and Guichen rendezvoused off the northern coast of Dominica. Guichen's ships escorted the rest of Solano's fleet to Santo Domingo, and it later made its way to Havana.

The Conquest of Mobile and Pensacola, 1780–1781

In the meantime, Bernardo de Gálvez had gone on the offensive in New Orleans. In less than a month, between August 27 and September 21, 1779, and with only a thousand men and scant artillery, he had taken the strongholds of Manchac, Baton Rouge, and Natchez, as well as the Amite River and Thompson Creek, removing the British threat from the lower Mississippi basin. Soon thereafter he launched the invasion of Mobile, which, together with Pensacola, represented the key to the Gulf of Mexico and British-held West Florida. Participating in this campaign were 3,348 soldiers, three ships of the line, four frigates, and twenty-two transport vessels. The fort at Mobile, which consisted solely of a garrison with three hundred men, surrendered on March 13, 1780.

Taking Pensacola, however, would be much more challenging for Gálvez. Following a disastrous scattering of his expedition by a hurricane on October 18, 1780, he once again set sail from Havana for Pensacola on

E. Carceller, *Portrait of José de Ezpeleta y Galdeano*, 1879 (copy of eighteenth-century original). Oil. Ezpeleta was governor of Mobile and collaborated with Bernardo de Gálvez in the conquest of Pensacola. (Courtesy Institute of Military History and Culture, Madrid, and Museum of the Artillery Academy, Segovia)

Artist unknown, *Portrait of José Solano y Bote*, late eighteenth century, oil. Solano was the first marquis of Socorro and captain general of the Spanish Royal Navy. He aided Bernardo de Gálvez in the siege of Pensacola. (Courtesy Ministerio de Defensa, Spain, Archivo del Museo Naval, MNM00437)

February 28, 1781. His war fleet was composed of a ship of the line, three frigates, and two minor vessels. The convoy was made up of eighteen transport vessels and two gunboats. A French unit, with one ship of the line and one frigate, was to join them. The troops in the expedition numbered only 1,543, a very small force considering the objective, although they were to be joined by a party of Choctaw allies. The British had a total of 2,679 troops garrisoned in Pensacola, including soldiers, sailors, free black volunteers, civilians, and Native American allies.

During the campaign, Gálvez was greatly assisted by Colonel José de Ezpeleta y Galdeano (then governor of Mobile), Field Marshal Juan Manuel de Cagigal, the royal commissioner Francisco de Saavedra, and Vice Admiral Solano himself. Between the landing on March 9, 1781, and Pensacola's surrender on May 9, the Spanish attack faced numerous difficulties, including its remoteness from the main operational base at Havana; the fact that the Florida coast has large sandbars and is vulnerable to storms; the enemy's wooden Red Cliffs fort, which controlled the mouth of Pensacola Bay; three other well-armed wooden forts that overlooked Pensacola; and thick forests, which the

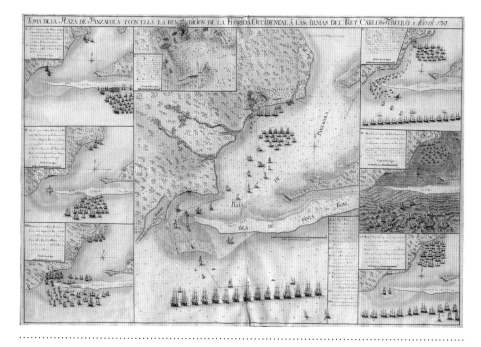

Plan of the Capture of Pensacola and with It the Surrender of Western Florida to the Army of King Charles III. Year of 1781. On this map are shown, from left to right, the different phases of Spain's conquest from March 9 to May 9. (Courtesy Ministerio de Defensa, Spain, Archivo del Museo Naval, 6-A-20)

British and their Native American allies used to great effect in guerrilla warfare. The arrival of Spanish reinforcements from New Orleans, Mobile, and Havana finally settled the issue: on April 18, Solano's fleet—carrying troops and composed of fifteen ships of the line, four frigates, and other, smaller vessels—arrived in Pensacola along with a French division of four ships, two frigates, and various smaller craft. Now the attacking force comprised 7,677 troops and had clear numerical superiority over the enemy.

On May 8, the powder magazine and munitions at Queen Anne's Redoubt, near Pensacola, exploded. The Spanish took advantage of the event and quickly captured the British position. The other two forts could no longer hold, and the following day the capitulation agreement was signed. The Spanish won a large booty of artillery, ammunition, and provisions. With the capture of Pensacola, Spain now controlled West Florida.

Central American Campaigns, 1779–1782

Central America also saw its share of Spanish victories, particularly under the leadership of Matías de Gálvez, captain general of Guatemala and the father of Bernardo de Gálvez, whose campaigns secured Spanish control of Central America between 1779 and 1782. Although his meagerly provisioned troops, both regulars and militia, faced tremendous obstacles in this immense territory, including mountains, rivers, jungles, swamps, and an unhealthy climate, they captured Fort George, Belize, and recaptured the fortress of Omoa, on the coast of Honduras, in 1779. Between 1780 and 1782, they destroyed the British establishments on the Mosquito Coast in Honduras, and they pursued Britain's Native American allies—the Miskito and Miskito Sambu—into the mountains. They also eliminated an enemy enclave in Costa Rica.

In April 1780, the British captured Fort Concepción, on the San Juan River in Nicaragua. This waterway gave access to Lake Nicaragua and to Granada, the former capital of the province, and Britain sought to take control of the area in order to reach the Pacific. Among the British expedition was a young naval officer named Horatio Nelson. However, Matías de Gálvez, after successfully defending the entrance to the lake from the San Juan River, managed to retake the fort in January 1781.

Another of Matías de Gálvez's operations was the capture of the island of Roatán in 1782. The island is located some forty miles off the Caribbean coast of Honduras, and its only stronghold was Port Royal, a hub for corsairs and smugglers. Its defenses included several forts and batteries manned by seven hundred soldiers, Native Americans, and African slaves. Matías de Gálvez sailed from Omoa on March 14 with three frigates, several smaller vessels, transports, and 1,600 soldiers. Port Royal capitulated on March 17.

The Bahamas and Jamaica, 1782

On May 6, 1782, the newly promoted Lieutenant General Juan Manuel de Cagigal attacked Nassau, the capital of the British-held Bahamas on the island of New Providence, with a convoy of fifty-seven transport vessels and 2,500 soldiers. The expedition was escorted by nine American vessels armed for corsair activity—meaning the capture of enemy merchant vessels and warships—and was under the command of Alexander Gillon, commodore of the South

Carolina navy, who knew the islands well. He launched the surprise attack from an unexpected direction: the channel northwest of New Providence. The British garrison of 612 men capitulated on May 8. The booty—artillery, armed ships, and merchant ships—was considerable. This action contributed to Spain's obtaining East Florida as part of the final peace treaty.

The final objective of the combined Spanish-French operation in the Caribbean was to capture Jamaica. Between January and March 1782, in Cap-François, Saint-Domingue (modern Haiti), Spain had been assembling a powerful naval and military force comprising warships, transports, and thousands of soldiers. The fleet of the French Admiral François-Joseph-Paul de Grasse, which sailed for Saint-Domingue from Martinique on April 8 with thirty-three ships of the line and 150 merchant vessels, was the second component of this expedition. But the French defeat in the Battle of the Saintes at the hands of Rodney's British fleet on April 12 paralyzed this ambitious plan, and the preliminary peace talks, which began in January 1783, put an end to the allies' ambitions to capture Jamaica.

Epilogue

In spite of the strategic errors mentioned above, the Treaty of Versailles, signed on September 3, 1783, was on balance favorable to the Spanish crown. Spain did not succeed in recovering Gibraltar and Jamaica, but the Spanish monarchy's sovereignty in Minorca, Florida, Campeche, and Honduras was secured, though it did have to make concessions to British trading interests in Belize. Also as a result of this treaty, the Spanish empire's continental territories in the Americas reached their maximum extent: more than six million square miles, stretching from San Francisco Bay to Tierra del Fuego.

Uniforms, Supplies, and Money from Spain

José M. Guerrero Acosta

> Critical Spanish assistance provided to the Americans during their Revolution included not only funding but also armaments, uniforms, blankets, and other supplies. — *Editors*

Most histories that discuss Spanish material aid to the Americans during the Revolutionary War have focused on the efforts of Bernardo de Gálvez, the governor of Spanish Louisiana, to supply arms and munitions to American troops fighting in the western theater, primarily along the Mississippi and Ohio rivers. For example, in October 1778, Gálvez provided three thousand barrels of gunpowder and other equipment to Oliver Pollock, the United States' representative in New Orleans, who sent them up the Mississippi River to Illinois troops under Lieutenant Colonel George Rogers Clark.

In fact, Spain's assistance to the Americans went far beyond the supplies sent up the Mississippi River. Much of Spanish aid was instead directed to the Continental troops who were fighting battles along the East Coast and doing so without adequate clothing or equipment. Most notably, from autumn 1777 until spring 1778, the Continental Army was encamped at Valley Forge, Pennsylvania. During those six months, the encampment was America's fourth-largest population center, with close to twelve thousand occupants, yet the army was almost completely without uniforms and equipment because American manufacturers could not begin to provide enough clothing. Instead, many of those supplies came from Spain.

Spanish *real* ("eight") coin, 1762. Silver. In its day this coin was worth about $24 in modern currency. Spain provided critical financial support, which included many such coins, to the American colonies during the Revolution. (National Museum of American History, NMAH 1992.0121.0021)

Translated by Larrie D. Ferreiro

Mary Daly, "Britannia's Ruin," 1779. Cartoon. This caricature shows Britannia lamenting that she has been "sold" by an American and "purchased" by France and Spain. The four men standing before her are (left to right) an American, a Frenchman, a Spaniard, and a Dutchman. (Library of Congress, Prints and Photographs Division, LC-DIG-ppmsca-10737)

Arthur Lee, the first representative of the Continental Congress in Spain, had foreseen the need for clothes and uniforms a year earlier and solicited these supplies from the merchant Diego de Gardoqui, whom King Charles III charged with managing this aid. After discussions in March 1777 in the city of Vitoria, Gardoqui began shipping blue and white cloth, metal buttons, thousands of blankets, and twenty-four thousand muskets to the Americans. Several months later, in November 1777, the Congress sent further urgent requests to its representatives in France and Spain for blankets and clothing.

Between July and December 1778, various ships departed Bilbao, Spain, for ports in New England, carrying a total of thirty thousand blankets as well as shoes, cloth, and uniforms. In September, more uniforms were shipped from France. But British blockades and the problems of shipping during wartime delayed the arrival of these supplies for many months. When they finally arrived in Boston and Portsmouth, New Hampshire, they were shipped by wagon to depots in Springfield, Worcester, and Hartford in Massachusetts. However, many other problems had to be overcome—including theft, apathy, and lack of coordination—before new uniforms reached the soldiers at Valley Forge and helped alleviate the harsh conditions there. (In May 1779, the Continental Army established that its uniforms would be blue with diverse trims of red, green, beige, or white according to the regiment. These were the colors used by the Spanish militias in America and in the cloth Spain delivered to the Continental Army.)

In July 1780, a French fleet carrying Jean-Baptiste Donatien de Vimeur, comte de Rochambeau, commander in chief of the French Expeditionary Force, landed in Newport, Rhode Island, to aid the Americans; the ships, however, brought along only a few of the new uniforms that the French had promised to the Americans. Several months later, in December 1780, the Spanish crown offered a new shipment to John Jay, the second Continental Congress representative in Spain. It consisted of six thousand complete British uniforms captured during a combined Spanish-French naval victory on August 9, 1780, under the command of Captain José Calvo de Irazabal, over a large British convoy off the coast of Portugal. Jay also received, via Gardoqui, a large sum of cash to pay for these uniforms, which consisted of red coats, shirts, shoes, hats, belts, and so forth. Jay's representative in Cádiz, the American merchant Richard Harrison, sent them aboard four vessels.

Two ships arrived on March 12, 1781, in Boston and Salem, another on March 30 in Boston, and the fourth on April 3 at Cape Ann, Massachusetts (or Alexandria, Virginia—sources do not clarify which it was). The unofficial Spanish representative in Philadelphia, Francisco Rendón, confirmed their arrivals in a missive to Madrid on April 27; on April 30, Harrison reassured an anxious George Washington that all the supplies had been sent, adding a list of the garments. In July, yet another Spanish ship arrived with more garments. Yet this would be the last shipment of new uniforms available to the American troops who were then marching toward Yorktown, because in May the merchant ship *Confederacy*, carrying twenty thousand suits to America from France,

had been captured by the British. The new Spanish uniforms were issued to
some of the Virginia troops as well as to the Invalids Corps. (Following the
Battle of Yorktown, the rest of the uniforms were transported in thirty-five carts
to Newburgh, New York, dyed brown, and distributed to four new regiments:
New Hampshire, Connecticut Line, New York, and New Jersey.)

Spanish financial aid also proved crucial to the final American and
French victory. Just weeks before surrounding the army of General Charles
Cornwallis, the French fleet under Admiral François-Joseph-Paul, comte de
Grasse, had brought 1.2 million pesos in silver coin (equivalent to $30 million
today) from Havana to pay wages to American soldiers and to procure supplies. Coming at a precarious time, when American discipline was almost at its
breaking point, the Spanish silver and Spanish uniforms breathed new life
into the American troops as they prepared for the decisive Battle of Yorktown.

PART II
AT THE EDGES

Tipu Sultan, leader of the Kingdom of Mysore from 1782 to 1799, commissioned this large mural to commemorate his victory in the Battle of Pollilur in 1780, Britain's worst defeat in India until that point. (Pictures from History / Bridgeman Images)

BRITISH GLOBAL AMBITIONS AND INDIAN IDENTITY

Richard Sambasivam

> The final battles of the American Revolution were fought not in North America but in India, another theater where Britain and France were vying for political dominance. In both the United States and India, as well as throughout the developing world, legacies of that distant war persist. — *Editors*

The independence of the United States of America is more or less contemporaneous with the loss of freedom by India.
Jawaharlal Nehru, *The Discovery of India*, 1946: 288

When France joined the war for American independence on the rebels' side in 1778, the revolution became a global conflict, one that spread to the Indian subcontinent. The French began contesting the British East India Company's position in India, and soon another enemy took advantage of Britain's defensive position: the Kingdom of Mysore. This South Indian great power challenged the British Empire at a difficult time and ultimately, if temporarily, set back British power in Asia.

The East India Company's failure to achieve victory against Mysore and the British loss in North America reinforced Britain's shift of focus toward what would eventually become the jewel in its imperial crown. This shift is seen most clearly in the career path of British officials: for example, a few years after his defeat at Yorktown, General Charles Cornwallis was installed as the company's governor general. He won a decisive victory against Mysore in 1792 that ensured later British control of the subcontinent.

This global war, coming at a time of instability and holdout resistance to British ascendance in India, had important implications for Indian identity, underscoring and deepening divisions that are still salient in Indian cultural

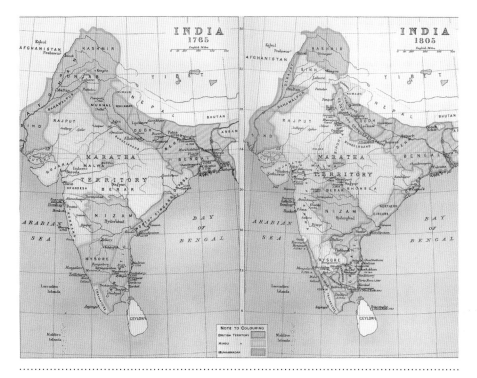

J. G. Bartholomew and Sons, Edinburgh, "Historical Maps of India, 1765 and 1805," 1931. These two maps illustrate the state of flux and competition that characterized the subcontinent in the eighteenth century. Note the growth of British territory, in addition to the change in Mysore's regime to a British-aligned Hindu ruler. (From *Imperial Gazetteer of India*, vol. 26, *Atlas* [Oxford: Oxford University Press, 1908]; map image courtesy Digital South Asia Library, http://dsal.uchicago.edu, University of Chicago)

debates today. As America asserted its new identity, the war raised new questions about the focus of the British Empire and the future of South Asia.

Tumult in India

In the eighteenth century, the Indian subcontinent was already in chaos, and the American Revolution provided the spark for renewed hostilities and for the increase of British dominance. During the millennia of its political history, the area that is today called India (to say nothing of the other countries of South Asia) had rarely been ruled by a single entity: the Mughal Empire, the last power to rule most of the subcontinent, began its decline in the 1700s. The one region that the Muslim Mughals did not control was South India, dominated by the Vijayanagara Empire, which in the sixteenth century itself

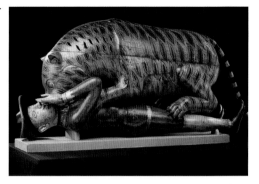

"Tipu's Tiger." Tipu Sultan, eldest son of Hyder Ali, succeeded him as ruler of Mysore. The British discovered this large wooden semiautomaton during their siege of Tipu's palace in 1799. The tiger is posed mauling what appears to be a British soldier, one of his family's worst enemies. Turning a handle caused the soldier's arms to move and the pipe organ in the tiger's side to make a moaning sound. (Victoria and Albert Museum, London, no. 2545[IS])

broke up into smaller kingdoms. The most politically and technologically advanced—and threatening—of these was Mysore.

Modern Mysuru, the kingdom's capital, lies a hundred miles west of modern Bengaluru, in the southwestern Indian state of Karnataka. The Kingdom of Mysore, ruled by a Hindu dynasty called the Wodeyars, became independent in the 1500s and subsequently increased its territory and cemented its power in the region. By the time of the American Revolution, the kingdom covered an area the size of Kansas and was home to six million people. Mysore's power reached its peak when Hyder Ali, a Muslim military commander in the service of the Wodeyars, usurped their power and founded his own ruling sultanate.

Hyder was one of the most challenging opponents the British ever faced, ranking alongside Napoleon, Erwin Rommel, and George Washington. Although illiterate, he was a brilliant tactician and administrator, having risen to the command of the Mysore army under the Wodeyars by defending the kingdom from northern invaders. He and his father pioneered the use of rockets in warfare, which were so devastating to the British that the British themselves later developed the Congreve rocket and used it in the wars against Napoleon and in the War of 1812 (in turn giving rise to the descriptions in "The Star-Spangled Banner," written at the Battle of Baltimore). Hyder also developed Mysore's navy, which offered foreign merchant ships protection against piracy. Though he increased the kingdom's status, his rule was not uncontroversial. Brutal to those who resisted his rule, Hyder ordered civilians mutilated and land laid waste. The English traveler Eliza Fay, imprisoned by Hyder in India after she had escaped trouble in Egypt, called him "a disgrace to human nature" (Fay [1817] 2010: 137).

Charles H. Hubbell, *Rockets at the Battle of Guntur*, 1939. Lithograph. Hyder Ali and Tipu Sultan improved the military use of rockets, including inventing the first iron-cased version. The British, initially rattled by the use of rockets on the battlefield, later adopted the technology themselves and used it against the Americans during the War of 1812. (National Museum of American History, Division of Armed Forces History)

Hyder challenged a number of rivals for regional domination. First he increased his own influence in the court of the Wodeyars, making the rajas mere figureheads. Declaring himself a sultan meant he had to carefully manage relations with the state of Hyderabad, a remnant of the Mughal Empire (and a periodic British ally) that claimed to rule all Muslim territories in the region. Administering the Carnatic region between Mysore and Madras was the nawab of Arcot, Muhammad Ali Khan, who, though nominally under Hyderabad's rule, also wanted to create an Islamic state, and he allied with the British to maintain his own sovereignty. The Maratha Empire, based near modern Mumbai, now controlled the largest area on the subcontinent and competed for more, fighting both Hyder and the British for most of the 1770s. Meanwhile, the raja of Thanjavur, on India's southeast coast, lobbied the British to keep the nawab of Arcot out of his territory. And then, of course, Hyder had to contend with the British, the preeminent European power in the region.

The Advance of Britain's Megacorporation

During the American Revolution, the British Crown did not directly control any territory in India. However, it held a substantial stake in the fortunes of the East India Company. Since its founding in 1600, the company had grown to become the predominant European trading power in Asia, where India and increasingly China were important sources of goods for Britain. Initially founded to explore trade with Southeast Asia, the company benefited from the rise of British naval dominance after the destruction of the Spanish Armada in 1588, a royally granted trading monopoly in Asia, and the development of its own effective fighting force on land and sea. Most important, ultimately, was the company's strategic importance to British power in Asia.

In the seventeenth century, the company established three major footholds — known as presidency towns — on the subcontinent: Bombay (now Mumbai) in the west, Calcutta (Kolkata) in the east, and Madras (Chennai) in the south. As the Mughal Empire crumbled, Delhi, in the north, began to fall under the company's influence too. During the eighteenth century, the company was on a path of rapid expansion with its large presidency armies, which were composed of Indian soldiers called sepoys. In June 1757, during the Seven Years' War, the company (under Robert Clive, whom the historian William Dalrymple called an "unstable sociopath" [Dalrymple 2015] for plundering Indian territory and causing famines) defeated the Mughals and their French allies at the Battle of Plassey, establishing company rule over Bengal and providing the company with substantial tax revenue beyond its normal profits from trade.

As the company advanced politically in India, it gained economic power over Britain and developed into an influential model for the modern multinational corporation, even issuing shares of publicly held stock, which created vested interests for shareholders as well as the state. (The Dutch East India Company became the first publicly listed company in 1602, which helped it to dominate trade in East Indies; the British East India Company followed suit in 1657.) In the late eighteenth century, Britain's economic strategy was still dominated by mercantilism, which emphasized the export of finished goods to the Americas and Asia. In addition, the company imported luxury goods such as silk and tea and strategically important goods such as saltpeter, required for the manufacture of gunpowder.

In addition to trade, the company played an outsized role in public finance. Around the same time that protests against taxation erupted in the American colonies, the tax revenue extracted from Bengal set off enormous debates in Parliament about whether there should be greater oversight of the company, which was not only governing foreign territory but also spreading corruption through the halls of Westminster by sending back newly enriched officials who bribed MPs and even bribed their way into office themselves. The financial burden of the Seven Years' War moved King George III to write that the wealth of India, in addition to taxes extracted from the American colonies, could preserve the "glory of this nation" by offering "the only safe method of extracting this country out of its lamentable situation owing to the load of debt it labors under" (letter to the Duke of Grafton, December 9, 1766, Fortescue 1928: 423–24). In the end, the British government compromised by allowing the company to continue to administer territory in exchange for a large annual payment to the royal treasury.

By now the company had become a firm "too big to fail," one whose misfortunes threatened to sink Britain's economy. In the early 1770s, with £1.5 million in debt and £1 million in unpaid taxes — roughly a tenth of annual British government revenues — the company's stock bubble burst. Defaulting on its obligations would impoverish the government and send shock waves throughout Britain's credit system. Afraid that, in the words of Edmund Burke, the "cursed" company would "be the destruction of the country which fostered it in her bosom," the government agreed to bail it out, loaning it £1 million in 1773 (Burke 1981: 392). Parliament then passed the Tea Act to sell off the company's massive inventory of tea to the irritable American colonists, who dumped more than three hundred chests of it into Boston Harbor to protest the associated taxes, needed to keep Britain financially sound.

The company's troubles were about to become more than financial, however. By this time, Hyder Ali saw the British as the greatest threat to Mysore's security and dominance in southern India. As in North America, the end of the Seven Years' War in India saw the French in retreat, though they maintained a number of port cities in India and continued to supply Hyder with arms. Though Hyder initially tried to ally with the British, in the late 1760s the nizam of Hyderabad manipulated the company and Mysore into a war to preserve his own power. In an unusual setback for the British, Mysore won a decisive victory. Hyder's opinion of the British continued to decline when they failed to uphold the terms of the 1769 Treaty of Madras and defend Mysore: he called them "the most faithless and usurping of all mankind" (Keay 2000: 396).

As Hyder predicted, the British remained wary of French involvement on the subcontinent. After its defeat in the Seven Years' War in 1763—and expulsion from its major holdings in India—France's policy was to maintain relations with anti-British Indian powers and encourage French mercenaries to serve in their armies in case France should undertake another invasion to expel the British. Therefore, British policy was to provide oversight and protection of the company in order to defend the country's stake in India from France. America created a trigger for renewed conflict with Britain's rival.

The Mysore Conflict Continued

In contrast to the American Revolution, there was no decisive victory in the Indian theater of the war. France's entry into the revolution on the colonists' side in 1778 led the East India Company's leadership in Calcutta to conclude that it was in the national interest to expel the French from India. In 1779, a British force captured the French port of Mahé, through which Hyder was receiving French supplies. Hyder then resolved to expel the British from the region. In the summer of 1780, he swept down with a large army on the plain outside Madras, burning villages and laying siege to British forts—a shock to the British leadership, who had believed peace would last at least until the end of the year.

As the British mobilized their own troops, Hyder dispatched a force led by his son, the thirty-year-old Tipu Sultan, to meet them in the Battle of Pollilur in September 1780. It proved to be one of Britain's worst defeats in India, with an army of thousands reduced to a few hundred captives. Moving on to take the British-allied Arcot, Hyder put the British once again on the defensive. Also at war with the Marathas, the British were at risk of losing their position in South India. An anxious company leadership, in directing its station in Bombay to sue for peace with the Marathas, wrote that in the Mysore war not only India was at stake but all of Britain's ambitions in Asia.

British fortunes turned under the command of a new general, the veteran Sir Eyre Coote, who in 1760 had established British supremacy over the

French in India at the Battle of Wandiwash. "Coote the Brave," as he was called in admiration by the sepoys he commanded, won a series of engagements against Hyder in 1781. While Cornwallis was surrendering in North America in October 1781, Coote's force took Negapatam (Nagapattinam), a Dutch holding along the Coromandel Coast, and forced Hyder back in one siege.

In February 1782, the French finally arrived to reinforce Hyder. In July, Admiral Pierre André de Suffren and Hyder met at Cuddalore, south of Madras, and agreed to establish a base there. Suffren, whom the famed naval historian Alfred Thayer Mahan termed a genius, went on to fight the British admiral Edward Hughes in a series of pitched battles at sea, which were indecisive but restored Hyder's confidence (Mahan [1890] 1918: ch. 12). However, despite naval support, Mysore suffered a serious setback: Hyder Ali died of cancer in December 1782, leaving the throne and his command to Tipu Sultan. Coote, too, was unwell and died of a stroke in 1783. General James Stuart took over for the British.

British fears of defeat did not die with Hyder: Tipu was just as threatening, if not more so, to the company. He was better educated than his father, and even more ambitious. He made further improvements to the military, adopting more French tactics and introducing iron tubes to the Mysore army's rockets, which gave them a longer range and more effective combustion than previous wooden or paper constructions. Tipu himself was a skilled rider and marksman. His state was developing a military machine, its resources enhanced by Hyder's improvements to tax collection and Tipu's establishment of a central bank, and the state began to produce its own high-quality arms rather than importing them from Europeans.

Tipu was also even more inclined to cooperate with France. On his deathbed, Hyder wrote to his son that "the English are today all powerful in India" and that it was critical to "put the nations of Europe one against the other" (Kaushik 2011: 73). Mysore had entered into partnership with France when Hyder enlisted French advisers and worked alongside French officers during his time as a commander in the 1750s. That cooperation continued in their joint opposition to the British. French mercenaries served alongside Hyder's armies, though they did not command regiments. In an unusual move for an Indian power, Tipu sent an embassy to Europe: his ambassadors arrived in

J. B. Morret, *Meeting of Bailly de Suffren and Haider-Ali-Khan*, 1789. Engraving. The French admiral Pierre André de Suffren is shown meeting the sultan of Mysore, Hyder Ali, upon Suffren's arrival in India in 1782. (Art Collection 3 / Alamy Stock Photo)

Portrait of Tipu Sultan in 1780. (David Pearson / Alamy Stock Photo)

Paris in 1788 and were noted with interest by a fellow Francophile, then the U.S. ambassador to France, Thomas Jefferson. Tipu's interest in France did not end with the demise of the French monarchy; after the French Revolution, he called himself Citizen Tipu and founded a Jacobin club with French support (in spite of the awkward contradiction of a French republic's embracing an autocratic sultan). The French-Mysorean alliance reached its peak when Napoleon, another great foe of the British, invaded Egypt in 1798 with the goal of cutting off his rival's trade, continuing to India, and linking up with Tipu to expel the British from the subcontinent.

However, the France-Mysorean relationship was limited on the one hand by France's internal turmoil and disappointments on the battlefield, and on the other by the fact that Tipu wanted French assistance but was not inclined to make commercial concessions—such as allowing the export of goods duty-free and the building of factories—that would grant the French East India Company the sort of market power the British held in their territories. Moreover, Tipu's diplomacy extended beyond France: he also sought the recognition and assistance of other Islamic states, such as the Afghan, Persian, and Ottoman Empires. Although these nations shared goodwill and maintained communication, they were too beset by their own issues to offer much aid to Tipu.

Solidarity also emerged between Mysore and the fledgling United States, both fighting British imperialism. Prior to the 1770s, Americans had supported British expansion into India and the goods it brought out of the subcontinent. From the Boston Tea Party onward, however, Americans began to see themselves as fellow victims of British oppression: John Dickinson, an impassioned member of the Continental Congress, claimed that the conduct of the East India Company in South Asia showed "how little they regard the laws of nations, the rights, liberties, or lives of men." The difference with America, he claimed, was that "we are not Sea Poys [*sic*], nor Marattas, but British subjects who are born to liberty, who know its worth, and who prize it high" (Dickinson 1895: 460).

American colonists recognized, however, that not all of India was acquiescing to the British: Hyder Ali and Tipu Sultan were fighting back. Yet the "alliance" between India and America was primarily one of goodwill. Unable to send troops to India to help the French, Congress encouraged its pirate navy to attack East India Company ships; Pennsylvania commissioned a ship named the *Hyder-Ally*; and Tipu is reported to have endorsed the Declaration of Independence along with the ideals of the French Revolution. Nonetheless, this friendship created little material advantage in the war; ultimately, the outcome in both countries resulted from the weakening of the British.

An Uneasy Peace

Like the start of the Revolutionary War, the peace that came with the Treaty of Paris in 1783 transformed the conflict in India. At the end of the naval campaign in India, Suffren defeated Hughes, paralleling the success of Admiral François-Joseph-Paul de Grasse in the Atlantic (see page 30). On Indian soil, the final engagement of this world war was at the Battle of Cuddalore, in June 1783. The British ended their siege of the French-Mysorean base on hearing of the peace. Frustrated by the French withdrawal, Tipu, too, decided to end hostilities with the British, signing the Treaty of Mangalore in 1784. The treaty, though it restored the prewar status quo, was notable for being quite favorable to the Indian ruler—primarily in its psychological impact, as Tipu dictated the terms and the British representative had to travel to reconquered Mysorean territory to sign it. The treaty would be the last of its kind; the peace following Mysore's next war would see half of Tipu's territory seized and his sons taken as hostages by the British, while treaties in other areas, such as the 1802 Treaty of Bassein with a Maratha ruler, stripped Mysore of both territory and sovereignty. Without the Treaty of Paris, the hostilities would have continued in India. Although the British were finished in the United States, their campaign in India was still under way. The conflict between Mysore and Britain simply had been put on hold.

At this juncture, the British assessed what had gone wrong. Still struggling to grasp the loss of America, Parliament took the East India Company to task. Deeply unhappy with the company's execution of the war and its administration of Indian territory, Parliament impeached the British governor general of India, Warren Hastings, and passed the 1784 East India Act, which created a board of control by which the government would administer Indian territory more directly.

It was also at this moment that Britain's imperial focus shifted from North America toward South Asia. The advantages of possessing India were not lost on the British: as the historian P. J. Marshall has pointed out, despite the government's grievances, the company paid for its own military costs, including royal reinforcements; employed executives responsive to London; boasted a professional administrative service; and, most important, established a well-developed revenue system that required no formal consent from the Indian population. In contrast, even when Britain had had control of its American colonies, the empire had no local armies (such as the Madras Presidency Army, composed primarily of Indians), and the troops it did have on American soil were difficult to support because funding them required consent from local assemblies. In a sense, the British came to prefer corporate autocracy in its rule over the Indians to controlling the ill-tempered democrats in America. Moreover, India was the future of British expansion: in Parliament's debate on the articles of the Peace of Paris, one of the chief ministers of the king, David Murray, Lord Stormont, said, "We might have found in the East Indies a recompence for all our losses in the west" (quoted in Marshall 2005: 270–71, 369). Whereas previously Britain had reduced its military support for the company after major conflicts, in this postwar period Britain maintained its naval force and a standing army for imperial purposes. India was of greater concern to Britain now than ever before.

India, meanwhile, continued to fight back. Mysore and Britain fought two more wars, with the next (1790–92) executed by Lord Cornwallis as governor general and resulting in a significant setback for Tipu and a weakening of Mysore, and the last (1798–99) resulting in a resounding victory for the British. Learning of Napoleon's intent to join forces with Tipu via Egypt in 1798, the British, with an army commanded by the Duke of Wellington, invaded Mysore one last time. Tipu died fighting at his palace at Srirangapatna on May 4, 1799. The British now looked for a loyal replacement. The maharani of Mysore, the widow of the raja deposed by Hyder Ali, had been in correspondence with the British and took this opportunity to return the Wodeyar dynasty to the throne. The British installed her adoptive grandson as ruler and made Mysore a princely state under British rule. One of the greatest threats to empire in India finally had been vanquished. With the defeat of the Marathas in 1818, all of India became British territory, and after the widespread but unsuccessful 1857 Indian Rebellion, the British government decided company rule was inadequate to manage its relationships on the subcontinent. In 1858, the East India Company was dissolved, and India fell under direct rule by the Crown as the Raj.

Auguste Jugelet, *Battle of Cuddalore, June 20, 1783*, 1836. Oil on canvas. The French fleet under Admiral Suffren sent the British into retreat at the Battle of Cuddalore in 1783. (RMN–Grand Palais / Art Resource, NY)

Richard Simkin, *The East India Company's European Regiment at the Battle of Cuddalore, 1st July 1783*, 1890. Watercolor. Mysore troops are shown fighting East India Company troops at the Battle of Cuddalore, the last battle of the Revolutionary War. The British siege ended after news of peace arrived on June 30, 1783. (Prints, Drawings and Watercolors from the Anne S. K. Brown Military Collection, Brown Digital Repository, Brown University Library)

Consequences

The conflict that the American Revolution sparked in India had vast consequences for the British Empire and for modern India. While the British initially viewed the West Indies as their most important colonies, the Anglo-Mysore Wars reoriented the British Empire toward the East and led to a new type of administration. The Mysore war of the 1780s not only changed colonial history but also shaped India's present-day culture wars, in which the protagonists of the war have become lightning rods for controversy.

The rule of Hyder Ali and Tipu Sultan in Mysore has had a lasting legacy in India. Mysore's ruling Wodeyar dynasty cemented its place under British rule, survived the transition to Indian independence, and persists to this day. It has been stripped of any official titles but not of its enormous wealth. Hyder Ali and Tipu Sultan remain controversial figures in Indian history, considered by some to be India's earliest freedom fighters — as acknowledged by the government of the present-day state of Karnataka, home to Mysuru — and by others to be brutal Islamic fanatics — an interpretation embraced by the East India Company in its propaganda against Tipu after his death. Of course, their views are more complex than either characterization suggests. Although, for example, Hyder Ali believed that the British problem extended across the entire subcontinent, he did not conceive of a united India that would free itself from British colonial rule. Just as the Americans initially believed that their states were practically independent countries, India may have been seen as one land and culture, but not as one political union. Had the British simply left India, the Marathas likely would have continued fighting Mysore, which would have continued fighting the nizam of Hyderabad, and so on.

Yet Hyder and Tipu were not the brutal zealots many imagine. Tipu may have played up his Islamic faith to other Islamic leaders, but he also endeared himself to his Hindu subjects, supporting their temples while reserving destruction and forced conversion for rebels. However, it is difficult to label Tipu a protonationalist as well: for example, he attempted to replace the local language, Kannada, with Persian. In reality, he was not much different from the British (and most other) rulers in that he was, above all, trying to cement his own power. "To live like a lion for a day," he philosophized, "is far better than to live for a hundred years like a jackal" (Embree and Lewis 1988: 104).

Thomas Gainsborough, *Charles Cornwallis, 1st Marquess Cornwallis*, 1783. Oil on canvas. This portrait was made before Cornwallis's posting to India, following his defeat at Yorktown in 1781. (© National Portrait Gallery, London, NPG 281)

Controversy over whether Tipu was "tiger or tyrant"—an early freedom fighter or a bigoted oppressor—continues in an increasingly nationalist India still affected by religious divisions.

Nevertheless, India was shaped by the permanent presence of the British on the subcontinent, which was brought about by three factors resulting from the American Revolution: the empire's loss of America, the relative strengthening of France, and the challenge of Mysore. All these factors moved Britain to complete its conquest of India in the nineteenth century. The lasting effects of British rule are evident in many ways: India's rail network, for instance, is a legacy of the British need to move troops quickly across the subcontinent, as in the wars with Mysore.

The mentality of the British during their fight with Mysore—one of deep insecurity—drove their grand strategy in protecting the Raj and their strategic advantages in Asia. In the 1790s, the East India Company, backed up by the triumphant Royal Navy, began shipping Indian-grown opium to the Qing Empire in order to pay the company's debts from its Indian wars and to secure Chinese tea for the British market, leading to new wars and imperialism in China. Fear of a Russian invasion of India induced the British to begin asserting influence in Iran in the 1800s and Afghanistan in the 1830s. Siam (Thailand) was used in the late 1800s as a buffer for British India against French Indochina (Vietnam). A similar logic drove Britain's dogged defense of Burma (Myanmar) against the combined strength of Japan, Siam, and the Indian National Army during World War II.

The consequences of the American Revolution, therefore, are felt around the world. The British exploited sectarian divides to increase their own power in India, emphasizing the negative attributes of rulers such as Tipu, while the actions of the East India Company brought into question the ethics of governance by a multinational corporation, and its ability to govern at all. In the twentieth century, the United States, a nation forged in this late-eighteenth-century global war, shaped the postimperial order. Although the newly formed United States left India to its fate after the revolution, near the close of World War II the administration of Franklin D. Roosevelt pushed the British to quit India, along with the rest of its empire. The common strategic interests of the United States and India, along with their shared modern identity as democratic states, have encouraged closer cooperation in recent years, providing echoes of their "alliance" of the late eighteenth century.

REVOLUTION IN AMERICA AND THE
DUTCH REPUBLIC

Alan Lemmers

> In December 1780, England declared war on the Dutch Republic. The Dutch had been supplying the Americans with arms, and now they would be drawn fully into the global conflict that the American Revolution had become. — *Editors*

America had held up a mirror to their own Republic in which they had glimpsed an idealised image of heroic patriotism. . . . The Dutch were on the point of inaugurating Europe's revolutionary generation.

Simon Schama, *Patriots and Liberators: Revolution in the Netherlands, 1780–1813,* 1977: 63

Essential to understanding the Dutch position during the American Revolution is the political standing of the Dutch Republic in Europe. At its core was the military alliance established with England in 1678, which had lasted more than a century and had cost the Republic significant military and financial strength. Dutch-English relations during this period deteriorated from uneasy to unfriendly, and the alliance gradually lost all substance because of unabated commercial rivalry between the two nations and their political divergence after 1713. The Dutch perspective on the American struggle for independence was further colored by a deep-rooted ideological controversy within the Republic, which made it receptive to the revolutionary wind blowing across the Atlantic. This essay first details the Anglo-Dutch alliance and the internal political tensions and then turns to the situation at the outset of the American Revolution, its consequences in Dutch foreign and domestic politics, and finally its relation to the end of the ancien régime in the Netherlands and Europe.

The Decline of the Dutch Republic

At the time the American colonists declared their independence from Great Britain, the Dutch Republic was a much-divided nation that had ceased to be the powerful state it had been in the seventeenth century. Since 1678, it had been in a military alliance with England that had proved ruinous both militarily and financially. The alliance stipulated that in combined naval operations, the English provided the majority of the ships and assumed command, while the Dutch Republic bore the greater burden in land operations. The Nine Years' War (1690–97) and the War of the Spanish Succession (1702–13), both fought alongside England against Louis XIV of France, completely exhausted the Republic's resources and brought it crushing debts from which it had not yet begun to recover by 1776. Even by the 1720s, Dutch armed forces had been reduced to a minimum for lack of funds. The tiny Dutch war fleet that remained was capable of only token convoy duties and rudimentary operations in the Mediterranean, meant to defend shipping against the plague of Barbary pirates. For decades, the Republic's army had been kept below its earlier peacetime strength. An exception was made for the War of the Austrian Succession (1740–48), in which the Republic sided with Austria and Britain against France, Prussia, and Spain. When that war ended, it was clear that the Republic was incapable of fulfilling any obligations to its British ally.

Its international impotence was reflected in and worsened by a domestic conflict that was rooted in one of the Republic's founding documents, the Unie van Utrecht of 1579. This text recorded the rights and duties of the members of the Republic, notably those involving national defense. The country was officially a federation of the Seven United Netherlands; that is, the seven voting provinces. Yet the real political power resided with the town councils and rural governments, which were dominated by rich and powerful men known as the *Regenten*, or Regency. From these local institutions, power was delegated to the states-provincial (provincial governments) and finally to the Estates General (congress) in the Hague. The Estates General was responsible for the union's foreign policy and appointed a supreme military commander, who was usually the *stadtholder* (governor) of the majority of the provinces. The provinces traditionally elected a *stadtholder* who was a descendant of Prince William I of Orange (who had led the revolt against Spain that won the Dutch Republic its independence in 1581). The provinces often chose the same candidate, who thus became a strong figure with national power. However, some of these princes of Orange had monarchist ambitions, and on several occasions they tried to enforce their will on civilian society by military means. After one such attempt in 1650, the Estates General decided not to replace the *stadtholder*: instead it assumed direct command of the military and thereafter appointed only temporary field commanders and admirals.

Meanwhile, the rule of the *Regenten* was resented by those excluded from power, who pinned their hopes on the house of Orange and seized upon every failure of the Regency as an opportunity to break the oligarchy. Thus, when in 1672 France and England invaded the Republic in a war of annihilation, William III (later also king of England) was called by popular acclaim to the office of *stadtholder* in six provinces. Reluctantly the Estates General subsequently made him supreme military commander for life. No one succeeded him after his death in 1702, but when the War of the Austrian Succession threatened to turn into a disaster for the Republic in 1747, popular pressure brought William IV, a distant relative of William I, to the position of *stadtholder* in all provinces and thus to supreme military command. This time, however, the office was made not merely lifelong but also hereditary, much to the horror of the republican Regency and its supporters. In their position as *stadtholder*s, William IV (1747–51) and William V (1751–95) steadily expanded their right to make civil appointments all the way down to the local level. This practice infuriated many who, excluded from the princes' favor, found careers in government closed to them. By the second half of the eighteenth century, the Orangist and republican factions were at each other's throats.

The conflict was further complicated by the question of national defense. With its diminished armed forces, the Republic had been reduced to a second-rate power with little or no influence in the European theater. For its maritime security, it relied almost entirely on British mastery of European waters, but this was an uncertain position because British and Dutch interests did not always coincide. In the Treaty of Westminster of 1674, which had concluded the Third Anglo-Dutch War, England granted the Republic the freedom of trade it wished. War supplies carried by Dutch or English traders to enemies of either nation were evidently excluded from this agreement and were considered contraband, but naval stores, such as timber, hemp, iron, and linen, were exempt. Dutch shipping could henceforward suppose itself safe from English seizure.

However, the love of money was too great. During the Seven Years' War (1756–63), in which the Republic remained neutral, Dutch trade tried to exploit the hostility between the warring parties. The British government, on the other hand, unilaterally broadened its definition of contraband to include naval stores. The Rule of 1756 instructed its navy and privateers to be ruthless in their seizure of Dutch ships. As a consequence, Dutch trade suffered heavily. Dutch merchants and shipowners were loudly proclaiming the need to have their convoys protected by the Dutch navy, but apart from a counterpiracy squadron in the Mediterranean, the Dutch war fleet had virtually ceased to exist. The official line of the Estates General, now dominated by the Orangist faction, was that Dutch merchant ships had nothing to fear from Britain as long as they complied with the definitions of legitimate cargoes in the Treaty of Westminster. And William V, who had family ties to the British crown, was disinclined to risk good relations with the Republic's most powerful ally by granting unlimited protection to Dutch convoys. Ships carrying naval stores and other goods prohibited by Britain would have to fend for themselves, and other convoy protection was kept at a minimum.

Measures to enlarge the Dutch navy were considered anti-British by the Orangist faction and, of course, by the British government. William V's advisers preferred to expand the army, which would strengthen the prince's position both nationally and on the European continent. Contrariwise, his opponents, notably the town of Amsterdam, regarded any increase in army expenditure as a hostile gesture toward France, Britain's main adversary but also a major outlet for Dutch trade. And trade, after all, was the main source of national income and as such indispensable to any defense effort.

The situation eased a little after the Seven Years' War, but the controversy over defense expenditures remained unresolved. Meanwhile the British and the French ambassadors in the Hague lobbied feverishly to limit defense spending in the Republic; from 1756 to 1778, neither the army nor the fleet was granted the funds necessary to expand (Bartstra 1952: passim). By then the international landscape was shifting once again, this time because of a rebellion in the American colonies.

The Caribbean and Atlantic Trade

The Dutch Republic had colonies in both the East and West Indies and maintained considerable shipping traffic with them. From its Caribbean settlements, Dutch traders also supplied foreign colonies, French and British ones in particular, at prices with which traders in their home countries could not compete because of colonial taxes. This trade, of course, was illegal but was also very hard to prevent: many British and French traders eagerly used Dutch trading channels to evade colonial levies. Wars between Britain and France, including the Seven Years' War, turned the Caribbean trade into a goldmine for the Dutch because the conflict brought French maritime transport to a stop. The French colony of Guadeloupe, for instance, was visited by only a handful of French ships each year, whereas more than three hundred ships arrived annually from the Dutch island of Sint Eustatius (also called Statia by the locals; Hartog 1976: 76).

Starting in 1774, when the British colonies no longer saw eye to eye with their mother country, they too became exceedingly profitable trading destinations. As long as Dutch ships stuck to permissible cargoes, there was little risk of British naval intervention, but as international tension increased, so did the temptation to profit from carrying forbidden military supplies. Dutch vessels began to transfer their loads to American ships off the east coast of North America, and American ships also called directly on Amsterdam (Schulte Nordholt 1979: 40; Huibrechts 2009: 140). In the Caribbean, Sint Eustatius became the center of a thriving trade in goods shipped to and from the American colonies, including slaves, sugar, naval stores, and even small arms and gunpowder. Gunpowder and arms could yield a profit as high as 400 percent for Dutch merchants, who received tobacco, rice, indigo, and other such wares in return. Ships of all nationalities traded through Statia, on average some three thousand a year, and from the mid-eighteenth century onward, French, Spanish, and English merchants even set up shops on the tiny island, often to the dismay of Statians and Dutch traders (Hartog 1976: 78−90; Attema 1976: 30−31, 37−38; Schulte Nordholt 1979: 40−41; Ferreiro 2016: 37−38). With business booming, it is not surprising that the island became one of the first targets in the Fourth Anglo-Dutch War (1780−84).

A. Nelson, *The Sint Eustatius Roads in 1774*, 1774. Watercolor. Among the ships at anchor are Dutch, French, and English vessels. By the 1750s, land reclamation aimed at accommodating the booming local trade had doubled the size of the boulevard seen here, and numerous warehouses had been constructed. (Collection Het Scheepvaartmuseum, Amsterdam, A.1029[02]1)

At first the British government merely protested loudly when confronted with evidence of Dutch ships' illicit trade with the American rebels. At Britain's request, the Estates General in 1775 urged the Dutch West India Company, which held the monopoly on Dutch trade in the Caribbean, to ban the weapons trade — for a year. But given the money that could be made, almost no one heeded such regulations, and anyone who did was regarded as a simpleton. Dutch traders, particularly those from Amsterdam, took no notice; nor did those far away in the West Indies, who thought themselves out of reach (Attema 1976: 31). However, British policy hardened after 1776 because of the "First Salute" incident at Sint Eustatius, when the island's Dutch governor fired a gun salute in recognition of an American warship. The incident was viewed by many as the first international recognition of U.S. independence. Britain's posture hardened still further when it went to war with France in June 1778 (Hartog 1976: 67–79; Schulte Nordholt 1979: 45–50; Attema 1976: 31; Tuchman 1988: passim). France, being in great need of shipbuilding timber, took a lenient view of trade in naval stores by ships from neutral countries, and despite the war, it instructed its navy and privateers to let such cargoes pass unmolested, even if they were destined for Great Britain. But such free trade was unacceptable to Britain, whose colonies by now were in open revolt. It reinstated the Rule of 1756, tightening its check on all shipping in Western European and West Indian waters, and Dutch (and other neutral) trade once

A. L. Brockman, *Johannes de Graeff*, 1834. Oil. Portrait after an earlier, lost likeness. On November 16, 1776, De Graeff (1729–1813), governor of the Dutch Caribbean colony of Sint Eustatius, returned the salute of the American merchantman *Andrew Doria*, which flew the striped flag of the Continental Congress. This gesture, seen by many as a recognition of the United States, provoked a furious outcry by the British government. (New Hampshire Statehouse)

again suffered heavily. As France had intended, this stance estranged Great Britain from other, neutral powers that wanted to trade freely; in 1780, on the initiative of Catherine the Great, Russia joined with Denmark and Sweden to form the League of Armed Neutrality, in which they pledged to protect one another's commercial shipping, predominantly against search and seizure by the British navy (Mott 1999: 31–48; Zwitzer 2012: 516–24).

Neutrality and Freedom

In 1775, when a large contingent of Britain's armed forces had been deployed to North America to quell the rebellion, King George III of England asked the Dutch government to lend its Scots Brigade. Although Prince William V and his close advisers were in favor of helping out the English king, many in the Republic were vehemently opposed. The young provincial representative Joan Derk, baron van der Capellen tot den Pol (1741–84), lashed out against Britain in a speech that was printed and widely distributed across the country, causing a sensation (Van der Capellen tot den Pol 1775). Besides pointing out that helping Britain would be a violation of Dutch neutrality and bring on war with France, Van der Capellen tot den Pol voiced his moral indignation at the

Mathias de Sallieth, *Johan Derk van der Capellen tot den Pol*, post-humous portrait, 1787. Etching. The public support offered by Van der Capellen tot den Pol (1741–84) to the American cause was hailed by Americans and won him a number of prominent American correspondents, notably William Livingston and Jonathan Trumbull. Publishing this correspondence made Van der Capellen tot den Pol even more famous, but as he subsequently was banned from office in the Republic, he became politically ineffective. (Rijksmuseum, Amsterdam, RP-P-1903-A-23375A)

idea that the Dutch people, once also enslaved and branded as rebels, would cooperate to oppress the Americans, whose freedom, like that of any other person, was a God-given right. In his reference to the Dutch past, he meant the Eighty Years' War (1568–1648), in which the Republic had freed itself from Spanish dominion.

His speech was not appreciated in Dutch government circles and cost him his seat in the Overijssel provincial parliament, but simultaneously it was widely acclaimed and sowed pro-American sentiments among large parts of the population. Although this was the first public call to defend the rights of the rebels, the atmosphere in many Dutch coffeehouses was already sympathetic to their cause. Besides, many Dutch eagerly anticipated the prospect of unrestrained trade with an independent American nation.

Yet William V was inclined to heed Britain's call, if George III would guarantee that deployment of the Dutch reinforcements would not increase the risk of the French waging war on the Republic. William also demanded financial compensation so that he could hire replacements for the duration of the Scots Brigade's absence. Faced with these conditions, George did not pursue his request (Schulte Nordholt 1979: 25–31; Zwitzer 2012: 498–503). By this point, Britain's patience with the Dutch Republic was wearing thin, and the short but acclaimed September 1779 visit of the American privateer John Paul Jones to Holland with a British prize (the ship *Serapis*) did not make things any better.

Simon Fokke, *The Squadron of Henry Fielding Intercepts and Seizes the Dutch Merchant Convoy Escorted by Admiral Lodewijk van Bylandt, 31 December 1779*, ca. 1779 – 80. Pen and ink. The seizure of this convoy for its disputed contraband resulted in the Dutch decision to join the League of Armed Neutrality and to expand its war fleet. War with Britain then became imminent. (Rijksmuseum, Amsterdam, RP-T-00-1587)

In Dutch domestic politics, several raw nerves had been touched by Van der Capellen tot den Pol's comparison of the American cause with Dutch history, which many felt the current political leadership was disregarding. William V's military authority, too, continued to be seen as a risk to civil liberties, which were exactly what the American rebels were fighting for. This mistrust was not alleviated by the prince's flirtations with Prussian concepts of a military society. William was a fan of Prussian military discipline and noted with approval the militarization of Prussian society; already he prioritized military courts over civilian courts in conflicts between the military and civilians, a practice that many criticized (Zwitzer 1987: 34, 36; Klein 1995: 170; Dorreboom 2000: 93 – 100). He had not made himself exactly popular with his usurpation of parliamentary rights and pro-British politics, and criticism grew as trade continued to suffer from restrictions and British assault while nothing was done to strengthen the Dutch fleet. While the Estates General did accord some "limited" convoy protection, which allowed for the free trading of naval stores except shipbuilding timber, on New Year's Eve 1779, a strong British squadron seized a large convoy escorted by five Dutch men-of-war under the command of Admiral Lodewijk van Bylandt, which caused outrage in the Republic.

When the British government shortly afterward once again demanded and was refused military assistance by the Dutch, Britain declared the 1674

Treaty of Westminster void, and matters really started to escalate. The Estates General now endorsed "unlimited" convoy protection, which included ships carrying naval and army stores "forbidden" by Great Britain, and voted for a program to expand the Dutch fleet to fifty-two men-of-war and fourteen thousand crew (Rodger 1999: 25; Zwitzer 2012: 514–16). A major building program was set in motion. By autumn, thirty-six ships were ready for service, but finding sufficient crew proved more difficult. The Dutch still did not feel strong enough to face the British fleet, so they looked abroad for assistance.

The Road to War

As described above, the Republic in this period was a thoroughly divided nation. Although the prince's faction dominated official policy, the liberal opposition, led by Amsterdam, was headstrong to the point of subversion. When France signed its Treaty of Amity and Commerce with the United States in February 1778, the enterprising province of Holland, led by Amsterdam, feared it would miss out on expanded trading opportunities and called for a similar treaty. But William V refused to countenance such a treaty, and even France discouraged it, as it needed shipbuilding timber supplied by a neutral Dutch Republic and did not want the Republic to enter into war with Britain. Open proposals to the Hague by American representatives in Paris for such a treaty all foundered amid diplomatic delaying tactics. Amsterdam, however, was not to be stopped by this setback; it concocted a secret "preparatory" treaty with the assistance of the U.S. commercial agent William Lee, based in Germany; this treaty, Amsterdam hoped, would be presented before the Estates General at the moment Great Britain recognized U.S. independence. The concept treaty was then sent secretly to the U.S. Congress for ratification (Schulte Nordholt 1979: 61–70).

On September 3, 1780, the American packet ship *Mercury*, sailing from Philadelphia to the Dutch Republic, was intercepted by HMS *Vestal*, captained by George Keppel. On board the *Mercury*, Keppel found Henry Laurens, the newly appointed U.S. envoy to the Republic, with a mission to secure a new trade treaty and a loan. As the *Vestal* hailed the *Mercury*, Laurens ditched a bag of papers overboard, which, though weighed down, failed to sink and was retrieved by the British crew. In it they found a draft of the secret treaty of Amsterdam.

Laurens was promptly rerouted to the Tower of London, while British rulers rubbed their hands in glee: the document proved that the Dutchmen had conducted secret negotiations with the American rebels, which, as the British minister David Murray, Viscount Stormont, wrote to Joseph Yorke, the British ambassador in the Hague, "give[s] the properest Direction to the War, by making it a particular Quarrel between Great Britain and Holland, in which no Neutral Power has any Concern" (Schulte Nordholt 1979: 138). Yorke was instructed, in the sternest language, to demand that William V seek out and publicly punish the culprits. But that was beyond William's power, and the Amsterdam burgomasters denied any wrongdoing given the provisional character of the document and their indispensable duty to guard the trade interests not only of their own town but of the entire country.

The Estates General formally decried their conduct but brought no charges, and only days later, on November 20, 1780, it decided that the Republic should join the League of Armed Neutrality. To prevent that from happening, Great Britain declared war on the Republic, with the Laurens Papers, as they became known, as *casus belli*. The declaration of war was signed by George III on December 19, 1780, and received ten days later by the Estates General (Schulte Nordholt 1979: 137–39; Rodger 1999: 25, 32; Zwitzer 2012: 516–24). Now at war, the Republic could no longer apply for membership in the League of Armed Neutrality; it stood alone.

Pieter Wagenaar II, *The Rape of Sint Eustatius by Admiral Rodney, 1781*, 1781–82. Pen and ink. En route to protect British Caribbean colonies from the French, Rodney stopped to plunder the Dutch colony of Sint Eustatius, which was known to supply arms and supplies to the Americans. According to some, Rodney's delay led to the loss of several British holdings to the French. (Rijksmuseum, Amsterdam, RP-T-00-1174)

War

The British fleet and British-employed privateers immediately clamped down on Dutch trade. They seized dozens of ships, including escorts that were not yet aware of the state of war. Almost all the West Indian colonies were conquered by Britain, as were the Dutch settlements on Sri Lanka and at Nagapattinam, India. Most noteworthy was the British depredation of Sint Eustatius by Admiral George Brydges Rodney in February 1781. Rodney was especially hard on the island's Jewish community and on the English traders he found there. In the opinion of some, his delay while plundering the island caused the loss of the British colonies (Rodger 2004: 348–49; O'Shaughnessy 2013: 308–13; Hartog 1976: 86–97).

At home, the Dutch fleet still was not ready to sail because of a lack of crew, victuals, and equipment. The building program eventually yielded forty-five brand new ships of the line (large warships), but most were not completed until 1782. The fleet commander, Vice Admiral Andries Hartsinck, was reluctant to venture out to the open sea because of the constant presence of British blockade squadrons. Given William's V neglect of the fleet in previous years, the public held him responsible for its ill-preparedness. Try as he might, the prince could neither shake off public anger nor whip the fleet into action. And without a military escort, no merchant ship could set sail. For months, the maritime sector lay idle. At last, on August 1, 1781, a convoy of seventy-one Dutch merchant ships sailed for the Baltic, escorted by seven warships. Near Dogger Bank, in the North Sea, they ran into a homebound British convoy, and the two escorting squadrons engaged in battle. After nearly four hours of fierce fighting, during which neither opponent managed to break the other's line of battle, the British ships withdrew. Both squadrons kept their position out of enemy range for another couple of hours before limping home. On the way back, the *Holland*, a sixty-four-gun Dutch ship of the line, sank.

While tactically the battle was a draw, like so many other line battles, the withdrawal of the British squadron was celebrated as a great moral victory in the Republic. Strategically, however, it was a defeat. The British merchant fleet had reached home safely, while the Dutch merchant ships had been forced to turn around and resume their inactivity. Given the number of damaged Dutch warships, another convoy was unlikely in the foreseeable future. Soon afterward the party mood faded, and criticism of William V and his political allies redoubled. He was even accused of betraying the Republic to the enemy.

Barely two months after the battle of Dogger Bank, an anonymous, widely distributed 143-page pamphlet (in truth authored by Van der Capellen tot den Pol) depicted William as the personification of all the evil that had befallen the Republic and a direct threat to civil liberties. It held the prince personally responsible for sabotaging efforts to reach a treaty with the Americans and with France and accused him of permitting Britain to recruit German mercenaries on Dutch soil and of granting them passage to the coast to embark for North America. Finally, the pamphlet called on Dutch citizens to arm themselves and train for service in local militias under their own freely chosen

C. Rochussen, *The Death of Rear Admiral Willem Crul, 1781*, 1886. Oil on canvas. When Rodney arrived at Sint Eustatius in 1781, he learned that a Dutch convoy of twenty-three merchant ships had just left for home. He had the convoy chased and seized. The commander of the convoy's escort, Rear Admiral Willem Crul, was unaware of the state of war between Britain and the Dutch Republic and was completely surprised by the attack. On deck in his best uniform to welcome his British ally, Crul was killed by a British musket shot. (Collection Mariniersmuseum, Rotterdam, 02744)

commanders, following the ancient example of the Swiss and the newer example of the Americans (Van der Capellen tot den Pol 1781: 82, 129, 143). The pamphlet caused an uproar. All over the country, "Patriot" militia organizations (*vrijkorpsen*) popped up, and "Patriotism" became the new name of the anti-Orangist movement.

The few Dutch successes during the war with Britain were due to privateers (Van Zijverden 1997: 193–94). William V, meanwhile, was incapable of stopping the developing political movement against him. In February 1782, a local governing body, the Frisian Provincial Estates, recognized John Adams as the United States of America's representative to the Dutch Republic; the

Estates General followed suit in April, and thus the Republic officially acknowledged U.S. independence.

It seemed as though the Republic's choice had been made, but when France proposed a joint naval expedition against the British Channel fleet that would also target the British merchant fleet returning from the West Indies, the Dutch government hesitated. Only in October did the Estates General agree to send the Dutch fleet to the French naval base at Brest, in Brittany, but just then word came that the British Mediterranean fleet was turning north. Most Dutch naval officers were opposed to the whole idea and argued that their fleet, then going into winter recess, was insufficiently supplied for such a mission. The general public went into a frenzy, however, when it learned the fleet would not sail: the decision cost the fleet commanders Hartsinck and Van Bylandt their jobs, but the obvious scapegoat was, again, William V. A squadron of six ships finally made a token sortie later in October, during which the brand-new sixty-four-gun ship *Unie* capsized and sank with all hands and another ship of the line was lost on a shoal. The misfortunes of the navy seemed endless.

In January 1783, the Republic, exhausted and beaten, made a truce with Great Britain. A peace treaty was signed in Paris on May 20, 1784. All the overseas properties that the Republic had seized were returned to Britain except for Nagapattinam, and British traders were granted access to the East Indian trade.

The recognition of the United States by the Dutch Republic, of course, had not come about without effort. In early 1780, John Adams had arrived in the Netherlands with the mission to secure funds and a trade treaty (he had been seconded to Henry Laurens, who was diverted from his mission and imprisoned in the Tower of London). One could fill a volume with the tedious negotiations Adams undertook to convince the various factions in the Dutch Republic to provide aid to the United States. In March 1782, an avalanche of requests and petitions from Dutch civilians (encouraged by Adams) as well as official institutions flooded the Estates General, crying for recognition of the United States (Schulte Nordholt 1979: 185–88). In the end, Adams succeeded in securing a sizeable loan (initially two million but finally eight million guilders) from Amsterdam entrepreneurs, which the American territories would be able to repay easily through trade. With Britain's 1780 declaration of war on the Republic and William V cornered at each turn, the recognition of U.S.

independence in April 1782 had been just a matter of time. When it came, the whole of the Dutch Republic erupted in festivities. In June 1783 (almost a year before the war with Britain was concluded, and well before Britain accepted U.S. independence), a small squadron carried the first Dutch ambassador, the Amsterdam statesman Pieter Johan van Berckel, to the United States—but this was yet another tragic episode, as one of the vessels sank during the crossing, with more than three hundred killed.

Revolution

With French, Spanish, and Dutch support, the Americans had won their revolution and independence, but the event also had wide-ranging repercussions in the Old World. The initial hesitance of European monarchs to aid the American rebels can be easily understood, as the American revolt could have set an example for revolutionary elements in Europe—as in fact it did. It certainly was a source of inspiration to the insurgency soon to erupt in the Dutch Republic.

Van der Capellen tot den Pol died suddenly in June 1784, but the Patriot movement by that time was in full swing. William lost one prerogative after another and in 1785 left the Hague to live in his palace in the country. The province of Holland alone counted more than two hundred *vrijkorpsen* militias carrying their own arms, and skirmishes with Orangist supporters became ever more frequent. After the prince used the army to suppress a Patriot uprising in two small towns in Gelderland in 1787, the province of Holland denounced him as a dictator, deposed him as its *stadtholder*, and deployed troops to guard its provincial borders. Unluckily for them, William's wife, Wilhelmina, was sister to Frederick II of Prussia, and when Patriots stopped her from traveling to the Hague, the Prussian king demanded satisfaction. When Holland denied any wrongdoing, a twenty-five-thousand-strong Prussian army crossed the border and invaded the province.

Patriot rule was wiped out everywhere in the country, and thousands of Patriots fled abroad, mainly to France. There they planned their return and the overthrow of William's reign, witnessing in the meantime the outbreak of the French Revolution in 1789. That year, too, the Belgians revolted against their Austrian monarch, Joseph II. Although the revolt, later called the Brabant Revolution, was short-lived (lasting only until 1790), it is telling that the Belgian revolutionaries called their freed nation the United Netherlands States. But the revolutionaries were badly organized and divided, and their movement swiftly collapsed when Joseph's successor, Leopold II, met his opponents halfway.

In France, meanwhile, the Dutch Patriots convinced their French corevolutionaries to help them "liberate" the Dutch Republic. The Batavian Legion—the first foreign legion in the French army—was formed, and in 1793, together with the French northern army, it invaded the Austrian Netherlands. These forces were repulsed by the coalition forces of Austria, Prussia, the Dutch Republic, and Great Britain. However, in 1794, the French armies returned and chased the coalition armies from the Belgian territories and across the Dutch border. When winter closed in, the rivers, usually a useful battle frontier, froze solid, and the Frenchmen and Patriots marched across them into the heart of the Republic: the Hague and Amsterdam. William V fled to England in a fishing boat. The rest of the old regime was sent home, and the country became the Batavian Republic; the Dutch Republic was no more.

Conclusion

The Dutch Republic's support for the American Revolution was relatively modest. France and Spain were at war with Great Britain from 1778 onward and thus contributed militarily to the American war effort; the Dutch Republic was never able to assist in a similar way, as it had little to no military presence in its colonies and its navy was insufficient. French support to the American revolutionaries far exceeded loans from the Dutch, and it came partly in the form of a gift or credit with the French arsenals (Mott 1999: 43–44). The Dutch loans from 1782 onward were monetary and granted by private bankers and local institutions, not by the state. Dutch trade and smuggling to the American colonies before 1780 had been very helpful but remained strictly business as well. William V, like most European monarchs, was unsympathetic toward civil revolt and clung to his British ally. Once at war with Britain, the Dutch navy was paralyzed by its inexperienced and reluctant senior officers. However, one can argue that the Fourth Anglo-Dutch War was in fact fought over the American insurgency, and that it forced the Royal Navy to divert some resources away from the American conflict to tie down the Dutch navy and Dutch trade.

Meanwhile, the enormous financial losses to Dutch trade due to the navy's inertia fueled popular anger in the Republic against the regime of William V. The Patriotic movement invoked the example of the American Revolution, calling for efforts to arm the citizens, protect and stimulate trade, and guard civil liberties. Patriot literature and iconography idolized America as Utopia, pure and untarnished, populated with honest, peace-loving, and heroic citizens—in short, an example for decadent Europe (Schulte Nordholt 1979: 200–07). The Republic's acknowledgment of U.S. independence in 1782 was seen as a Patriotic achievement. The Americans' success very much inspired the Patriot Revolution of 1787—as well as the Brabant Revolution and the French Revolution two years later—and it heralded the downfall of William V in 1795 and the end of the ancien régime in the Republic.

Thomas Buttersworth, *The* Bon Homme Richard *and HMS* Serapis, ca. 1830. Oil on canvas. (National Museum of American History, gift of CIGNA Museum and Art Collection, 2005.0279.034)

JOHN PAUL JONES

The most famous naval battle of the Revolutionary War was fought on September 23, 1779, off Flamborough Head on the Yorkshire coast. The battle, between Captain John Paul Jones's ship *Bonhomme Richard* (United States) and Captain Richard Pearson's HMS *Serapis* (Britain), was part of an elaborate ruse by the French navy meant to distract the British from the planned French-Spanish invasion of the British coast.

Back in June 1779, Antoine Raymond Jean Gualbert Gabriel de Sartine, the French naval minister, had asked Jones to send his squadron around the British Isles to attack British shipping. Jones finally got under way in August with his converted merchant ship and several smaller vessels, and by late September he was off the Yorkshire coast. There he spotted an inbound British convoy under Pearson's command, escorted by a frigate and a converted merchant ship. While ordering the rest of his convoy to safety, Pearson maneuvered his ship to intercept Jones.

The fighting began as the sun was setting, so most of the battle was fought by moonlight. HMS *Serapis* was a newer, faster, and better-armed ship, with a more thoroughly trained crew, and in the ensuing gun battle *Serapis* tore apart *Bonhomme Richard* faster than the Americans could damage their opponent. Jones saw that his only chance was to have his crew grapple and lash the two ships together so that Pearson could no longer run out some of his cannon.

But even after more than two hours, the battle was clearly going in Pearson's favor. He called to Jones, "Have you struck?" Jones fired back, "I may sink, but I'm damned if I'll strike!" It was clear indeed that *Bonhomme Richard* was settling lower in the water, and that time was running short. Half of each ship's crew lay dead or wounded. Just then, one of Jones's sailors crawled out along *Bonhomme Richard*'s yards and threw grenades onto *Serapis*'s deck, one of which bounced through a hatch and ignited gun cartridges below. The resulting explosion and deflagration ran the length of the gun deck, killing or wounding fifty of the men crammed there and putting the rest of the guns out of action. By 10:30 p.m., Pearson decided to strike his colors. Jones took possession of *Serapis* and sailed it to neutral Dutch waters, after which he was hailed in both Europe and America as a naval hero. Pearson, having saved his convoy, was later knighted for his actions.

THE INTERNATIONAL WAR ON THE GULF COAST

Kathleen DuVal

> The global dimensions of the American Revolution were particularly relevant to those living along the Gulf Coast, as their perspective contrasted sharply with those of the British colonists in the rebelling colonies along the East Coast. — *Editors*

The Gulf Coast and Mississippi Valley should be parts of the story of the American Revolution that everyone knows, but they are not. This region saw important battles of the Revolutionary War, and its history during and after the Revolution is central to understanding how the young republic expanded across North America and became a cotton empire that would, within a couple of generations, nearly destroy itself in the Civil War.

Few people know about the role of the Gulf South in the American Revolution because they do not see it as a world war. There was never a significant rebel movement in the colonial towns of Pensacola, Mobile, or New Orleans. The battles there were between the British and the Spanish. Most of the population was American Indian, and few Indians, Europeans, or Africans in the region were particularly interested in the squabble over taxation and representation in the eastern colonies.

Yet war came to the Gulf Coast. Ultimately it would draw the attention of Spanish, British, French, and American Indian military strategists and pull in local people whether they were interested or not. When France and Spain entered the Revolutionary War, they made it a world war, and one in which Britain stood to lose not only the thirteen rebelling colonies but also power and imperial wealth around the globe. Ultimately, the international fight for the Gulf Coast was pivotal to the outcome of the American Revolution and the future of the hemisphere.

The Gulf South in 1763

The Gulf South was an international place, ruled by several empires and many Native nations. Three large Indian polities dominated the region: the Creeks, Choctaws, and Chickasaws. The Creeks, in a loose confederacy of towns, lived in the river valleys of the region that would become the states of Alabama and Georgia. The Choctaws controlled the territory to the west, north of Mobile and parts of present-day Mississippi. Farther north, the Chickasaws lived in what is now Mississippi and Tennessee. In addition, there were dozens more Native nations in the Gulf South, speaking different languages, ruling themselves independently, and having their own histories and hopes for the future.

By the 1760s, the colonial population (Europeans, slaves, and free people of color) was nearly equal in size to the Indian population in the eastern half of the Mississippi Valley but still greatly outnumbered in the western half. A few small European settlements and trading posts hugged the Gulf of Mexico and the Mississippi, but, despite claims on paper, European holdings amounted to less than one hundred square miles of territory in the Mississippi Valley and Gulf Coast, compared to some three hundred thousand square miles controlled by Indians.

Before the Seven Years' War, France had claimed the entire Mississippi Valley as its colony of Louisiana, but the war had dramatically reapportioned colonial claims. Having lost the war, France surrendered to Britain the half of Louisiana that lay east of the Mississippi River, including Mobile, Pensacola, Natchez, and Baton Rouge. The British called its new colony West Florida. Britain also gained East Florida, Spain's former colony on the Florida peninsula, including St. Augustine. Spain received the western half of French Louisiana, plus New Orleans, at the mouth of the Mississippi. Still called Louisiana but now half its previous size, Spanish Louisiana connected Spain's western colonies of Texas, New Mexico, and California with the East.

The colonial towns on both sides of the Mississippi River were international places. Most of the colonists there in 1763 were French, some of them

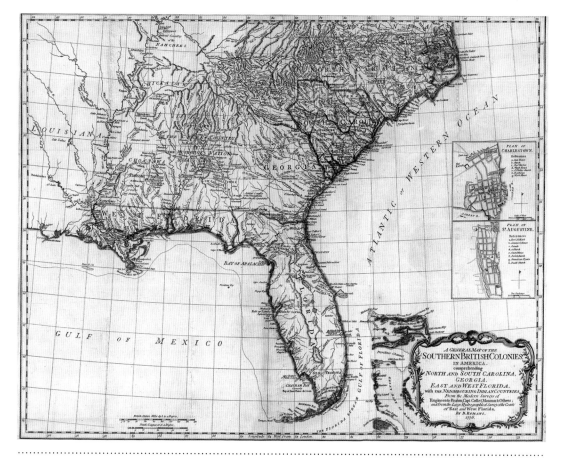

Map of the Southeast, from Bernard Romans, *A General Map of the Southern British Colonies in America*, 1776, showing the division of the Gulf Coast after the Seven Years' War. (Library of Congress, Geography and Maps Division, G3870 1776 .R6)

descendants of those who had established the colony; others were recent Acadian refugees, French Canadians who had fled to Louisiana when the British took Acadia (and renamed it Nova Scotia). Britain gave lands in West Florida to veterans of the Seven Years' War, and its population increased with the arrival of English and Scottish immigrants. In both Spanish Louisiana and British West Florida, colonists took advantage of the lower Mississippi Valley's fertile climate and the international slave trade to build plantations, so the enslaved population of both colonies grew dramatically.

The War on the Gulf Coast

To people on the Gulf Coast and decision-makers in France, Spain, and even Britain, the rebellion of the thirteen colonies was simply a spark. The real war was the global one. While the Americans valued the assistance of powerful France and Spain because it made their independence effort more viable, most people saw the conflict as a rematch of the Seven Years' War. It would either restore the French and Spanish to their previous imperial prominence or solidify British dominance and expansion. In fact, Spanish correspondence tended to refer to the conflict as "the war between France and England," making no reference to the rebelling colonies (Bernardo de Gálvez to Josef de Gálvez, August 17, 1779, quoted in Gálvez 1777–81, vol. 3, 345–46).

In theory, the alliance between the Spanish king, Charles III, and the French king, Louis XVI, obligated Spain to join the war against Britain once France did. But Charles took some persuading that this rebellion within the British empire offered any true opportunity for Spain. France promised that the war would give Spain Gibraltar and East and West Florida and that France would prevent U.S. expansion into Spanish territories. Having little interest in siding with rebels against an empire, Spain did not officially ally with the United States but declared war directly on Britain in 1779. In no way seeing the

Revolutionary War as a war against empire, Spain fought to expand its own imperial territory. In North America, the effort was led by the governor of Louisiana, General Bernardo de Gálvez.

Although many Louisiana colonists hoped war would not come to their colony, the new Acadian residents were an exception. In the previous war, the British had killed, captured, and exiled tens of thousands of Acadians, and those who made it to Louisiana had not forgotten. One young boy named Amand Broussard and his parents and siblings had been forced from the wooded highlands of his Canadian homeland at gunpoint by British forces. The British had imprisoned his family in Halifax for three years before forcing them into exile. In 1775, Broussard married sixteen-year-old Anne Benoît, born in Maryland during her parents' own journey of exile from Acadia to Louisiana. By the time of their marriage, the couple owned land in the settlement of Attakapas, Louisiana, and were becoming prosperous selling cattle to the urban population in New Orleans. When the Spanish called on the people of Louisiana to take up weapons against the British, the Acadians did not forget that the British were their enemies and the Spanish had saved them.

British colonists would have to make decisions, too. Although revolutionary history highlights "the thirteen colonies," in fact Britain had twice that many colonies in North America, extending from the Canadian colonies to the islands of the West Indies, and British administrators were at least as keen to keep the nonrebelling colonies as the rebelling ones (O'Shaughnessy 2000).

James and Isabella Bruce, two of many Scottish residents of West Florida, saw themselves as British subjects whose prosperity lay within the empire, even if their ancestors had long ago rebelled against it. For James's service during the Seven Years' War, the British Crown granted him four thousand acres of land in Britain's new colony of West Florida. He and Isabella established themselves in Pensacola and began buying slaves in order to grow and export indigo, hemp, and rice.

When Parliament passed the Stamp Act in 1765 to tax the colonies, the Bruces and other colonists in West Florida were no happier about it than people in Boston or Barbados. As in other British port cities, people in Pensacola wrote letters of complaint, protested when the stamps arrived, and called the stamps "badges of slavery" (George Johnstone to John Pownel, February 26 and

April 1, 1766, quoted in Starr 1976: 38–39). But later in 1765, when delegates from nine colonies sent a resolution to Parliament and the king protesting the Stamp Act, West Florida did not join them; nor did it join the Revolution or the independence movement that followed. People like the Bruces felt they owed their newfound wealth and prominence to the British Empire and that it would be crazy—and treasonous—to try to leave it. Moreover, they were sure the rebels would lose a fight against the most powerful empire in the world.

The enslaved men and women on whose backs ambitious colonists like the Bruces were building their fortunes took advantage of living in a borderland under wartime conditions. In one of countless similar occurrences, in May 1780, three young men named Jacob, Matthieu, and Christophe ran away together from their masters in New Orleans and fled to Mobile, hiding in a canoe in the bayous along the way. They presented themselves to the Spanish commander at Mobile, telling him that their masters had "punished them much" and volunteering their service. The commander wrote his superior to ask if they could stay, stressing the abuse they had suffered and the fact that he had "very few blacks here for the many jobs for which they can be used" (José de Ezpeleta to Bernardo de Gálvez, May 22, 1780, in Papeles Procedentes de Cuba, legajo 2, reel 165, frame 1005). In Mobile, an enslaved man called Petit Jean, who knew the bayous and trails of the Gulf Coast from his work as a cattle driver, took advantage of the wartime need for his skills and expertise to leave his master and become a courier and spy for Spain (DuVal 2015).

American Indians made their own decisions about the war, as individuals and as nations. Their varied histories would take up many books. This essay now turns its focus to two Native nations involved in the conflict on the Gulf Coast: the Chickasaws and the Creeks.

British officials knew they would need Native allies in the American Revolution, and they assumed the Chickasaws would be first to volunteer. The British and Chickasaws had fought side by side against the French and the Choctaws for most of the eighteenth century and had been important trading partners for just as long. By the time of the Revolution, British officials saw the Chickasaws as "generous friends . . . whom neither dangers could startle nor promises seduce from our interest" (Report of the Congress at Mobile, March 26, 1765, in *Mississippi Provincial Archives: English Dominion* 1911: 219).

Chickasaw Indian. Illustration from Bernard Romans's *A Concise Natural History of East and West Florida*, 1775. (Library of Congress, Prints and Photographs Division, LC-USZ6-680)

Characteristick Chicasaw head

But previous wars had been hard on the Chickasaws, even though they usually won, and now many of them wanted peace. Warfare had killed many, others had died from diseases brought to the Americas after 1492, and many Chickasaws had fled to other places to escape the conflict. As a result, the Chickasaw population in their homeland had declined from around 5,000 at the start of the eighteenth century to only 1,600 by the time of the Revolution, and they lived clustered together in one large fortified town rather than spread out in towns and farms across their land (Cegielski and Lieb 2011: 33, 35, 40–42). So when their enemy France lost the Seven Years' War, the Chickasaws seized the opportunity to make peace with their old Native enemies and establish good relations with Spain. Their desire for peace conflicted with the British assumption that the Chickasaws would fight on their side.

At the start of the war, the Creeks were more inclined than the Chickasaws to join the British effort. A powerful confederacy of around ten thousand people, they saw the revolution as a conflict between land-hungry settlers and an empire that sought to keep them in check. Most Creeks chose the empire. The Creek leader Emistisiguo explained in 1776, "I have sat quietly a long time without joining either party, but the Virginians are now come very near my

John Trumbull, *Creek Leader Hopothle Mico*, 1790. Pencil. This sketch shows the headman of the Upper Creek town of Great Tallassee, also known as Tallassee King or Tame King. (Charles Allen Munn Collection, Fordham University Library, Bronx, New York)

nation and I do not want them to come any nearer" (Emistisiguo to John Stuart, November 19, 1776, in *Documents of the American Revolution, 1770–1783*, 12: 250). In general, the Creeks believed it was Britain's job to control its rebellious colonies, but many of them were willing to join the fighting to protect their country, as long as they could fight in their own way.

Britain needed Indians on its side but wanted them to fight against the targets that the British selected: rebel leaders and the Continental Army, not settlers. Attacks on settlements might convert nonpartisans into rebels. The Crown wanted the settlers to remain loyal or return to its fold in order to rebuild the colonies after the war.

How the Gulf South Changed the War

Decisions made in and regarding the Gulf South would shift British priorities and change the course of the war. When the French and then the Spanish declared war, Britain's troubles grew from a problem of governance to one of worldwide risk and opportunity. Along the Gulf Coast, Spain took the offensive; its forces took posts along the lower Mississippi River in 1779 and then at the port of Mobile in 1780.

Britain also discovered that the Native American forces it had counted on were not at its disposal. According to British military plans, the Chickasaws were to guard the Mississippi River from attack by rebels on the Ohio River, while a "general confederacy" of Chickasaws, Choctaws, Quapaws, Cherokees, and Creeks was to be at the ready "to act as shall be judged best for His Majesty's Service" (John Stuart to William Howe, March 18, 1777, Records of the British Colonial Office, class 5, microfilm reel 7, frame 609). When the Chickasaws did nothing to stop James Willing from leading a semiofficial American expedition down the Mississippi to seize British forts on the east bank of the Mississippi, British officials began to worry that, as the British deputy superintendent Alexander Cameron put it, the Chickasaws "did not seem to approve of taking any active part in the war" (Cameron to George Germain, August 1780, Records of the British Colonial Office, class 5, microfilm reel 8, frame 589).

At first more eager to fight than the Chickasaws, the Creeks grew frustrated at British fecklessness. After many delays, British forces finally opened a southern campaign at the end of 1778. British ships sailed with over three thousand troops from New York and took Savannah, where they joined with two thousand regular and loyalist militia forces from British East Florida. From there, they planned to secure all of Georgia and then move north to the Carolinas and choke off rebellion. Indians were essential to the plan. Creeks were to attack from the west and Cherokees and Ohio Valley Indians from the northwest, while the British navy blockaded the Atlantic ports. Creek leaders assembled war parties and headed toward Georgia. But British ignorance of the time required for communicating and organizing across the vast territory prevented Indian forces from arriving before British forces had retreated.

This kind of miscommunication and resulting mutual blame occurred each time the Indians and British tried to work together. When Spain invaded British territory from the west in 1779, the British desperately needed Indian allies. In September, the British general John Campbell sent word that the Chickasaws and Choctaws were "to march where ordered" (Campbell to Charles Stuart, September 9, 1779, Carleton Papers, microfilm reel 7). Instead, a delegation of Chickasaws traveled to Spanish New Orleans to solidify their alliance with Spain. When Spanish forces attacked Mobile, more than two thousand Creeks and Choctaws came to Britain's aid, but they did not arrive before

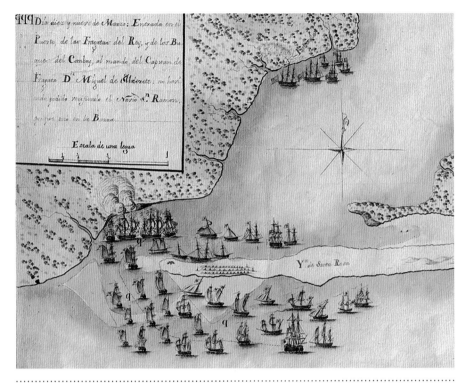

"Map of the Siege of Pensacola," 1781. From *Toma de la plaza de Panzacola y rendición de la Florida Occidental a las armas de Carlos III* (Ministerio de Defensa, Spain, Archivo del Museo Naval, 6-A-21)

Campbell surrendered Mobile. Rather than give them a feast and supplies to reward their effort, Campbell just told them to go home.

The Spanish general Bernardo de Gálvez was more than happy to hear of Indians' disgust with the British. Large delegations from various Native nations, including the Chickasaws, Creeks, and Choctaws, traveled to New Orleans and other Spanish posts to conduct diplomacy and receive supplies. In Mobile alone in the summer of 1780, the Spanish gave Creeks 160 barrels of rum, 50 pounds of gunpowder, 100 pounds of musket balls, 100 gun flints, 55 barrels of cornmeal, 132 pounds of sugar, 235 pounds of tobacco, 34 pounds of fresh meat, and 276 pounds of bread, plus assorted knives, salt, shirts, and vermilion paint (José de Ezpeleta to Bernardo de Gálvez, July 12, 1780, Papeles Procedentes de Cuba, legajo 2, reel 168, frames 2483–88). And Spain got little

George Gauld, *A View of Pensacola*, ca. 1770s. Etching and engraving. (Library of Congress, Prints and Photographs Division, LC-DIG-pga-06781)

in return. The Native nations were not switching sides from Britain to Spain: they were using the Spanish-British rivalry to whatever advantage they could.

As a result of British bumbling, only a few hundred Native fighters were in Pensacola when Gálvez's fleet began its siege in early March 1781. The Creek leader Alexander McGillivray finally rode into Pensacola in early April with about forty Creeks. Eventually another forty Creeks, ninety Choctaws, and fifty Chickasaws showed up. Still, they numbered less than a quarter of those who had responded to Campbell's first call, a far cry from British expectations. In addition, the likely presence of Choctaws and even Creeks in the Spanish camp kept those with the British forces from making an indiscriminate attack on the Spanish. Indeed, there is no evidence that Indians killed one another at all in the Pensacola conflict.

If all the Indians whom British officials assumed to be their allies had fought on their side, the war might have turned out differently. However, Indians felt no more bound by British loyalty than certain British colonists did, and of course they had less reason to follow the orders of an empire not their own. Ultimately, this was not their fight.

While Spain and France sent reinforcements to Gálvez's siege, no new British forces arrived. The governor of Jamaica, John Dalling, had sent only two ships to aid Pensacola, both with crews so undependable that they attacked and looted rival ships and never made it to Pensacola at all. Britain had few forces to spare. A hurricane the previous fall had damaged the British fleet and killed more than twenty thousand people in the Leeward Islands alone. British troops at Jamaica were suffering from disease. Dalling and Admiral Peter Parker were focused on fighting the French and Spanish in the Caribbean, Honduras, and Nicaragua and protecting the prized colony of Jamaica from attack by the French, Spanish, and now the Dutch. As for the British army in North America, General Charles Cornwallis was trying to conquer Virginia, and General Henry Clinton was defending New York against the combined forces of George Washington's Continental Army, the French troops of General Jean-Baptiste Donatien de Vimeur, comte de Rochambeau, and the French navy. The secretary of state for the colonies, George Germain, refused Campbell's request for aid and optimistically assured him that Indian assistance and Pensacola's seaside fortifications should suffice for its defense.

They did not suffice. By May 7, the Spanish had advanced their trenchworks to within two hundred yards of the redoubt that held the fort's main artillery. General John Campbell wrote to Germain, "Our fate appears inevitable. We are attacked by an armament that shows the importance of the conquest in the estimation of Spain." In contrast, he noted, British Pensacola had "been neglected." He was going to hold out as long as he deemed reasonable, but he suspected that his next letter would be "the unpleasing and disagreeable task of reporting the triumph of Spain and their acquisition of a province under their dominion" (Campbell to Germain, May 7, 1781, in *Documents of the American Revolution, 1770–1783*, 20: 138).

Indeed, the following day a Spanish shell blew up the British powder magazine within the redoubt, killing nearly a hundred British soldiers and sailors. Spanish troops occupied the remains of the redoubt, and General Campbell decided British defense was futile. He surrendered Pensacola and the entire colony of West Florida to Spain.

The surrender's repercussions were quickly apparent. The British had lost a colony that had not rebelled, and they could vividly see that the war's risks extended far beyond the Atlantic coast. After the surrender, Spanish ships rushed from Pensacola out into the Gulf of Mexico and the Caribbean to protect French ports. This move freed the French admiral François-Joseph-Paul de Grasse to head for Yorktown to join with Washington's Continental Army and French land forces to force Cornwallis's surrender five months after Pensacola. The Spanish took the Bahamas and Minorca and conferred with the French on where to send their ships next—St. Augustine? Halifax? Or Jamaica, the crown jewel of the British sugar islands? Foreseeing an attack on their most valuable colony, and without forces to fortify it, the British agreed to peace.

The War's End

Actions and decisions in the Gulf region helped doom the British attempt to force the rebelling colonies back into the empire. Now those colonies were their own nation—the United States—which would become the determining force in North America. Yet at the end of the Revolutionary War, U.S. dominance seemed unlikely. While there were some in the Spanish monarchy who saw the United States as a potential threat, things generally looked good for Spanish expansion. The Continental Congress was a weak and underfunded central institution trying to coordinate thirteen extremely independent-minded states. Spain's victories on the Gulf Coast promised a strong and growing Spanish presence in North America.

Although James and Isabella Bruce left West Florida and returned to Britain, other colonists—English, French, and Spanish—accepted Spain's offers to stay. Amand Broussard and Anne Benoît lived and prospered in the expanding Spanish empire.

After the war, at least a thousand enslaved men and women in Spanish Louisiana and the Gulf Coast freed themselves by purchase, taking advantage of Spanish slave laws and their wartime opportunities. Petit Jean and his wife gained their freedom by insisting on a reward for their service to the Spanish. In this era, enslaved people and their loved ones spent at least $250,000 buying freedom ($5 to $10 million in today's dollars), and they would form a population of free people of color even as slavery increased around them. The Creeks were soon soliciting Spanish assistance in fighting settlers who threatened to move west from Georgia, but they were confident that they would prevail. The Chickasaws seemed to have established the peace they had sought. Those who had

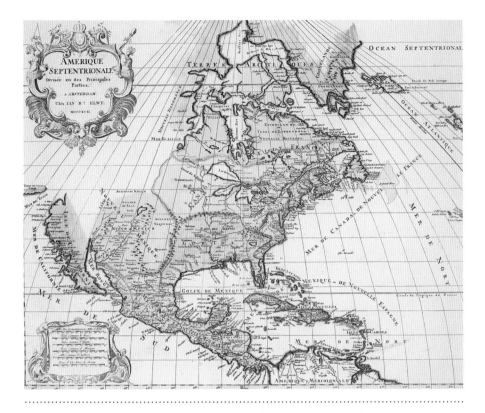

Map of North America, 1792, showing the large extent of Spanish claims after the Revolution. From Jan Barend Elwe, *Amerique septentrionale* (Amsterdam: Jan Barend Elwe). (Courtesy Lionel Pincus and Princess Firyal Map Division, New York Public Library, image ID 434864)

taken refuge in the fortified town were able to leave its protection and return to smaller towns and farms in Chickasaw country. Chickasaws who had moved away entirely were able to return home, and with their return, the population rebounded to over three thousand by 1790 (Cegielski and Lieb 2011: 33–35, 42). As Chickasaw leaders put it, "We increase and live in peace and plenty" (Chickasaw Talk to the Rebels, May 22, 1779, Papers of the Continental Congress, reel 65, frames 41–42).

All this was to change as people from the United States sought land in the West and access to world markets via the Mississippi River. They brought their guns and slaves and transformed the region into the cotton-growing South of the nineteenth century. That antebellum history would erase the international history of the earlier era, when empires and Native nations ruled over the land.

LAFAYETTE

Patrick Villiers

> Lafayette's role in the American Revolution was different from the way he portrayed it in his autobiographical *Memoirs*; it was more complex, more intertwined with other characters, and more intriguing than either his book or the standard histories have depicted. — *Editors*

Gilbert du Motier, marquis de La Fayette, wrote very little about his exact role in the War of American Independence. As Étienne Taillemite, inspector general of the Archives of France, would later note in his book *La Fayette*, the marquis's autobiographical *Memoirs* served to "sculpt his own statue, trying to persuade his readers that everyone opposed his project, which was completely wrong" (1989: 22). Neither was Lafayette (as he later Americanized his name) one of the first French officers to come to the assistance of the American insurgents, as is often insinuated by popular historians of the Revolution. He fails to mention in his *Memoirs*, for example, the crucial roles of King Louis XVI and his ministers Antoine Raymond Jean Gualbert Gabriel de Sartine and Charles Gravier, comte de Vergennes, in the war. However, the archives of Lafayette's maternal family and new research have granted us fresh insight into his role in the American Revolution, in which he stood shoulder to shoulder with the emerging United States.

Like his father and a great-grandfather before him, Lafayette had always wanted to become an army officer. In ancien régime France, as in most European nations of the day, army officers bought their commissions (and

Translated by Larrie D. Ferreiro

accompanying regiments) from the Crown. A colonelcy was particularly dear, costing one hundred thousand *livres* (the equivalent of over half a million dollars today), assuming that the king agreed to grant one. For most young men of the lesser nobility, a lack of money meant little hope of a military career unless they entered a specialist school, where studies were paid for by the Crown. One such specialist school was the French Royal Corps of Engineers, where, after 1751, admission was contingent on passing a rigorous examination.

Lafayette's father, Michel de La Fayette, belonged to the impoverished nobility of Auvergne, in central France, so it was only by acquiring a hefty dowry that the young Lafayette could buy a regiment. In 1757, the elder marquis married Julie de La Rivière, daughter of the very wealthy marquis de La Rivière and the granddaughter of the well-to-do comte de La Rivière, an army lieutenant general and commander of the prestigious Black Musketeers. Michel de La Fayette was thus able to become a colonel of grenadiers. The younger Lafayette was born later in 1757.

Lafayette's father was killed in 1759, during the Seven Years' War, while leading his regiment of the King's Grenadiers at the Battle of Minden in Prussia. His mother sent the young Gilbert to be raised at the Château de Chavaniac in Auvergne by his grandmother and aunts. The deaths of his maternal uncles soon thereafter made his mother a potentially rich heiress, and she sent Gilbert to Paris in 1768 to receive an education reserved for the highest nobility. In 1770, the unexpected deaths of both his mother and his maternal great-grandfather suddenly made Gilbert one of the richest orphans in France, with an estate of three million livres (the equivalent of about $20 million today).

Gilbert wanted more than anything to be an army officer like his father. One of his great-grandfathers, the comte de La Rivière, who resided in the royal Luxembourg Palace, assured the young man's entry into the Corps of the Black Musketeers in April 1771. Now the trustee of Gilbert's fortune, the comte de La Rivière quickly arranged his marriage into the celebrated Noailles family, led by the old maréchal-duc de Noailles, whose eldest son, the duc d'Ayen-Noailles, had five daughters to marry off. The dowry of Adrienne, the second daughter, was worth only two hundred thousand livres, but this would be enough to buy young Lafayette a lieutenancy in the well-known regiment of the Dragons de Noailles.

Louis Leopold Boilly, *Lafayette in the Uniform of the Dragons de Noailles*, 1788. Oil on canvas. In this portrait, Lafayette is shown in the uniform of his regiment, alongside a fine horse. The French army reforms of 1776 disrupted Lafayette's dreams of becoming a great military officer, and to attain his goal he had to fight overseas. The comte de Broglie, who bought the vessel *Victoire* and its cargo of munitions, offered him the route to that dream. (© RMN-Grand Palais / Art Resource, NY)

The Noailles family was among those closest to King Louis XVI. The duchesse de Mouchy, Gilbert's aunt by marriage, was nicknamed "Madame Etiquette": she had been charged with initiating Marie Antoinette, a member of the Austrian Hapsburg ruling family and the wife of Louis XVI, into the strict conventions of life at the Bourbon court of Versailles. Gilbert soon became part of Marie Antoinette's intimate group of confidants, but he turned out to be a poor courtier, dreaming only of military life.

From 1774 to 1776, Gilbert participated in each of the major annual maneuvers of his regiment at the garrison city of Metz, where Charles-François, comte de Broglie, was both military governor and grand master of the Free-masons. In September 1775, the eighteen-year-old Gilbert was promoted to second captain of the Noailles regiment, but the reforms imposed in May 1776 by Claude Louis, comte de Saint-Germain and French minister of war, abruptly halted Gilbert's rise in rank. These reforms included a reduction in the number of troops, slashing each regiment from two companies to one, which effectively eliminated the need for a second captain. On June 11, 1776, Lafayette was "reformed" out of his position as second captain, which in modern parlance meant that he was placed in the reserves. Instead, he resigned from his regiment and returned to life at the Versailles court.

But Lafayette wished to remain a military officer, and the only way to do so was to fight overseas. The only field of battle open at that moment was alongside the American insurgents (as the French press liked to call them). Unofficial French aid to the American Revolution in the form of arms and munitions was being provided in secret, but Louis XVI had already set the wheels in motion to prepare France to enter the war against Britain: on April 22, 1776, he ordered the rearmament of the entire French Royal Navy, which then had only 60 ships of the line to face down the British Royal Navy, armed with 120 powerful ships. In fact, France required the support of an additional fifty ships of the line from Spain in order to effectively confront Britain. The comte de Vergennes, France's minister of foreign affairs, was the key player in this French-Spanish alliance. In June 1776, he negotiated the payment of three million livres from the French and Spanish courts (as well as from private investors) to the French merchant Pierre-Augustin Caron de Beaumarchais (see page 67) to enable Beaumarchais to create a shell corporation, Roderigue Hortalez et Compagnie, that would sell arms and munitions to the Americans. Beaumarchais chartered eight vessels to carry thirty thousand muskets, one hundred thousand cartridges, two hundred cannon, and other war materiel across the Atlantic. Meanwhile, on July 17, 1776, de Broglie's private secretary, Guy Dubois-Martin, introduced Vergennes to Silas Deane, the newly arrived American envoy in Paris. This meeting was fruitful: on August 15, Deane wrote to the U.S. Congress's Committee of Secret Correspondence to tell them that he had begun to recruit French officers to the American cause.

At the heart of this French engagement with the American insurgents was the comte de Broglie, often operating in secret through Dubois-Martin. It is impossible to summarize here de Broglie's accomplishments from 1763 to 1777 in preparation for a war against England, but is essential to try (see Villiers and Lemineur 2016 for more detail). The younger brother of one of France's most senior military leaders, the maréchal de Broglie, the comte de Broglie was recruited in 1752 by Louis XV to head the Secret du Roi, or the French secret service. It was the comte de Broglie who subsequently recruited both Vergennes and Beaumarchais into the service's operations. De Broglie (whose originally Italian family name fittingly translates as "conspiracy") was a ferocious enemy of England: in 1763, just after France's humiliating defeat at the end of the

Seven Years' War, he ordered plans to be drawn up for a potential invasion of the English coast on the Channel, which he would reprise in its general form in 1779.

De Broglie had been governor of Metz since 1774 and could judge Lafayette's performance during the army maneuvers of 1774 and 1775. He had more than a passing interest in the young officer: he had been with Lafayette's father when he was killed at the Battle of Minden in 1759. Now de Broglie was actively promoting the recruitment of French officers by Silas Deane. Initially, Deane overlooked the credentials of the officers who were motivated to join the fight, and many proved to be more ambitious than competent. But the Continental Congress now asked for engineering officers specializing in artillery and fortifications. Deane recruited and dispatched one group, under the artillerist Tronson du Coudray, most of whom sailed aboard Beaumarchais's ship *Amphitrite*. Deane later sent a second group of four engineers, headed by Louis Antoine Jean Le Bègue de Presle du Portail (later Americanized as Duportail), who would become an American general and the founder of the U.S. Army Corps of Engineers.

Thanks to a recent book by Serge Le Pottier, we know quite a bit about the recruitment of Duportail and his companions (Le Pottier 2011). Louis XVI authorized the four officers from the engineering school at Metz to take leave from the French army to join the Americans, with the promise that they would be reintegrated on their return to France. All four officers had gone through their military education and training after the Seven Years' War, passing through four years of schooling and two years of field training. Duportail was promoted to captain in 1775, and in 1776 the minister of war, Saint-Germain, requested that he reform the artillery corps. Saint-Germain then suggested that Benjamin Franklin, who had arrived in Paris after Deane, consider recruiting Duportail, but because Franklin's French was poor and Duportail spoke no English, many misunderstandings arose between them. The contract for the French officers that Franklin, Duportail, and Saint-Germain eventually agreed on stipulated the following:

> It is well understood that the officers are free to return to France when they wish, as long as it is not in the middle of a campaign or the

Charles Willson Peale, *Major General Duportail*, 1780. Oil on canvas. Duportail is shown in the uniform of an American general but wears the French Cross of Saint-Louis, a decoration awarded by the king for exceptional service. (Courtesy Independence National Historical Park, National Park Service)

construction of works. Of course, the high regard for honor still practiced by French officers will dictate their actions in this regard. For its part, the American government will also be free to dismiss these officers if it so desires. The risk of being taken prisoner was also mentioned: in case of capture or imprisonment by the English, Congress shall be completely committed to do the maximum to obtain an exchange of prisoners. (Le Pottier 2011: 38)

Like his companions, Duportail had little money, so he requested a commission at the rank of lieutenant colonel with a promotion to colonel, and proposed that his three companions be given the rank of captain, with promotion to lieutenant colonel. Congress would reimburse them for the purchase of the engineering instruments necessary for their profession. They departed Nantes by ship in March 1777, but because of the British blockade of the American coast, Duportail and the others had to disembark at Cap-François, in Saint-Domingue (today's Haiti), and then take one of Beaumarchais's ships to New River, North Carolina, where they landed on June 3. They arrived in Philadelphia on foot on July 5 and met George Washington on July 29.

Charles Willson Peale, *Frederick William Augustus, Baron von Steuben*, 1782–84. Oil on canvas. Steuben was a Prussian officer who systematically trained the amateur American troops in military discipline and successfully prepared them to meet the professional British forces head on. Oil on canvas. (Courtesy Independence National Historical Park, National Park Service)

Even though the two men had much in common, the recruitment of Lafayette was notably different from that of Duportail. Lafayette, unlike Duportail, was still considered a minor when he joined the Americans: in the French order of things, he would not reach his majority until 1782, when he turned twenty-five. Until then, his entire fortune was being managed by his family lawyer, Jean Gérard, an onerous guardian who was the only person authorized to release funds for expenses approved by the family council, headed by Lafayette's great-grandfather and father-in-law. Quite contrary to Lafayette's assertion in his *Memoirs* that he had escaped to America on his own, everything was organized by the comte de Broglie and the duc d'Ayen-Noailles.

In September 1777, de Broglie tasked the former Prussian army officer Baron Johann de Kalb with promoting his scheme to take command of the American forces to the Continental Congress. De Kalb was not an aristocrat like de Broglie, having been born into a peasant family in the Bavarian town of Hüttendorf. He had been recruited into the French army by the de Broglie family of officers. Impressed with his competence, they paved the way for his promotion to lieutenant colonel in 1761 and his ascendancy to a baronetcy in 1763. In 1767, on the recommendation of the comte de Broglie, the French foreign minister, Étienne François, duc de Choiseul, sent de Kalb (who spoke

English) on an espionage mission to America to gauge its readiness for a revolution against Britain. De Kalb returned to France the following year, convinced of the inevitability of American independence.

De Broglie's scheme was based on his misguided notion that the young United States needed a strong, experienced European leader to conduct its military affairs. De Broglie was certain that the Congress would be dazzled by his reputation as a chief of France's secret service and as a brilliant tactician in France's fight against Prussia, but he also knew that the parlous state of American finances would not permit his recruitment. Probably based on advice from Beaumarchais, he envisaged buying arms in France and sending them for resale to the American states and Congress at a great profit, which would pay for his services and those of his staff. Silas Deane accepted de Broglie's scheme at face value, and de Kalb submitted it to Franklin in December 1777. While awaiting Congress's reply, de Broglie and de Kalb both embarked on Beaumarchais's ship the *Seine* at Le Havre, but within days the British ambassador, David Murray, Viscount Stormont, had persuaded the French government to embargo their departure.

It was then that Lafayette managed to convince de Broglie that he, and not de Broglie, should leave for the United States with de Kalb and the other officers now prevented from embarking on the *Seine*. Enthusiasm was one thing, however; organizing a passage to America was another. Lafayette, both in his *Memoirs* and in his various letters, wrote so many contradictory accounts of his departure that we must refer to indisputable sources, the account books of Lafayette and the archives of the Admiralty of Bordeaux. First, Lafayette had to convince his wife, Adrienne (then the young mother of a two-year-old), as well as her parents, the duc and duchesse d'Ayen, to agree to his departure. On December 15, de Kalb presented Lafayette to Silas Deane and signed his contract. Contrary to Lafayette's assertions, the Noailles family was well aware of his plans, because only the family council could authorize the lawyer Gérard to pay the bills of exchange for the ship and the cargo.

But all the initial preparations were made by de Broglie. In France, following the naval ordinance of 1681, only a licensed merchant could purchase a vessel and recruit a crew and a captain. The archives of the Admiralty of Bordeaux prove that on February 22, 1778, the merchant-ship owner Pierre

Reculées de Basmarein, a relation of Beaumarchais, bought the 278-ton ship *Clary* for twenty-nine thousand livres. It was renamed *Victoire* on March 7. Now de Broglie had to repay Basmarein and also buy the arms he planned to resell. The bill of exchange for these was signed by François Augustin Dubois-Martin, an impoverished second lieutenant of the regiment of Port-au-Prince. He happened to be the brother of Guy Dubois-Martin, de Broglie's private secretary and the real source of the funds. Meanwhile, Lafayette went to London at the beginning of March with an uncle, the marquis de Noailles, the French ambassador to Britain, in order to divert attention from his plans for America.

From late 1777 until the summer of 1778, the merchant shipping firm Basmarein, Raimbaux et Compagnie dispatched sixty-five ships (thirteen thousand tons total) to America and the West Indies, armed with 381 cannon and carrying 1,550 crewmen. Thirty-eight of these ships never returned: they were either shipwrecked or captured by the British. Like all shipowners, Basmarein had bought all or part of the cargo on speculation with its own funds. Through the Admiralty archives, we know that the cargo of the *Victoire* was worth more than eighty-five thousand livres (almost half a million dollars today) and included probably five to six thousand surplus M1766 muskets that the French army was replacing with newer models. Some of these rifles were stored in Bordeaux at the Château-Trompette, whose governor, the duc de Mouchy, was another of Lafayette's uncles by marriage. Lafayette, although rich, borrowed 43,500 livres from Beaumarchais. When he arrived in Bordeaux, he paid 4,412 livres to Basmarein and 53,000 to Dubois-Martin to pay de Broglie's account. Lafayette thus owned about 80 percent of the cargo of the *Victoire*. According to his friend, shipmate, and fellow army officer Charles-François, chevalier de Dubuisson, Lafayette hoped to sell that cargo in Charleston, South Carolina, at a profit of 300 to 400 percent. To further increase the profitability of the operation, the duchesse d'Ayen also suggested purchasing a shipload of rice in Charleston for 100,000 to 150,000 livres, which Basmarein would then resell in Saint-Domingue (Larquier-Rochefort 1987: 53ff.).

After a stopover at the Spanish port of San Sebastián, probably to load a complement of weapons, Lafayette and his two servants, de Kalb, and thirteen French officers set sail on April 26, 1777, for a crossing of fifty-four days, during which time the marquis fought against seasickness. Gifted in languages, he quickly learned English. To evade the British blockage on Charleston, Lafayette, Dubuisson, and de Kalb landed on June 13 in South Inlet near Georgetown, South Carolina. Lafayette later wrote, "Rowing upriver by canoe, I finally felt the American soil, and my first words were an oath to conquer or perish with this cause" (Lafayette 1837–38: 1: 16).

When he landed in Charleston on June 18, Lafayette received a disappointing welcome, but everything changed when he learned that the *Victoire* had arrived and that the shipment of arms had been sold by the banker John Cripps (the Charleston agent for Basmarein) with the expected profit, more than 150,000 livres (over $1 million today). The shipment of rice for Saint-Domingue had also been purchased and stowed aboard the ship. Lafayette then donated twenty-seven thousand livres to the governor of Charleston, reimbursed de Kalb for twenty-seven thousand livres, and bought horses and carriages, because there was still a distance of nine hundred miles to cover to reach Philadelphia. Lafayette, though still a foreigner, was now a financially independent one. In Philadelphia, Cripps connected him with Robert Morris, the great financier of the American Revolution, who would also serve as Lafayette's banker. On July 27, Lafayette declared before Congress, "I come to serve at my own expense," which meant serving without pay, although he requested the rank of general (Lafayette 1837–38: 1: 19). He disavowed any further ties with the comte de Broglie's scheme to take command of the American forces, which de Kalb also abandoned and which never came to fruition. For his part, de Kalb declared in Congress: "I would like to serve, if the Congress will have me, as a major general. . . . The French minister and his officers will find it very strange, and, I think it entertaining, to see me under the command of the marquis de Lafayette" (Chatel de Brancion and Villiers 2013: 78). In the event, both were given the rank of major general.

Introduced to Washington and invited to review the troops, Lafayette declared, "I am here to learn": an adroit move, as he had never received formal training in a military school (Villiers and Lemineur 2016: 16). At his secondary school, the Collège Duplessis, Lafayette had received only a classical literary education, although he had learned cavalry maneuvers in the regiment of the Dragons de Noailles. The Battle of Brandywine, which was fought on

John Vanderlyn, *Washington and Lafayette at the Battle of Brandywine*, late eighteenth or early nineteenth century. Oil on canvas. This work exemplifies the myth of Lafayette (right), a brilliant horseman and friend of George Washington (left). (Gift of Thomas Gilcrease to City of Tulsa, 1955; © Gilcrease Museum, Tulsa, Oklahoma, 0126.1018)

September 11, 1777, in an ultimately futile attempt to stop the British from invading Philadelphia, showed Lafayette in his element: daring and dismissive of his wounds, but above all a source of courage for American soldiers who had abandoned hope when they were pushed back by the British troops. After recovering from his injuries and carrying out various other missions, he also won hearts and minds at Valley Forge. Along with de Kalb, the Baron Friedrich Wilhelm von Steuben, and Duportail, he helped transform the disparate Patriot militias into a unified army able to fight against the professional British troops. He warned, for example, against placing American soldiers in needless danger, given the problems of recruiting and training new troops. This advice Washington followed.

France and the United States signed the Treaty of Amity and Commerce in February 1778. Sensitive to the fact that the Americans had fought the French in the Seven Years' War (also known as the French and Indian War) just a decade earlier, Lafayette played a vital role in bringing together these former enemies in an alliance against Britain. The French fleet of Vice Admiral Jean-Baptiste Charles Henri Hector, comte d'Estaing, arrived off New York in July, but lacking accurate charts and experienced pilots, he was unable to attack the port, much to Washington's disappointment. But the marquis, from Auvergne like d'Estaing, formed a strong bond with him and attempted to gain the initiative by hurrying an amphibious assault on British-held Newport, Rhode Island. However, a great storm blew up, scattering both the French and British fleets to sea and preventing d'Estaing from winning a decisive victory over the Royal Navy. He brought his battle-damaged fleet to Boston for repairs, but as winter approached, he left to defend the strategic French sugar islands in the West Indies from likely British assaults.

With France now officially in the war, Lafayette, who was suffering from illness, returned to his native land in January 1779. Queen Marie Antoinette appointed him a colonel and allowed him to buy his regiment for one hundred thousand livres. However, most of the other French volunteers remained in America, including Duportail, who convinced the Continental Congress to create the Corps of Engineers, modeled after the French system, and to appoint him its chief engineer.

Jean-Baptiste Donatien de Vimeur, comte de Rochambeau, was appointed commander of a new French expeditionary force to give direct military support to the Americans, which set sail in early 1780. Lafayette returned to the United States aboard the frigate *Hermione* to announce Rochambeau's arrival and was reinstated as an American major general. As soon as the French troops disembarked in July, Lafayette tried to push Washington and Rochambeau to attack New York, but the two commanders refused to do so and accused him of trying to divide them. Washington instead assigned him to lead an offensive in Virginia.

The entire southern campaign had been plagued by setbacks. Duportail was sent to Charleston to defend against a British siege but was captured when the city fell in May; de Kalb was killed at the battle of Camden in August. With his Virginian troops, the marquis practiced guerrilla tactics instead of fighting the superior British forces in European-style lines of battle. He adopted the philosophy of Horatio Gates on commanding the militia: "They must be led, not driven" (Villiers and Lemineur 2016: 159). Lafayette was able to slow down

Artist unknown, *Vice Admiral d'Estaing in Uniform*, ca. 1776–80. Print. Having battled corsairs in the Indian Ocean as an army colonel, Jean-Baptiste Charles Henri Hector, comte d'Estaing, later transferred into the navy. He was promoted to lieutenant general and then vice admiral, even though he had little experience at sea. His campaign in the United States was not decisive, as he failed in his attempts to drive the British from Newport and Savannah. Nevertheless, he and Lafayette became brothers in arms. (ART Collection / Alamy Stock Photo)

the British general Charles Cornwallis in Virginia in 1781, preventing him from moving farther north and following him to Yorktown. This was a key element in the plan of the comte de Grasse, who had coordinated with Washington and Rochambeau to bring his fleet from the Caribbean to surround the British in Chesapeake Bay. De Grasse defeated a British fleet at the Battle of the Chesapeake on September 5, 1781, which paved the way for his blockade of Cornwallis at Yorktown. Lafayette led his Virginian force to Yorktown to begin the landward side of the siege, and there found Duportail (recently paroled by the British), who, under Washington's orders, directed the plan of attack on the fortifications as troops under Rochambeau and Washington were marching south from Newport and New York.

Lafayette recruited the enslaved American James Armistead to spy on Cornwallis's camp, and Armistead returned with detailed information on weaknesses in the British defenses. Lafayette was at Washington's side, in his American uniform, when Cornwallis's second in command, Brigadier General Charles O'Hara, offered his surrender to the French and American forces. Lafayette then returned to France to participate, with d'Estaing, in the planned

French-Spanish invasion of the British naval stronghold at Jamaica. When Lafayette, then at Cádiz, Spain, received word of the provisional peace treaties in February 1783, he immediately left for Paris to take possession of his *hôtel particulier* (townhouse) at 183 rue Bourbon, which he had bought the previous September for two hundred thousand livres ($1.2 million). He dubbed his residence the embassy of the United States in Paris. From there he fought for the abolition of slavery. Earlier he had petitioned Washington: "Let us Unite in Purchasing a small Estate Where We May try the Experiment to free the Negroes, and Use them only as tenants" (Lafayette to Washington, February 5, 1783). On October 20, 1783, he received the noted British abolitionist William Wilberforce and Prime Minister James Pitt for further discussions of the subject. He also attended lodge meetings of the Freemasons. The ideas of the young American democracy had left an indelible impression on this French officer, which led him to think deeply about the natural rights of man.

Lafayette's return trip to the United States in 1784 allowed him not only to see the country at peace, but also—and especially—to talk to Washington about the constitutional problems of the young republic. On his return to France, Lafayette launched himself into the game of domestic politics there. He played a decisive but controversial role at the beginning of the French Revolution, where, with Jean-Sylvain Bailly and others, he helped publish the Universal Declaration of the Rights of Man and the Citizen. Despite warnings from Washington and the ambassador to France, Gouverneur Morris, he believed he could tame the tiger of the French Revolution. However, like his friend Duportail, whom he had urged to become one of the last ministers of war under Louis XVI, Lafayette was impeached and sentenced to death. Both fled the country but were captured and held in Austria. Their flight from France, while certainly not glorious, allowed them to escape the guillotine. Duportail returned to the United States, became a farmer, and later died, apparently of a burst appendix, aboard a ship taking him back to Napoleonic France.

Lafayette was more fortunate. He was eventually released from his Austrian prison, thanks in part to the negotiations of his wife, Adrienne, and managed to return to the family castle of Lagrange in France. Lafayette would make one more triumphant return tour around the United States in 1824–25 before he died on May 20, 1834, at the age of seventy-six, known forever more as the "Hero of the Two Worlds."

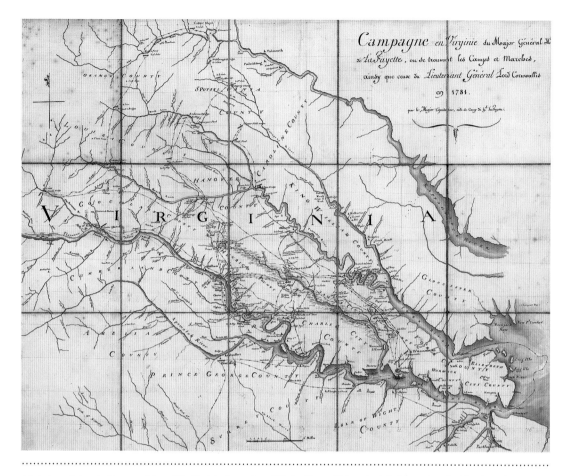

Michel, capitaine du Chesnoy, *Map of the Virginia Campaign of Major General Marquis de Lafayette in 1781, Showing His Encampments and Movements as Well as Those of Lieutenant General Lord Cornwallis*, 1781. Capitaine du Chesnoy was Lafayette's aide-de-camp. (Library of Congress, Geography and Maps Division, LCCN 00558784)

Jean-Baptiste Lepaon, *Lafayette and Armistead at Yorktown*, 1783. Oil. Lafayette used the services of the enslaved American James Armistead to spy on the weaknesses of General Cornwallis's defenses at Yorktown, and later Lafayette helped to obtain Armistead's freedom from William Armistead of Virginia. (The identification of Armistead in this portrait is uncertain.) (Lafayette College Art Collection, Easton, PA; gift of Helen Fahnstock Hubbard in memory of her husband, John Hubbard, Harvard University [class of 1892], ca. 1941)

HORATIO NELSON

When Spain entered the war in 1779, it was determined to drive Britain from its dominions in Nicaragua and Honduras around the Gulf of Mexico, where for over a century the British had maintained logging colonies that supplied mahogany for shipbuilding and logwood for making dye. Britain was equally determined to maintain and expand its presence there. The Spanish governor of the region, Matías de Gálvez (the father of Bernardo de Gálvez), correctly divined the British strategy: a two-pronged attack to cut the Spanish empire in half. In September and October 1779, the governor of Jamaica, John Dalling, sent Captain William Dalrymple to capture the northern port of Omoa on the Gulf of Honduras, but the following month, Gálvez counterattacked and recaptured it.

The British and Spanish next turned their attention to the south, where in April 1780 Dalling sent another force of a thousand men to capture the Inmaculada Concepción fortress on the San Juan River, which was the primary access to Lake Nicaragua. Disease and sickness took their toll on the troops, including a young navy captain named Horatio Nelson, who had taken the lead in the expedition before dysentery laid him low and forced him to return to Jamaica. After a two-week siege marked by both artillery salvos and hand-to-hand combat, the Spanish surrendered. Gálvez, meanwhile, had hastily constructed a new fort on Lake Nicaragua at the mouth of the San Juan River, effectively bottling up the British troops and preventing their planned assault across the isthmus. Central America was in a stalemate that would not be broken until the end of the war, when the peace treaty acknowledged Britain's logging rights in Honduras.

John F. Rigaud began this portrait of Nelson in 1777, three years before the actual assault on Fort San Juan, depicted in the background. He did not finish it until the year after Nelson returned from the Nicaragua campaign.

....

John F. Rigaud, *Captain Horatio Nelson, 1758–1805*, 1781. Oil on canvas. Nelson had hoped to follow his hero James Wolfe into immortality by leading a daring attack like the one in which Wolfe seized Quebec in 1759, but Nelson found only disease and disaster on the hostile San Juan River. (© National Maritime Museum, Greenwich, London, BHC2901)

War Supplies from the Low Countries

Marion Huibrechts

Merchants in neutral nations and states became crucial sources of war supplies to the American colonies during the American Revolution. Most of these supplies passed through trade routes in the West Indies, which became an extremely active but highly contested region. — *Editors*

One major issue that globalized the American Revolution was the arms trade. Having few domestic sources for weapons, gunpowder, and ammunition, the American rebels had to find various suppliers in Europe. Because British and French arms manufacturers at the time were producing muskets mainly for their own armies, the Americans had to search for supplies elsewhere.

At the close of its long and successful fight with Spain (1568–1648), the Dutch Republic had prospered conspicuously, and it monopolized the carrying trade of the world. The city of Amsterdam, in the province of Holland, became a market for war supplies. Throughout the seventeenth century, several Dutch cities—The Hague, Delft, Dordrecht, Rotterdam, Maastricht, Groningen, and Nijmegen—produced small arms. Because of the absence of raw materials in these locales, production primarily involved assembling parts manufactured elsewhere. Musket barrels and locks were imported from the prince-bishopric of Liège and fitted together with locally made stocks and mounts. Yet during the eighteenth century, Dutch production of muskets came to a halt because of a slump in demand from the very weak Dutch military forces and competition from Liège merchants. Even domestic demands had to be met from other sources.

Still, arms had arrived in the American colonies along with the first settlers. They were used for hunting and protection and as gifts for American Indian chiefs, who cherished the "thundersticks" as status symbols. Nearly every family in the expanding frontier area possessed at least one musket and often more. Military-style muskets arrived with the British and French armies during the colonial wars of the seventeenth and eighteenth centuries. During the Seven Years' War (French and Indian War; 1754–63), military supplies for the American colonists had come almost exclusively from the British Isles. At the time of the first skirmishes of the Revolutionary War, there were not enough skilled artisans available to make or oversee the making of American small arms. Arms production in colonial America was essentially limited to repairs.

As tensions rose, the British administration progressively reduced transports of weapons and gunpowder to its colonies. The rebels were now forced to organize themselves to procure arms and ammunition from elsewhere. In the colonies, that amounted to securing arms from the provincial armories. Overseas, the Dutch Republic, France, Spain, and Portugal allowed war supplies to leave from their ports. Thus, during the summer of 1774, American vessels appeared in European waters, and the Americans started buying arms and ammunition in the Dutch Republic. By the end of 1774, movements of military equipment for the American colonies were reported, sailing through the English Channel. The traffic was closely watched, not only by British agents but also by maritime powers who were attentive to its political and commercial implications.

The battle for arms and ammunition was fierce. Despite British attempts to seize American and neutral vessels suspected of transporting war supplies, a lively trade was carried on. Piracy and privateering flourished. American privateers brought the American Revolution to Europe, forcing the British navy to protect its own ships carrying military stores to the British forces in the colonies.

An order in the Privy Council of October 19, 1774, prohibited the exportation of gunpowder, weapons, and warlike stores from Great Britain for six months. Other orders were to follow. In January 1775, the British administration launched a worldwide naval and diplomatic campaign to prevent shipments of military supplies to its rebellious colonies. British naval vessels appeared in the English Channel; they also patrolled outside Spanish, French, and Dutch ports in Europe and the West Indies and along the American coastline.

Amsterdam was by far the busiest market for military stores in Europe, offering a means of obtaining whatever wares the American insurgents might require. Because only gunpowder was manufactured within the Dutch Republic, Dutch merchants turned to Liège arms makers to fulfill the orders for muskets. With British naval vessels cruising the North Sea, marine transportation became hazardous. Moreover, the Dutch "Plakkaat" (proclamation) of March 20, 1775, effected a six-month ban on the exportation of war supplies from Dutch ports by British ships (as well as the lading of such supplies by other ships) without the consent of the local admiralty. Transport routes shifted from Amsterdam to the North Sea ports of the Austrian Netherlands (the region south of the Dutch Republic, roughly the area of modern-day Belgium and Luxembourg, then ruled by the Hapsburg dynasty). Eventually the Dutch West Indies island of Sint Eustatius became the hub of the contraband trade. On the day the Fourth Anglo-Dutch War was declared (December 20, 1780), Vice Admiral George Brydges Rodney was given the order to capture the island. On February 3, 1781, Sint Eustatius, ironically unable to defend itself despite its massive supply of arms, was taken by the British.

The call for war supplies from the colonies boosted the fortunes of the Liège arms industry. The geopolitical position of landlocked Liège, and the jeopardization of trade routes through the Dutch Republic because of the latter's treaty obligations to Great Britain, also created opportunities for the politically neutral Austrian Netherlands.

The Arms Industry of Liège
Over the centuries, Liège had become one of the most important arms manufacturing centers in Europe. Craftsmen or pieceworkers dispersed over a large geographic area produced musket parts in workshops in their own homes, with each producer specializing in a specific part. Merchants collected the parts for assembly by ironmongers. Liège never developed its own model of musket: it was famous for copying foreign weapons. This unusual system protected the Liège arms industry from competition. All weapon models were available. The government's role in the trade was limited to enacting the legislation needed to support and benefit the private enterprises. The River Maas was the main transportation artery, linking Liège to France upstream and to the province of Holland downstream. From there, Liège firearms were transported to nearly every region of the world.

Robert Daudet le fils, *Vue de la Ville et du Port d'Ostende Dédié à Leurs Altesses Royales Dame Marie-Christine, Princesse Royale de Hongrie / et Monseigneur Albert-Casimir, Prince Royale de Pologne*, 1784. Copper engraving on paper after a lost painting by Balthasar Solvijns. The port of Ostend was a strategic location on the North Sea from which Liège arms were shipped to Dutch, French, and Spanish ports and then on to the Caribbean and North America. (Courtesy City of Ostend, Belgium)

From 1776 onward, orders for arms from the Dutch Republic, France, and Great Britain were considerable. Thousands of Liège-made flintlock muskets, produced according to the British and French patterns provided by foreign commissioners, left Liège by road for the North Sea ports of the Austrian Netherlands: Ostend, Nieuwpoort, and Antwerp. They were transported to French, Portuguese, and Dutch ports. From there, they were carried across the Atlantic Ocean to the French and Dutch West Indies, and, ultimately, the shores of the rebelling British colonies. In 1776, muskets were commissioned from Holland with the stamp *Pro Libertate*, an incontestable proof that these arms were destined for the American insurgents. Liège arms merchants placed heavy production demands on their artisans, and the streets of the city were reportedly filled with cases of arms.

By the summer of 1777, the bulk of the muskets had gone to France, filling orders placed by the commissioners of Nantes, Dunkirk, and other French ports. The arms had to be shipped in small cases to facilitate transport over land and loading onto ships.

The Geopolitics of the Arms Trade

The government of the Austrian Netherlands stimulated commerce by constructing a network of roads and waterways leading to Ostend, the gateway of a transportation network that linked the hinterland to the sea and thence to the rest of the world. It also facilitated trade by lowering customs duties, including those on arms. Because there were few arms manufacturers in the Austrian Netherlands, there was no reason to restrict the transit of arms from Liège. Because of the tolls charged on the River Maas and the longer route to the sea, it became cheaper and safer to carry goods from Liège to the Dutch Republic through the Austrian Netherlands.

When the Dutch Republic, under diplomatic pressure from Great Britain, issued its Plakkaat prohibiting the export of war supplies, Liège arms traders saw their business slow. They started distributing arms to France and Portugal via Ostend.

The fate of the American merchant brig *Charming Peggy* illustrates the complexities of the trade and transport of arms. The ship sailed from Philadelphia in September 1775, with a cargo of flaxseed to be sold in Europe. Captain

Gustavus Conyngham and Jonathan Nesbitt, the "supercargo" (an officer on a merchant ship who superintends sales and has charge of the cargo), planned to return with a shipload of military supplies. Because no war supplies were available in the French port of Dunkirk, Nesbitt went to Amsterdam, where he bought 589 barrels of cannon gunpowder, 71 barrels of saltpeter, 30 barrels of sulfur, and 9 barrels of flints. A Dutch smack brought the cargo to Nieuwpoort, in the Austrian Netherlands, some seventeen miles from Dunkirk. The cargo was transshipped on April 5 and 6, 1776, officially destined for Sint Eustatius. At the request of John Peter, the British consul in Ostend, the brig was detained. The case turned into a civil litigation between the "rebel supercargo" and the British consul. The case was decided in favor of Nesbitt, and the consul was held liable for damages.

Initially, Britain did not attempt to intervene in the arms trade from these ports because it did not consider the Austrian Netherlands to be a maritime power. On April 27, 1776, however, following a request from London, a one-year ban on the exportation of war supplies by sea to the British American colonies was issued in the name of Empress Maria Theresa of Austria. Article 1 of the ordinance forbade "all our subjects" from furnishing supplies to the Americans. Cargoes whose papers indicated other destinations easily acquired authorizations from the Financial Council. Strictly interpreted, the ordinance was not meant to keep other countries from supplying the Americans with Liège arms. A second ordinance was issued on April 17, 1777, but a new request by the British ambassador in April 1778 was refused. By then France was at war with Great Britain, and the British were also buying arms from Liège.

Trade through the West Indies

After the closure of the port of Boston, the Continental Congress enforced its demands on the mother country with a "peaceable measure"—a trade boycott known as the Continental Association, which banned the importation and consumption of all goods from Great Britain, Ireland, and the West Indies, effective December 1, 1774. It included a provision banning all exports from America to Britain starting September 10, 1775, if the Americans' demands were not met.

In revenge for the American boycott, George III prepared the Prohibitory Act. It suspended all trade and commercial ventures between Great Britain and the rebelling colonies. Despite fervent opposition from many parliamentarians, who predicted the ruin of the West Indies plantations, George III signed the act on December 23, 1775.

On the islands of the British West Indies, all arable land was used for the cultivation of sugar cane and spices. Plantation owners there depended on the American colonies to supply food for their numerous slaves and the lumber necessary for storage of sugar, rum, syrups, and other products. By the end of spring 1775, some islands petitioned for dispensations from the Continental Congress to safeguard them from the effects of the boycott.

The requests from the West Indies reached Philadelphia just as the news from the Battle of Bunker Hill (June 17, 1775) convinced Congress of the importance and urgency of war supplies. Benjamin Franklin immediately submitted a resolution to Congress to allow exports from the colonies in return for cargoes of arms and ammunition. On Saturday, July 15, 1775, the Second Continental Congress adopted a resolution allowing American vessels to export indispensable foodstuffs to the West Indies in exchange for arms and ammunition. The resolution made a simple point: no war supplies, no food.

The resolution offered an indirect but clear incentive for other European countries with holdings in the West Indies (France, Spain, the Dutch Republic, and Denmark) to offer military supplies in exchange for American produce. The Americans sent small and fast vessels to the West Indies. These smaller boats could not only outmaneuver pursuing British cruisers on the open sea but could also sail through the Caribbean rather than out into the Atlantic Ocean, making their way up the creeks and small rivers of the mainland without having to approach the colonies by way of major ports or rivers.

From the beginning of 1776 onward, significant quantities of war supplies reached the colonies through the West Indies. From Europe to the islands, French vessels carried cargoes to the French West Indies and Dutch vessels to the Dutch West Indies. The transports thus had the character of trade operations, and interference by the British navy constituted an obstruction of national commerce.

Arms and ammunition came principally through the French and Dutch islands (notably Sint Eustatius), while other equipment and supplies, such as sails, came through the Danish islands. The practice of packing the arms in small cases in Liège made it easier and quicker to transship the cargoes onto American boats in the West Indies.

If the British government intended to stop contraband trade, it had to be done in the West Indies. The routes of Europe were too well established to be impeded.

PART III

LEGACIES

Portraits of four of the leading diplomats who negotiated the several peace treaties that ended the American Revolution. Clockwise from top left: David Martin, *Benjamin Franklin (1706–90)* (detail), 1767, oil on canvas, for the United States (White House Historical Association, gift of Mr. and Mrs. Walter H. Annenberg). Antoine-François Callet, *Charles Gravier, Comte de Vergennes, Ministre d'État des Affaires Etrangères (1719–87)* (detail), ca. 1774–87, oil on canvas, for France (© RMN-Grand Palais / Art Resource, NY). Jean-Laurent Mosnier, *William Petty, 2nd Earl of Shelburne (1737–1805)* (detail), 1791, oil on canvas, for Britain (ART Collection / Alamy Stock Photo). Pompeo Batoni, *Don José Moñino Redondo, Count of Floridablanca (1728–1808)* (detail), ca. 1776, oil on canvas, for Spain (Art Institute of Chicago / Art Resource, NY)

HESSIAN SAVAGES, FROG-EATING FRENCHMEN, AND VIRTUOUS AMERICANS

Robert A. Selig

> Americans struggled in their dealings with the foreigners whom war brought to their country—both the German soldiers hired by Britain, and the French. In the course of the war, however, personal contacts eroded prejudices to the degree that some Germans and French elected to desert and remain in America. — *Editors*

The years between 1776 and 1783 constitute the only time in the history of the United States when large numbers of foreign troops fought on its soil. Britain's German auxiliaries and the U.S. Congress's French allies arrived at different points during the war, and they came with varied goals and mixed expectations about the people and country they would encounter.

Britain's German auxiliaries, who began to arrive in 1776, were collectively known as Hessians, though they hailed not only from the principalities of Hesse-Kassel and Hesse-Hanau but also Brunswick-Wolfenbüttel, Ansbach-Bayreuth, Anhalt-Zerbst, and Waldeck. They constituted a comparatively homogeneous group. Eventually numbering just over thirty thousand, these troops spoke the same language and overwhelmingly professed the Protestant faith.

The roughly 5,300 French forces who stepped ashore in Newport, Rhode Island, in July 1780, and the almost 700 who arrived in Boston in June 1781, both under the command of Jean-Baptiste Donatien de Vimeur, comte de Rochambeau, represented a much more diverse group. One of the four infantry regiments, the Regiment Royal Deux-Ponts (with about a thousand men), hailed from Zweibrücken (Deux-Ponts), a duchy in the Holy Roman

---

Unless otherwise indicated, all translations are the author's.

Hessian recruitment poster, November 1776. It states, in part: "By special order of . . . Prince Friedrich, Landgraf of Hessen . . . we officially announce publicly that [we seek] . . . qualified foreigners for military service, who wish to serve as part of Great Britain's military corps. . . . [R]ecruits will receive a signing bonus in addition to a salary and the necessary uniform, [and] . . . English pay." (Collection of Robert A. Selig)

Empire of the German Nation that bordered France. Its soldiers, almost half of whom were Lutheran or Reformed Church members rather than Catholic, spoke German rather than French. The same was true of most of the roughly six hundred infantry, artillery, and cavalry serving in the Volontaires Étrangers de Lauzun, generally known as Lauzun's Legion after its commanding officer, Armand Louis de Gontaut, duc de Lauzun. This was a mixed unit thrown together less than a month before Rochambeau's departure for America because the duke wanted to go and needed a unit to command. It was dissolved and reorganized into the Fifth Regiment of Hussars as soon as it returned to France in 1783.

The Americans would have preferred not to host either the Germans or the French. Americans' preconceived notions about them — sometimes decades in the making — shaped the initial tone of interpersonal contacts. The response of settlers to the soldiers at their doorsteps depended on the Americans' religious and cultural backgrounds, family traditions, prior personal

Anonymous, *Carte Militaire des Troupes de France* (detail), 1775. Thousands of French soldiers came to fight in the American war. More than three thousand lost their lives. (Reproduced by permission of the Society of the Cincinnati, Washington, DC)

Anonymous, *Colonel de Hussard de Lauzun*, ca. 1783. Print. (Brown University, Anne S. K. Brown Military Collection, bdr:237269)

experience, and political loyalties. Yet as Americans got to know the Hessian and French troops, and vice versa, perceptions changed, and they began to see the foreigners more as individual human beings than as enemies or allies.

The Hessians

When news reached London of the bloodshed at Lexington and Concord on April 19, 1775, King George III decided to force his disloyal subjects into submission. Faced with a shortage of manpower, his government decided to hire foreign troops. Although the practice was common, many Englishmen found this decision abhorrent. Speaking in the House of Commons in February 1776, Richard Bull exclaimed: "Let not the historian be obliged to say that the . . . German slave was hired to subdue the sons of Englishmen and of freedom"

The REPRESENTATIVES of the UNITED STATES of *America*, in CONGRESS affembled,

To the PEOPLE in general, and particularly to the Inhabitants of *Pennfylvania*, and the adjacent STATES.

FRIENDS and BRETHREN,

WE think it our Duty to addrefs a few Words of Exhortation to you in this important Crifis. You are not unacquainted with the Hiftory of the Rife and Progrefs of this War. A Plan was carried on by the Britifh Miniftry for feveral Years in a fyftematic Manner to enflave you to that Kingdom. After various Attempts in an artful and infidious Manner to bring into Practice the laying you under Tribute, they at laft openly and decifively afferted their Right of making Laws to bind you *in all Cafes whatfoever.*

Oppofition was made to thefe Encroachments by earneft and humble Petitions from every Legiflature on the Continent, and more than once by the Congrefs reprefenting the whole. Thefe were treated with the utmoft Contempt. Acts of the moft unjuft and oppreffive Nature were paffed and carried into Execution, fuch as exempting the Soldiers charged with Murder in America from a legal Trial, and ordering them to be carried to Britain for certain Abfolution; as alfo directing Prifoners taken at Sea to be entered on board their Ships, and obliged either to kill their own Friends or fall themfelves by their Hands. We only mention thefe from among the many oppreffive Acts of Parliament as Proofs to what horrid Injuftice the Love of Dominion will fometimes carry Societies as well as Men. At the fame Time to fhew how intenfible they will be to the Sufferings of others, you may fee by the Preambles to the Acts and Addreffes to the King, that they conftantly extol their own Lenity in thofe very Proceedings which filled this whole Continent with Refentment and Horror.

To crown the whole, they have waged War with us in the moft cruel and unrelenting Manner, employing not only the Force of the Britifh Nation but hiring foreign Mercenaries, who, without Feeling, indulge themfelves in Rapine and Bloodfhed. The Spirit indeed of the Army in general is but too well determined, by their inhuman Treatment of thofe who have unhappily fallen into their Hands.

It is well known to you, that at the univerfal Defire of the People, and with the hearty Approbation of every Province, the Congrefs declared the United States free and independent ; a Meafure not only juft, but which had become abfolutely neceffary. It would have been impoffible to have refifted the formidable Force deftined againft us laft Spring, while we confeffed ourfelves the Subjects of that State againft which we had taken Arms. Befides, after repeated Trials, no Terms could be obtained but Pardon, upon abfolute Submiffion, which every public Body in America had rejected with Difdain.

Refiftance has now been made with a Spirit and Refolution becoming a free People, and with a Degree of Succefs hitherto which could fcarce have been expected. The Enemy have been expelled from the northern Provinces where they at firft had Poffeffion, and have been repulfed in their Attempt upon the fouthern by the undaunted Valour of the Inhabitants. Our Succefs at Sea, in the Capture of the Enemies Ships, has been aftonifhing. They have been compelled to retreat before the northern Army. Notwithftanding the Difficulty and Uncertainty at firft of our being fupplied with Ammunition and military Stores, thofe we have now in Abundance, and by fome late Arrivals and Captures there is an immediate Profpect of fufficient Clothing for the Army.

What we have particularly in View, in this Addrefs, is not only to promote Unanimity and Vigour through the whole States, but to excite the Inhabitants of *Pennfylvania*, *New Jerfey*, and the adjacent States to an immediate and fpirited Exertion in Oppofition to the Army that now threatens to take Poffeffion of this City. You know that during the whole Campaign they have been checked in their Progrefs, and have not till within thefe two Weeks ventured above ten Miles from their Shipping. Their prefent Advances are owing not to any capital Defeat, or a Want of Valour in the Army that oppofed them, but to a fudden Diminution of its Numbers from the Expiration of thofe fhort Enliftments which, to raife the People, were at firft adopted. Many have already joined the Army to fupply the Deficiency, and we call in the moft earneft Manner on all the Friends of Liberty to exert themfelves without Delay in this preffing Emergency. In every other Part your Arms have been fuccefsful, and in other Refpects our facred Caufe is in the moft promifing Situation. We think it proper to inform and affure you that effential Services have already been rendered us by foreign States, and that we have received the moft pofitive Affurances of further Aid. Let us not then be wanting to ourfelves. Even a fhort Refiftance will probably be effectual, as General LEE is advancing with a ftrong Reinforcement, and his Troops in high Spirits.

What Pity is it then that the rich and populous City of *Philadelphia* fhould fall into the Enemy's Hands, or that we fhould not lay hold of the Opportunity of deftroying their principal Army now removed from the Ships of War, in which their greateft Strength lies.

It is certainly needlefs to multiply Arguments in fuch a Situation. All that is valuable to us as Men and Freemen is at Stake. It does not admit of a Queftion, what would be the Effect of our finally failing. Even the boafted Commiffioners for giving Peace to America have not offered, and do not now offer any Terms but Pardon on abfolute Submiffion. And though (bleffed be God) even the Lofs of *Philadelphia* would not be the Lofs of the Caufe—Yet while it can be faved, let us not, in the Clofe of the Campaign, afford them fuch Ground of Triumph ; but give a Check to their Progrefs, and convince our Friends, in the diftant Parts, that ONE SPIRIT ANIMATES THE WHOLE.

Confiding in your Fidelity and Zeal in a Conteft the moft illuftrious and important, and firmly trufting in the good Providence of God, we wifh you Happinefs and Succefs.

Given at Philadelphia, December 10, 1776.

By order of Congrefs,

JOHN HANCOCK, *Prefident.*

Continental Congress broadside warning about foreign mercenaries, December 10, 1776. In this public announcement, Congress warned that Britain was waging war not only with great cruelty but by "hiring foreign Mercenaries, who . . . indulge themselves in Rapine and Bloodshed." (Library of Congress, Rare Books and Special Manuscripts Division, bdsdcc 01801)

("Debate in the Commons, February 29, 1776," in *Parliamentary History of England* 1813: vol. 18, col. 1185). On March 5, 1776, in the House of Lords, William Pitt, the First Earl of Chatham, labeled the plans a "sale of human blood," calling the soldiers "devoted wretches thus purchased for slaughter" ("Debate in the Lords on the Duke of Richmond's Motion for an Address to Countermand the March of the German Troops, and for a Suspension of Hostilities in America, March 5, 1776," in *Parliamentary History of England* 1813: vol. 18, col.

1223). Eighteen months later, in November 1777, an irate Pitt decried the hiring of Hessians as the bond that would unite Americans in their opposition to the Crown. "If I were an American as I am an Englishman, while a foreign troop was in my country, I never would lay down my arms; never, never, never" ("William Pitt in the House of Lords, 18 November 1777," in *Parliamentary History of England from the Earliest Period to the Year 1803* 1814: vol. 19, col. 363).

Across the Atlantic, proindependence radicals in Congress used these reports of the Crown's hiring foreigners to fight its own subjects as proof that Parliament had no real interest in negotiation. A writer in the *Pennsylvania Journal* in February 1776 lamented that the king had hired the Hessians to bring tyranny and despotism to his American colonies and to enslave his own subjects. In the writer's view, American colonists were dutiful subjects who asked for nothing more than their rights, yet the king had hired foreign mercenaries "to kill, lay waste, and spread desolation, by fire and sword, from one end of the colonies to the other" ("Johannes in Eremo" 1776).

Writing under the pseudonym "Cato" in March 1776, William Smith said of the American colonist, "Even the wife of his bosom, and the daughter of his affection, are not safe from the unholy violence of mercenary soldiers, rioting through every corner of a land not their own, insolent in victory, and barbarous in defeat" ("Cato" 1776). British treaties with Frederick II of Hesse-Kassel, William of Hesse-Hanau, and Duke Charles I of Brunswick-Wolfenbüttel opened the doors for Hessian troops to be deployed to the United States. For many Americans, these treaties removed the last doubts about declaring independence.

As they arrived in the New World, the Hessians' view of America and its rebellious inhabitants favored the British perspective. How could it be otherwise? Loyalty to hereditary princes was their lodestar. The Americans were ungrateful rebels opposing their rightful king. Did he not have the divine right, even the obligation, to reestablish the God-given order by forcing his subjects into submission? As Lieutenant Andreas Wiederhold, of the Hesse-Kassel Regiment von Knyphausen, wrote to his friend Georg Ernst von und zu Gilsa in April 1776, on the eve of Wiederhold's departure for the New World: "My profession and my duty demand of me to risk my life in the service of my master, and I am ready to fulfill this duty" (Wiederhold 2010: 89). A small intellectual

Dutch soldier from the Graafschap Beverwyk. Print. (Brown University, Anne S. K. Brown Military Collection, bdr:231035)

elite did oppose German participation in the war, not because they disagreed with its goals but because their rulers had contemptuously sold their subjects to fight in America.

Extant letters and notes by enlisted soldiers headed for America indicate that they understood little about why, where, or whom they were fighting. Twenty-two-year-old Stephan Popp of the Ansbach-Bayreuth troops wrote simply: "Since my youth I had had a desire to see the world" (Popp 1953: n.p.). The Hessian grenadier Johannes Reuber, on receiving live ammunition for his musket, "looked around in bewilderment, and each one saw that this was serious" (quoted in Burgoyne 2012: 16). The surgeon Julius Wasmus of the Brunswick troops recorded in July 1776: "Our men . . . firmly believe that Spain borders on America. They confuse the European Spain with the American and think it possible to get from Spain to France . . . to Germany by land. This

Leib Grenadier Regiment. Every Hessian regiment included black soldiers recruited in America. While most were laborers, some were children, age eleven to thirteen, who served as drummers or fifers. (Brown University, Anne S. K. Brown Military Collection, bdr:249643)

erroneous belief tempted some to desert, but they could not even get out of Canada" (Wasmus 1990: 26).

After they arrived in America, the Hessians bore the brunt of months of debate and propaganda vilifying them. As he was marching across Massachusetts in August 1777, Wasmus, who was taken prisoner at the Battle of Bennington, recorded that in Williamstown, "Our landlady had a child . . . that she was carefully hiding. . . . She had heard the Germans were cannibals, slaughtering children &c. . . . When we expressed our astonishment . . . she asked whether we . . . believed that God was our creator and Christ our Saviour. She had been reliably assured that we were the savages of Germany" (Wasmus 1990: 76). Even in Boston, "almost daily, people come from distant places to look at us. They are quite surprised that we are in form just like American men but regret that we had come to America for killing them and their children and for making them slaves" (Wasmus 1990: 79).

As they marched across New Jersey in the fall of 1776, some Hessians lived up to the evil reputation ascribed to them by American propaganda, but some, at least, were doing so with the encouragement of British officers. A letter by an unidentified author, presumably a Scottish officer in a regiment of Highlanders, published in the Worcester *Massachusetts Spy* in September 1776, reported that during the Battle of Long Island on August 27, 1776, "The Hessians and our brave Highlanders gave no quarters; and it was a fine sight to see with what alacrity they despatched the Rebels with their bayonets after we had surrounded them so they could not resist. We took care to tell the Hessians that the Rebels had resolved to give no quarter to them in particular, which made them fight desperately and put all to death that fell into their hands" ("Extract of a Letter from an Officer in General Frazier's Battalion" 1776). An American soldier seems to confirm this claim, writing that "our wounded were mostly put to death by the bayonet. An [American] Soldier near me fired on one of those murderers and brought him down" (quoted in "Recollections of the Revolution in Long Island" 1869).

In the course of the war, atrocities were committed on all sides. Many Americans were ready to give the savage Hessians the treatment they believed the mercenaries deserved. Looking back in the 1830s, Nathaniel Barnett remembered that the day after the Battle of Bennington in August 1777, "Mr. Barber . . . used to relate, that the action was in a clearing, where the stumps were still standing. . . . [E]very stump had on it the head of a Hessian soldier—& on some stumps were 2 & 3 heads, cut off by the Green Mountain boys, such was the animosity felt towards these mercenaries" (quoted in Fitch n.d.: vol. 4, entry 1540 [ca. 1873]).

Still, the success in painting the Hessians as inhuman monsters seems difficult to comprehend, given the German population of the colonies. Germans living in America made up around 275,000 of the roughly 2.5 million colonists, constituting the largest non-English group. Pennsylvania and New York alone were home to about 225,000 German speakers, who generally had been welcomed by the Crown as frugal, hard-working taxpayers. Government tolerance, however, had not translated into full acceptance by their English neighbors, some of whom resented what they perceived to be German clannishness and refusal to integrate. Benjamin Franklin, one of the more famous exponents of this position, complained in 1751, "Why should Pennsylvania, founded by the English, become a Colony of Aliens, who will shortly be so numerous as to Germanize us instead of our Anglifying them, and will never adopt our Language or Customs, any more than they can acquire our Complexion?" (Franklin 1755: 10).

How did German Americans feel about the revolution? Some were Loyalists, for they feared their royal land grants could be taken away by a new republican government. Others felt continuing gratitude to the British Crown for their opportunity to live in a free society. That gratitude was felt especially among pacifist groups such as the Dunkers, Mennonites, Amish, and Moravians in the Mid-Atlantic states who had been forced from their homes by religious persecution in Germany and whose refusal to take up arms made them even more suspect to their fellow Americans.

But these pacifist groups constituted barely 10 percent of all German Americans, most of whom supported the revolution early on. On October 31, 1774, Joseph Hewes, a signer of the Declaration of Independence and a North Carolina delegate to Congress, informed James Iredell that "the Germans who compose a large part of the inhabitants of this province are all on our side; the sweets of liberty little known in their own country are here enjoyed by them in its utmost latitude" (Hewes to Iredell 1774, in Smith et al. 1963: 1: 83). In an attempt to prove their Americanism, German Americans outdid each other to "insult and berate us with the vilest words," Captain von der Malsburg wrote home to Hesse (quoted in Kipping 1971: 24). Jäger Captain Johann von Ewald (a member of the light infantry) bore the brunt of an elderly woman's wrath when he asked her for a glass of water. The woman berated him "in a true Palatine dialect," saying that the "Germans come here to suck us dry and drive us out of house and home" (quoted in Ewald 1976: 91). Thousands would serve in the Continental Army, sometimes even in German-speaking units.

The French
Inviting French land forces to assist Americans in their struggle for independence was discussed even before the Declaration of Independence was signed, but the idea was initially rejected out of hand. Once independence was declared, however, Congressional leaders had to face the fact that they had started their

fight with Britain penniless and lacking the arms, equipment, and expertise needed to win. They knew that the only sources of such assistance were the two Bourbon kings, Louis XVI of France and Charles III of Spain. They also knew that this aid could be obtained only if they declared the colonies an independent nation—in other words, if they portrayed their rebellion as a war between nations rather than a civil war, and cast Britain as a common enemy.

Initially, Americans' willingness to accept French assistance did not extend to accepting French soldiers on American soil. Many Americans, according to the historian Samuel F. Scott, saw the French as "the adherents of a despicable and superstitious religion, as the slavish subjects of a despotic and ambitious prince, as frivolous dandies lacking in manly virtues, as physical and moral inferiors whose very dress and eating habits evidenced this inferiority" (Scott 1984: 45).

As Samuel Breck wrote about his fellow Bostonians in the 1770s, "Before the Revolution the colonists had little or no communication with France, so that Frenchmen were known to them only through the prejudiced medium of England. . . . When, therefore, the first French squadron arrived in Boston, the whole town, most of whom had never seen a Frenchman, ran to the wharves to catch a peep at the gaunt, half-starved, soup-*maigre* [skinny] crews. How much were my good townsmen astonished when they beheld plump, portly officers and strong, vigorous sailors!" (quoted in Scudder 1877: 24–25).

American prejudices against the French need to be understood in their broader historical, religious, and cultural context. Settlers to the New World had taken the English tradition of French-bashing with them across the Atlantic. Reflecting on his journey to England in the 1750s, Louis Charles Fougeret de Monbron informed his French readers, "We are the only nation in the universe that the English do not despise. They rather do us the honor of hating us with all the heartiness possible. Their aversion against us is a sentiment with which they are inculcated from the cradle. Before they know that there is a God to worship, they know that there are Frenchmen to be detested" (Monbron 1757: 52). This fundamental prejudice had been strongly reinforced during the French and Indian War (1754–63), when Americans along the western frontier had renewed their hatred of the French for inciting Native Americans to raid their homes and settlements.

In spite of these common prejudices among the general population, American leaders knew well that they needed French money, supplies, weapons, ships, advisers, and troops to win their independence. In February 1778, France, which had been supporting the rebels clandestinely since the spring of 1777, signed the Treaty of Alliance with the United States, recognizing its independence. Britain responded by declaring war on France. In 1779, France dispatched a fleet under Admiral Charles Henri Hector, comte d'Estaing, to cooperate with the Americans. However, after joint attacks against Newport, Rhode Island, in 1778 and Savannah, Georgia, in 1779 failed, d'Estaing returned to France. His hapless foray into the American theater had strained the young alliance. In November 1778, d'Estaing complained to the naval minister, Antoine Raymond Jean Gualbert Gabriel de Sartine: "One must also fawn, to the height of insipidity, over every little republican who regards flattery as his sovereign right, . . . hold command over captains who are not good enough company to be permitted to eat with their general officers (one must be at least a major to enjoy that prerogative), and have some colonels who are innkeepers at the same time." D'Estaing continued, "It is his knowing how to turn all that to advantage, to put it in its place and remain in his own that has most impressed me in the difficulties that the marquis de Lafayette has overcome" (d'Estaing to Sartine, in Idzerda et al. 1979: 2: 202–03).

French leaders reluctantly agreed that they needed to make a greater investment in the American war if it were to have a chance of success. In 1780, Louis XVI decided to deploy an expeditionary force under the direction of Jean-Baptiste Donatien de Vimeur, comte de Rochambeau. Given the widespread anti-French prejudice in America and d'Estaing's earlier failure, it is not surprising that the welcome of French forces as they stepped ashore in Newport, Rhode Island, was not quite as friendly as Rochambeau's men had hoped. Lieutenant Comte de Clermont-Crèvecoeur believed that "the local people, little disposed in our favor, would have preferred, at that moment, I think, to see their enemies arrive rather than their allies." He thought the British were to blame. They "had made the French seem odious to the Americans . . . saying that we were dwarfs, pale, ugly, specimens who lived exclusively on frogs and snails" (quoted in Rice and Brown 1972: 1: 21). These wild ideas were soon dispelled by personal contact between French and American soldiers. Closer acquaintance also corrected the impression many French officers had of America as a continent inhabited by noble savages and of its wilderness as a tabula rasa where the ideals of humanity formed in the minds of *philosophes* might be realized.

One of the characteristics that exploded this myth was Americans' seemingly inherent love of money. Rochambeau felt himself "at the mercy of usurers" (quoted in Scott 1983: 91). His aide-de-camp, the Swedish count Axel von Fersen, wrote, deeply disillusioned, in January 1781 that "the spirit of patriotism only exists in the chief and principal men in the country, who are making very great sacrifices; the rest who make up the great mass think only of their personal interests. Money is the controlling idea in all their actions." Americans "overcharge us mercilessly . . . and treat us more like enemies than friends. . . . Their greed is unequalled, money is their God; virtue, honor, all count for nothing to them compared with the precious metal" (Fersen 1879: 371).

Nevertheless, many French enlisted men found alluring the degree of equality they encountered in America. As he was marching from Newport, Rhode Island, to White Plains, New York, Private Georg Daniel Flohr of the Royal Deux-Ponts marveled at a country where "all inhabitants are wealthy and well. One does not see a difference between rich and poor. . . . [O]ne does not see a difference between the Sunday clothes and their workday clothes," and women were "always dressed like ladies of the nobility." Looking around, he realized that this prosperity was created by a relatively equal distribution of wealth and free ownership of land, while the absence of tenancy, at least in those parts of America that he saw, leveled social distinctions based on noble privilege. Americans were "not haughty at all. They talk to everybody, whether he be rich or poor," while common folk live "more ostentatiously than the nobility in Europe" (Flohr 1784: n.p.). Not haughty, but not deferential either.

Flohr's admiration for New England society was matched, however, by his abhorrence of Virginia's slaveholding economy. "We also saw that these black people, something that perplexed me very much again, are kept like cattle, and that the young ones of these blacks are raised as much in a state of nature as young cattle; the more young ones they make the more the master who owns them likes it. In various ways they are kept in a state of nature, something that I do not want to describe here in too much detail because it is completely against human nature" (Flohr 1784: n.p.).

By 1781, as the French joined their American allies on the march to Yorktown, many more Americans met French soldiers for the first time, and the "getting to know you" experience repeated itself a thousandfold. The successful partnership that brought the stunning victory at Yorktown and led to independence created a bond between the French and American people that has never been broken. As the French marched north between July and December 1782, the nation celebrated a people whom many had previously reviled and misunderstood.

Deserters

The experience of fighting in America convinced some French and German soldiers that they might be better off if they took the risk of deserting to build a new life in the upstart nation. The New World of German-speaking Pennsylvania—a country without nobility, tithes, or unpaid labor obligations, and offering minimal taxes, an abundance of land, and unlimited opportunities to make one's fortune—exerted a powerful pull on the sons of impoverished German-speaking French peasants.

Of 316 deserters from Rochambeau's corps who avoided recapture, 104 came from the Royal Deux-Ponts alone. Another 186 were German-speaking subjects of the king of France, mostly soldiers from the provinces of Alsace and Lorraine serving in Lauzun's Legion. The remaining three "French" infantry regiments and the artillery accounted for the remaining eighty-one deserters. Flohr claimed that Americans made a distinction between French and German troops serving in Rochambeau's army. As they entered New Jersey from Suffern, "the inhabitants would ask you if you wanted to stay with them and promised to hide you until the French were gone" (Flohr 1784: n.p.), but this does not fully explain the low desertion rate of French-speaking soldiers.

Wherever he went, no Frenchman could say, like Baron Ludwig von Closen (a German officer in the Royal Deux-Ponts), that the environment "recalled to me my dear native land" (quoted in Acomb 1958: 116). Though they had come as allies "to lend a strong hand," French-speaking soldiers simply did not operate in a very hospitable environment, even if interpersonal contact corrected the caricature that had dominated American views of the French.

Traveling across Connecticut in June 1781, Louis François Bertrand Dupont d'Aubevoye, comte de Lauberdière, stopped at Canterbury, where he "passed a fairly pleasant evening with a country squire. . . . He had a preconceived idea of the French" and told Lauberdière

> that I could only be Scottish, that I was [too] white for a Frenchman, that the people of [France] were not usually so polite, so well behaved as I seem to be. . . . I responded that my freshness was not surprising because I was only twenty years old and that all my compatriots had the same kind manners for everyone. . . . He told me that it would be very easy, when he returned home, to deceive his neighbors about what they thought of us, that he was happy to give us justice and that he always wanted to forget the false notions he had of us. We left very good friends. (Dupont d'Aubevoye 1781: cahier 2, 65)

French-speaking deserters found few compatriots to help them adjust to their new surroundings or blend in sufficiently to evade authorities looking for deserters. Complaining about unjust treatment, the *chasseur* Jean-Claude Passant, born in Franche-Comté and serving in Lauzun's Legion, told his commanding officer that he "would rather stay with his girl-friend [*maîtresse*] in a country that offered him the sweetness of liberty" than return to France (quoted in Massoni 1996: 161). Yet when the time came for his unit to depart from winter quarters in the town of Charlotte Court House in rural Virginia, in June 1782, Passant did not act on this assertion but returned to France. Ten of his German-speaking comrades and a lone Frenchman granted themselves leave and remained behind.

Thousands of Hessians, too, deserted so that they could remain. The United States could hardly encourage the troops of its French allies to desert or offer land bounties to them, but no such limitations applied to the Hessians. In the summer of 1776, George Washington had already suggested that Congress encourage Hessians to desert as a means of weakening British forces, but British military success and the American propaganda painting the Hessians as savages and devils brought this plan to naught. Within a few months of

France's entry into the war in February 1778, the political and military situation had changed fundamentally. As British forces abandoned Philadelphia, the changing fortunes of war brought about a considerable increase in desertions from Hessian units. By then the United States also held thousands of prisoners of war, who over the next few years became targets of Congressional propaganda encouraging them to desert. Those efforts, however, were never as successful as Congress had hoped.

The reasons why a soldier deserts are as varied and deeply personal as those that persuade a person to emigrate. The decision depends more on a welcoming environment than on government incentives. By the spring of 1778, many Hessian officers had learned some English, while personal encounters between Hessians and Americans had proved American propaganda wrong. In late 1776, Captain von der Malsburg could already report that the people in New Jersey "have lost much of their initial reserve and shyness toward us after they found out that many of their ideas about us were wrong" (quoted in Kipping 1971: 30). Official figures list 2,949 deserters from Britain's German auxiliaries, but the total number of deserters was much higher. More than two-thirds of the approximately six thousand Hessians who made the United States their new home came from Hesse-Kassel (figures based on Atwood 1980: 254; Kipping 1971: 9). Many prisoners of war had been farmed out and could not be located when the time came for them to march to New York City to embark for Europe. Many others did not want to be found, and their officers did not search very diligently for them. In January 1783, Markgraf Karl Alexander of Ansbach-Bayreuth granted a discharge to all soldiers who wanted to remain in the United States. Landgraf Frederick II of Hesse-Kassel ordered all soldiers discharged who were not his subjects. Such an arrangement helped all sides, except maybe the soldier stuck in the United States. But Britain was looking for settlers in Canada, and Hesse, a poor, mountainous state, was glad for every soldier who did not return.

Conclusion

The responses of Americans both to the War of Independence and to the foreign troops at their doorsteps were deeply personal. Some German Americans became Loyalists, and others joined the Patriot side. Some communities emerged strengthened from the war; others fell apart. For example, half of Londonderry, South Carolina, joined the Loyalist side out of gratitude to Britain, and their descendants still live in Nova Scotia. The other half joined the Patriot side; their descendants now live all across the United States. All that is left of Londonderry itself is a historical marker. Some Americans were pacifists, and some fought in the Continental Army. Others wanted only to be left alone.

The Hessian and French soldiers had similarly diverse experiences and attitudes. Some were anxious to return home, while thousands of Hessians, and hundreds of primarily German-speaking soldiers in Rochambeau's army, decided to settle in the United States. Whatever their motivations for remaining behind may have been, they and their descendants all continue to contribute to the mosaic that forms the United States of America.

FRANCIS PEIRSON

Although histories of the Revolutionary War record mainly the major battles, there were also countless small-scale skirmishes fought throughout the war, and the Isle of Jersey, in the English Channel, was the site of two such conflicts. Jersey is a Channel Island that belongs to Britain, even though it is only fourteen miles from France and visible from the French coast. On May 9, 1779, the French navy staged a small amphibious assault on the island as a diversion in advance of a planned, much larger French-Spanish invasion of the British coast; fleets were then assembling off Spain. In the end, the British army and militia prevented the mainland invasion from taking place.

Yet France continued its plans to retake the Channel Islands. Jersey in particular was important: it sat near the supply route to the French navy base of Brest, and so it was essential during French-British conflicts. Privateers based on the island harassed French shipping as well. In January 1781, France launched a much larger attack on Jersey, planning to mass two thousand troops on the island. Storms, however, scattered half the French fleet, and only about 1,400 troops managed to come ashore in separate landings, led by the baron Philippe de Rullecourt.

Undetected, they entered Jersey's capital, Saint Helier, in the early hours of January 6. The island's governor, Moses Corbet, was captured, so the British defenses were led by twenty-four-year-old Major Francis Peirson, who rallied a successful counterattack but died from a musket ball to the chest. The black soldier to the left, firing a musket to kill Peirson's assassin, was actually a servant of a fellow officer. The French commander, Rullecourt, died of his own wounds later that night. The British captured six hundred French troops, and the survivors of the failed invasion quickly retreated to France.

....

John Singleton Copley, *The Death of Major Peirson, 6 January 1781*, 1783. Oil on canvas. (© Tate, London, 2018, N00733)

Saint-Domingue's Free Men of Color

John D. Garrigus

The French army that fought in the Revolutionary War included free men of color from Saint-Domingue, in the Caribbean. They played an important part in the attack on Savannah, Georgia, in 1779. Later, some of these men became leaders in the fight to win Haitian independence. — *Editors*

In 1779, 545 free men of color sailed from the French Caribbean colony of Saint-Domingue (modern-day Haiti) to fight in the American Revolutionary War. They were members of a fleet aiming to capture Savannah, Georgia, from the British. The expedition was the beginning of their efforts to link military service with civil rights. For decades after the Battle of Savannah, Saint-Domingue's free black militiamen argued that their military service qualified them for French citizenship. In 1790 and 1791, they began to pressure the white local colonial government for civil rights. It is no exaggeration to say that the participation of Saint-Domingue's free black people in the American Revolution helped bring about the Haitian Revolution of 1791.

Involvement by free men of color in the Savannah expedition began in March 1779. When France formally joined the North American war, it sent a naval fleet to the Americas under Admiral Charles Henri Hector, comte d'Estaing. He sailed first to the Caribbean. Fifteen years earlier, he had been governor of Saint-Domingue, France's most valuable colony. During that tenure, d'Estaing established a military unit of free men of color to replace the unpopular white militia. His experiment failed, but in 1779 the admiral created two new forces in Saint-Domingue to join his North American expedition. One, for free men of color, was called the Chasseurs Volontaires; the other, for whites, was named the Grenadiers Volontaires.

Artist unknown, *Plan of the Siege of Savannah . . . 9th October 1779*. This drawing by a British officer details the failed attempt by American and French forces to recapture Savannah from British troops. (University of Georgia, Hargrett Rare Book and Manuscript Library, hmap1779p4)

Soon after he arrived in Saint-Domingue as an admiral, d'Estaing publicly embraced free black military veterans and urged younger men of color to enlist (Moreau de Saint-Méry 1797: 1: 230). The honor of military service would allow patriotic volunteers to reject racial prejudice, he said. Within weeks, over a thousand such men had enlisted. Those who did not volunteer faced official pressure. Saint-Domingue's governor ordered free black militiamen to enlist in the Chasseurs or spend three months in the rural constabulary (orders of March 30, April 13, May 3, June 26, and July 30, ANOM Series F, F³188, 1779; "Lettres du Gouvernement sur les chasseurs volontaires des 18 septembre et 8 octobre," ANOM Series F, F³189, 1779). Many free men of color were skeptical about leaving home for military service. Only about half of those who enlisted actually sailed with the fleet in August. However, the free black force was roughly four times larger than its white counterpart, which had only 156 participants. Both groups were a small but symbolic component of d'Estaing's overall force, which included 3,186 European soldiers (muster records, ANOM Series D, $D^{2c}41$, n.d.; "État comparatif des forces françaises, américaines et anglaises devant ou dedans Savannah," ANOM Series F, F^3189, 1779; Lawrence 1951: 49).

In early September, the French fleet arrived at Savannah and joined the American rebel forces laying siege to the British fort there. As civilian volunteers, the Grenadiers and Chasseurs dug trenches and built siege works. On October 9, French and American troops stormed the fort. The British held their ground and counterattacked, driving the attackers out of their trenches. The French suffered 521 dead and wounded, compared to American rebel and British casualties of 231 and 57, respectively. One Chasseur died, and seven were wounded in the trench fighting (Lawrence 1951: 107). D'Estaing's fleet left the Georgia coast and split up, sailing for various destinations.

The siege of Savannah lasted less than two months, but many of Saint-Domingue's free black volunteers did not return home for two years, because imperial officials were eager to have free black soldiers. Such men often survived the tropical diseases that decimated European units, and they cost little to recruit and equip. One Chasseur company of sixty-two men escorted casualties from Savannah to Charleston, South Carolina, and was the only French force serving during the siege of that city in the spring of 1780. Another unit fought at the Battle of Pensacola. Four hundred Chasseurs may have been stationed in Martinique with regular troops (Voelz 1993: 142). Others were garrisoned in Guadeloupe in 1780. Roughly one-fourth of the Chasseurs were sent to Grenada in the eastern Caribbean and stayed there until at least 1782 (*Affiches américaines,* December 14, 1779, May 2, 1780).

Inspired by d'Estaing's creation, in late March 1780 Saint-Domingue's governor, Jean François de Reynaud de Villevert, created a new troop of free men of color, the Chasseurs Royaux (Moreau de Saint-Méry 1786: 6: 22–30). Reynaud did not even pretend that his was a volunteer unit; he planned to conscript men of color. So many men fled their homes to escape this draft that influential colonists complained to Versailles. They claimed that by alienating these men, Reynaud jeopardized Saint-Domingue's free black constabulary, which hunted escaped slaves, thereby helping thirty thousand white colonists hold roughly four hundred thousand people in slavery. Fearful of losing this valuable tool, Versailles disbanded the Chasseurs Royaux (ANOM Series E, E310, n.d.).

For individual free men of color, the Savannah campaign was a disappointment. Those who volunteered learned that officials valued their low cost, not their idealism. However, the governor's failed attempt to create a conscripted version of the Chasseurs revealed how much the colony depended on the military service of free men of color. Their support was critical to the slave plantation regime.

Militia service became a political asset for men of color in 1789, when the French revolutionaries in Paris decreed that men who served in a local militia uniform were qualified to vote. Saint-Domingue's free men of color seized on this new rule as applicable to their own situation. Free black militiamen across the colony claimed voting rights and formed local national guard companies, sometimes calling themselves *chasseurs*. Veterans of the Savannah campaign, such as André Rigaud and Jean-Baptiste Chavannes, were prominent among the leaders of these units (Thésée 1982: 43; Saint-Rémy 1854–57 [1956]: 67).

In 1790, a man of color named Vincent Ogé returned to Saint-Domingue from Paris with a French militia uniform in his baggage. Ogé had not been a Chasseur, but he demanded that the governor allow free men of color to vote based on the laws of the French Revolution. He seems to have seen his militia uniform as proof of his eligibility. Veterans of the Savannah campaign, such as Chavannes, flocked to his side, along with several hundred militiamen of color. After Chavannes's men disarmed local whites and killed at least one, the governor declared that the free people of color were in revolt. Colonial troops attacked and dispersed Ogé's group. Ogé and Chavannes were eventually captured and brutally executed in February 1791 (Garrigus 2011: 54–62).

This so-called Ogé revolt began the destabilization of colonial society that culminated in the slave uprising of August 1791. As free men of color fought for political rights after Ogé's death, their absence weakened the slave control system. Participation in the American Revolution's Battle of Savannah had taught Saint-Domingue's men of color that their military service was a valuable bargaining chip for civil rights, and in this way it opened the door to the Haitian Revolution.

CRAFTING THE PEACE

David J. Hancock

Although American diplomats were deeply involved in crafting the treaties that ended their Revolution, the principal decision-makers were Britain's Lord Shelburne and France's comte de Vergennes, who were in truth more concerned with the balance of power in Europe than with American independence. — *Editors*

The treaty signed in Paris on September 3, 1783, by representatives of Great Britain and the new United States formally ended a grueling seven-year war. Negotiations over the contours of American independence among the two British and four American representatives had dragged on since April 1782.

The Pennsylvania-born artist Benjamin West sought to capture their achievement. Soon after preliminary articles of peace were signed in early 1783, he began work on a group portrait of the negotiators (see facing page). Seated at the table are John Adams on the left; Benjamin Franklin in the center, staring straight out at the viewer; and Henry Laurens, whose head rests wearily on his hand, on the right. John Jay stands on the left side of the canvas, above Adams, pointing to Franklin, the most senior member of the delegation, while Franklin's secretary and illegitimate grandson, William Temple Franklin, stands between him and Laurens. Documents crowd the table. Behind them, a window draped with thick curtains of a muddy chartreuse color opens onto a landscape with a white house in the background and an intense blue sky above it.

But the right side of the canvas is empty. West's portrait of the peacemakers proved impossible to finish, despite the fact that, living in London, he was well situated to capture the characters of all concerned. Britain's principal representative, the merchant Richard Oswald of London and Auchincruive in

Benjamin West, *American Commissioners of the Preliminary Peace Negotiations with Great Britain*, 1783 (unfinished). Oil on canvas. (Winterthur; Department of State, Diplomatic Reception Rooms, Washington, DC)

Scotland, and his secretary Caleb Whitefoord, do not appear: both Scotsmen were reluctant to be memorialized as the men who gave away the bulk of Britain's North American colonies, especially after Parliament's hostile reception of the preliminary articles struck on November 30, 1782. Always sensitive about his looks (some thought him ugly; he was certainly vain, needing spectacles and an ear horn but loath to use them in public), Oswald actively resisted sitting for West. Admittedly, it might have been inconvenient, as he resided in France and Scotland much of the time, but he also refused to allow the only portrait he had of himself—a primitive 1750 marriage portrait that he disliked intensely—to be used as a model. Just over a year after the signing of the definitive articles of the treaty, he died at his seat in Ayrshire.

Gilbert Stuart, *Caleb Whitefoord, Secretary*, 1782. Oil on canvas. Whitefoord was one of Lord Shelburne's representatives in the Paris peace negotiations. (Montclair Art Museum, 1945.110)

West held on to the unfinished oil sketch until his own death in 1820. Thereafter it passed through the hands of several collectors, including J. P. Morgan and H. F. du Pont, who made it a centerpiece of his new Winterthur Museum. Two copies survive—one in the diplomatic reception rooms of the U.S. Department of State in Washington, D.C., and another on a wall of the John Jay Homestead in Katonah, New York. The U.S. Postal Service clumsily reworked West's image in a stamp issued to commemorate the 1983 bicentennial of the peace.

According to some historians and art historians, the absence of the British negotiators from West's depiction symbolizes either the division between the mother country and its former colonies or an assertion of American independence and will. These conclusions are implausible. We know the omission was not West's intention. More likely, the British negotiators' nonappearance reflects their view that the former colonists were simply not the most important parties to the peacemaking—hard as that is for subsequent generations of Americans to fathom.

More striking in the lush visual depiction of the negotiations is the absence of the true architects of the peace: Charles Gravier, comte de Vergennes, Louis XVI's chief minister; and William Petty-Fitzmaurice, second Earl of Shelburne, George III's prime minister. Too easily forgotten, these two political leaders deftly directed—and often micromanaged—the negotiations.

Antoine-François Callet, *Charles Gravier, Comte de Vergennes, Ministre d'État des Affaires Etrangères (1719–87)*, ca. 1774–87. Oil on canvas. (© RMN–Grand Palais / Art Resource, NY)

Jean-Laurent Mosnier, *William Petty, 2nd Earl of Shelburne (1737–1805)*, 1791. Oil on canvas. (ART Collection / Alamy Stock Photo)

Historians often describe the peace the two ministers constructed in 1782 and 1783 as Britain's caving in to the United States. Britain gave away so much, it is said, because the North American insurgents had won the war and then, with more wily and moralistic representatives, the negotiation; Americans gained so much because weak, gullible, and corrupt British ministers and negotiators had steered the ship of state to financial weakness and defeat. Historians treat Britain's separate negotiations with France, Spain, and the Dutch Republic, as well as the United States' dealings with them, as second-order diplomacy. This narrative is driven on the one hand by triumphalist American historians writing a victors' account of the war and its aftermath, as those in any country are wont to do, and on the other hand by defeatist British historians who did not see much to extol in the huge losses of men and land (except for the expansion of territorial empire in Asia), and who saw in the loss of America a prefiguration of further decline two centuries later.

Through a twisting of historical sense, West's painting can be made to fit the American narrative of superiority and dominance. But the reality is a much more complicated story, one that has to do with the British and European personalities involved in the peacemaking process; their philosophies, programs, and aspirations; and their need to consider one another's motives—not just those of the Americans—in crafting the diplomatic outcome. That is to say, the British negotiators had more to consider than just the territory of the United States, its wily and moralistic negotiators, and American concerns. It was the British working in concert with the French who really commanded the peacemaking, and their leaders were, despite having been on opposite sides of the conflict, more united than divided.

Historians have looked at the negotiations variously. British historians such as Vincent Harlow in the 1950s argued that the peace was shaped by overseas and, to a lesser extent, domestic developments. The Crown and ministers preferred trade over territory, as exemplified in the "swing to the East" that supposedly recentered their empire in Asia during and after the loss of America. In contrast, American historians like George Bancroft in the 1870s and Samuel Bemis and Richard Morris in the 1930s and 1960s, respectively, adopted a moralistic and patriotic stance. For them, the peace was an unequivocal moral and strategic win for clever, superior Americans and a total loss for inept, inferior, and corrupt Britons.

However expansive their outlook, historians in both camps largely ignored what was going on in Europe, Africa and India. As the historian Andrew Stockley has suggested in the most thorough recent analysis of the peace, earlier scholars have failed to take account of the simultaneous discussions and negotiations being conducted between and among Britain, France, Spain, the Dutch Republic, Austria, Switzerland, Sweden, and Russia. There is another way to tell the story of the peace, Stockley suggests: analyzing its outcome as the product of more international, multivariant factors. Shelburne in London may be the most important party, inasmuch as he was the mastermind and midwife of four separate treaties.

Who Was Lord Shelburne?

Shelburne's life, personality, and philosophy decisively shaped the diplomacy of 1782 and 1783, and he contributed to the highly interconnected European, Atlantic, and often global endeavor. While he was commonly referred to as a "friend to America" throughout the revolutionary period, when crafting and selling the terms of peace Shelburne did not consider or deal only with the former colonies and their negotiators. Indeed, his correspondence reveals that France loomed larger and more continuously in his mind, and other European states weighed on it heavily as well. In crafting the treaties, he adroitly balanced the desires and needs of the French, other Europeans, and Americans with those of Britain and its empire. In crafting solutions, he combined an idealistic, cosmopolitan philosophy and outlook with a pragmatic approach to problem solving that, at least in the short run, maintained the balance of power in Europe.

Shelburne was one of the most influential leaders of the late-eighteenth-century anglophone world. His family had lived in Ireland since the twelfth century and had adhered to the Catholic faith until the 1690s. He would inherit vast estates in Ireland, England, and America. He studied for several years at Christ Church, Oxford. He served as a volunteer military officer with the British army in France and Germany in the late 1750s. Although elected to the House of Commons in 1761 at age of twenty-four, he never took his seat: on the death of his father, he was elevated to the House of Lords, and there he sat for the next forty-four years, towering above his peers as one of the Whigs' great orators and head of one of their many factions. An avid, informed

"Improver," he tinkered not only with soils and crops on his many Irish and English estates but also with economic, social, political, and religious practices throughout all of Britain in attempts to better his estate, his nation, his continent (for he thought of himself as also a citizen of Europe), and his empire. He died in London in his palatial Berkeley Square home in 1805.

Shelburne was a formidable intellectual and cosmopolitan figure who sought to advance literature, science, arts, religion, and society. He read and collected books in seven languages (of which he spoke four), amassing one of the largest and most influential private libraries in Britain. He visited Paris nearly every other year, purely for personal enjoyment. Abroad and at home, he gathered around himself some of the era's greatest free thinkers, encouraging, imbibing, and promoting their work; to them, he evangelized about his belief in the unity of European and American culture.

The record on Shelburne's personality is mixed. He was both much despised and much loved. He was called a Jesuit, or at least Jesuitical, a modern-day Malagrida (a Jesuit missionary who exerted great influence at the Portuguese court and whose name came to signify a smooth, informed but specious interlocutor). Because Shelburne was able to talk on any side of any issue, he was seen as insincere. To many, he appeared to possess no principles at all. He experienced frequent and often unpredictable changes of opinion and looked to others to influence him. He was accused of being a knave and a liar, deceitful, deceiving, or misleading. More, he was accused of double dealing, working to people's disadvantage behind their backs. He also attracted and consciously gathered about himself not aristocratic peers but "the middling sort"—educated and professional men such as Adam Smith, Richard Price, Jeremy Bentham, Francis Baring, John Dunning, and Samuel Garbett.

After Shelburne became the prime minister in 1782, his contemporaries found new traits to decry. He was seen as having a "passionate or unreasonable . . . temper and disposition," alternating between violence and equanimity (Rose 1860: 1: 25). He frequently exhibited whimsical behavior. As one observer noted, he possessed "an inequality of temper" that made him difficult to please (Knox 1902: 6: 283).

But was it true? Was this the same man who commandingly moved the items in negotiation like so many pieces in a cool game of chess? Along with his detractors, there were those who praised him—many in private but a few in public. As James Boswell observed toward the close of his *Life of Samuel Johnson*, "Man is in general made up of contradictory qualities, and these will ever show themselves in strange succession" (Boswell 1826: vol. 4, 389). Shelburne was no different. But most of his peers and political contemporaries were not men of much introspection, and the roughly dozen highly damning traits stuck to his name, regardless of reality or relevance.

Greater insight into Shelburne and his dealings with fellow peers, politicians, and diplomats in 1782 and 1783 comes from realizing that he suffered from an inability to connect with others. Initially, his upbringing and his parents' treatment of him left him feeling alone and unsure of himself. He suffered emotional trauma after the deaths of his three sisters during his childhood and the later loss of his two young wives, his second-born son, and his only daughter. Moreover, from birth, he coped with chronic eye and ear diseases. Finally, he experienced serious financial problems, always spending more than he earned and having to mortgage and remortgage his properties. He died a bankrupt (Hancock, forthcoming).

Detachment greatly overshadowed anxiety in Shelburne's psychological makeup. In particular, the effect of having two emotionally distant parents continued to affect his behavior even as an adult. Many of the traits identified by his political foes in 1782 and 1783 can be seen as those of someone who had for decades tried to keep people at a distance.

Shelburne as Peacemaker

The dislike and envy felt by contemporaries, and Shelburne's detachment from them, shaped his peacemaking probably more than anything else. By temperament, he was a lifelong compromiser. Throughout his long career in politics, he was willing to change his mind on particular matters when given more or different information. Unsurprisingly, this trait created difficulties for him by giving others the erroneous impression that he sought only to please others and exercise power. But in almost all cases, the turn had to do less with ingratiating himself with others than with confronting and embracing new information or a situation different from the one he had expected.

On occasion, Shelburne would concede on a matter of principle. From the start of the peace negotiations in 1782, for instance, he had wanted to defer the acknowledgment of American independence until the final terms had been crafted and confirmed—not, as the Americans wished, to recognize it as a condition for treaty making, for he believed such a position would not wrest the Americans from their reliance on the French. Yet by August 1782, he had conceded the issue in order to move the process forward and to draw the Americans to his side, or at least away from the French.

On material matters, Shelburne made repeated concessions to the United States and France: he was pilloried at home for giving away too much. The loser in the war for America, Britain had little bargaining power over the victors: even so, Shelburne did not give everything away, and when he did make a concession, he did it to gain a complementary advantage on some other front. He refused to cede Canada to the United States, for instance, as Franklin had proposed in April and again in July. On this point Shelburne was supported by Vergennes. Both men wanted some check on American imperial ambitions.

Shelburne and Vergennes struck a similar accord over their overlapping and competing interests in the Newfoundland fishery. France wanted a French fishery on the northwestern, western, and southern coasts of Newfoundland, as sanctioned by the Treaty of Utrecht. Britain refused to cede the southern coast but construed the western coast as 130 miles longer than under the French definition and understanding. France also wanted exclusive fishing rights in the areas granted, not the concurrent rights Britain proposed. Shelburne resolved the matter with ambiguous language, thereby conceding nothing. With respect to the reclamation of France's Indian possessions, France wanted some area granted around its trading posts in India to supply and protect them and also wanted to strengthen the forts. Britain refused these requests, allowing only the construction of a sanitation ditch encircling Chandannagar and an armistice for French allies on the subcontinent, thus retaining the upper hand. Finally, while entertaining Vergennes's *premier commis* (first secretary) Joseph Matthias Gérard de Rayneval at his Wiltshire country seat and his London townhouse in mid-September, Shelburne called for economic cooperation in the form of freer trade between the two powers, a position with which Vergennes agreed. By early October, he and Vergennes had agreed that the time was not right for negotiating political and commercial amity and that the status quo should remain. Shelburne preferred that it do so for only a few years, whereas the French wanted to set no deadline for reaching agreement. Shelburne won the point.

Shelburne compromised with Spain as well. While he implied in mid-August 1782 that he would consider handing over Gibraltar to Spain, he later withdrew the offer. It is not clear whether it was ever meant in earnest or just as a ploy to bring the parties to the negotiating table. With the success of the British navy's final relief of Gibraltar on October 10 and the failure of the subsequent Spanish siege, British desire to keep the peninsula grew stronger, and the cabinet opposed ceding it. Accordingly, Shelburne abandoned the idea in early December.

The Dutch posed a different challenge. With them, Shelburne worked out an agreement on the terms of peace. His long-time personal and political enemy Charles James Fox, as secretary of state for foreign affairs under the prime minister, the second Marquess of Rockingham, had agreed in April to allow the Dutch the freedom of navigation that had been stipulated by the 1780 League of Armed Neutrality. But when Shelburne replaced Rockingham at the latter's death on July 1, 1782, Shelburne rescinded the offer. The Dutch were also demanding the restoration of colonies and the compensation of losses. In response, Shelburne demanded the retention of Trincomalee, the main port town of Ceylon (modern Sri Lanka), which Britain had captured during the war, as well as of Demerara and Essequibo, two valuable sugar colonies on the north coast of South America. Vergennes, who had more or less pushed the

Dutch aside and negotiated on their behalf, balked at this proposal. Throughout December and January, the two ministers wrangled. Shelburne settled for possession of Nagapattinam on India's Coromandel Coast, as well as the British right to navigate freely (but not to trade) in the Dutch East Indies, while the Dutch held on to Trincomalee and the right to trade in their own zone.

Could these demonstrations of concession and compromise induce Europeans and Americans to promote greater international harmony and balance? Shelburne and Vergennes thought so: indeed, it was their ultimate goal.

In resisting, conceding to, and compromising with France, Shelburne was ever the idealist. He believed strongly in partnership among civilized nations. He resolved the dilemma of negotiating with France by following the fashionable, enlightened precepts of cosmopolitanism, an ideology that competed with the creeds of patriotism and nationalism. A collector and reader of all the works of the new Enlightenment ideology, Shelburne hoped that a more sophisticated understanding of the nature of polity, the extension of the principle underlying constitutionalism, economic and social development, and the equivalence of belief systems would bring Britain, Europe, and America closer together, politically, practically, and morally. While separate, Britain and France were also joined by a common culture, and Shelburne the peacemaker worked to recognize and perpetuate the ties between them. He hoped that by working together, they would establish the rules that the other European states would have to follow.

It is hardly surprising that Shelburne readily found common ground with Vergennes. From his time at Oxford and his first visit to France from 1757 to 1760, through the darkest days of the French Revolution, he never wavered in his admiration of French culture and thought. Nearly a third of his library of nine thousand volumes consisted of works of French history, politics, and literature.

Thus, beginning in 1782, a friendship based first on admiration, then on trust, developed between the two chief ministers. Before Shelburne and Vergennes ever corresponded, they had been in agreement in their desire to avoid the co-mediation of their disputes by Austria and Russia. In the ensuing months, they jointly and individually worked to keep Canada from the United States, keep Gibraltar from Spain, and keep the Dutch from exerting absolute control over trade in the Dutch East Indies. Shelburne's complementary ideas of amity, union, and balance became the watchwords of his negotiations, much as they had guided his earlier political career. Continually the negotiators emphasized consideration, respect, moderation, and justice. Shelburne and Vergennes strove to preserve a balance of power between small and large states, in particular by keeping Russia and Austria from expanding at the expense of Turkey and the Crimea. Both wanted France and Britain to work harmoniously together to keep the peace in Europe.

In seeking cooperation and rapprochement, Shelburne was not merely indulging his appreciation of the French way of life and his admiration of some of its ministers: he was moved by pragmatic considerations as well. His rather small following and weak support in Parliament counseled for an early resolution to the negotiations, as did the dwindling finances of the treasury he managed.

Even so, Shelburne's effort to achieve peace and establish real harmony in 1782 and 1783 was also motivated by a philosophical and sentimental belief in "solid friendship"—certainly with the United States, but even more so with France. His service in the Seven Years' War, first on the battlefield and then as the emissary of the prime minister John Stuart, third Earl of Bute, in some of the peace negotiations, had convinced him of the necessity of rapprochement with France. During his several tours of France in the 1770s, he was struck by the cultural affinities between the two polities, and he argued to no one in particular that the two countries should not be in opposition. Indeed, as recently as June 1780, he had lamented in the House of Lords that Britain had missed an earlier opportunity of reconciliation with France (Hancock, forthcoming).

While it is easy to see with hindsight that Britain could have survived a few more years of struggle, many well-informed individuals at the time thought otherwise. As the British treasury dwindled, a resolution to all the conflicts seemed urgent. Moreover, Shelburne's ministry had only a five-month window while Parliament was not sitting in which to construct a peace without impedance from lesser politicians and special interests, and without hectoring and badgering from Parliament, to derail their progress.

By 1782, American independence was a foregone conclusion, even if Shelburne wanted to delay acknowledging it. The prospect of a stable Europe was not. From the voluminous documentation produced by the peacemakers, supporters, and opponents, it is evident that Shelburne's stance on the new

EN CE BÂTIMENT
JADIS HOTEL D'YORK
LE 3 SEPTEMBRE 1783

DAVID HARTLEY,
AU NOM DU ROI D'ANGLETERRE,

BENJAMIN FRANKLIN,
JOHN JAY, JOHN ADAMS,
AU NOM DES ETATS-UNIS D'AMÉRIQUE,
ONT SIGNÉ LE TRAITÉ DÉFINITIF DE PAIX
RECONNAISSANT L'INDÉPENDANCE
DES ETATS-UNIS.

Plaque commemorating signing of the Peace of Paris on September 3, 1783. (Photograph by David K. Allison, 2016)

republic was taken with an eye to both advancing the desired reconciliation with France and getting France to deal with other states in Europe. "It was a very deep game," he told his wife (letter from Shelburne to Lady Shelburne, ca. January 1783, Bowood Archives). The compromises he struck were intended primarily to further Britain's position with respect to France, even if they also concerned the new United States.

While he was able to effect an end to a war that had significantly reduced the British empire, he could do little to guarantee peace in the future, especially given the internecine warfare of British politics and the social and economic discontents in France that would boil up into the French Revolution. It would soon become clear that the governments of Britain and France could neither legislate and impose free trade for all nor keep the peace in Europe. Even so, Shelburne and Vergennes created at least for a few years an amity among the powers in Europe and a balance of power between large and small states. At the war's end, amity and balance in Europe were just as important (to all but the treaties' American architects) as American independence.

Since his days on the Continent as a military officer, Shelburne had felt that Britain should not be implacably opposed to France and its European allies. An uneasy, uncertain combination of idealism and realism, of philosophy and personality—traits shared by Shelburne and representatives of Britain, Europe, and America—shaped the entry of the new United States onto the world stage.

REIMAGINING THE AMERICAN REVOLUTION

David K. Allison

> Full historical reinterpretation of the American Revolution as a world war requires rethinking not only narrative accounts of the conflict but also the visual imagery that epitomizes it in texts, exhibitions, and national buildings. —*Editors*

[A] compleat History of the American War . . . is nearly the History of Mankind for the whole Epocha of it. The History of France Spain Holland, England and the Neutral Powers, as well as America are at least comprized in it.
John Adams to the abbé de Mably, Paris, January 15, 1783

Images, like facts and stories, shape our understanding of important historical events. Circling the rotunda of the U.S. Capitol building in Washington, D.C., are eight grand historical paintings, each eighteen feet wide by twelve high. Four were commissioned by Congress in 1817 and painted by one artist, John Trumbull. They commemorate events that he believed summarized the essential history of the American Revolution: the Declaration of Independence, the surrender of General Burgoyne, the surrender of Lord Cornwallis, and General George Washington resigning his commission. Trumbull intended them as symbolic statements more than as factual representations; like his artistic contemporaries (and indeed like modern movie directors), he strove to present aesthetic "truth" and ascribed greater importance to his own artistic judgment than to historical accuracy. His images unquestionably reveal cultural biases characteristic of the era. Yet over the past two centuries, they have exerted a lasting influence on how Americans visualize key moments in the founding of their nation.

Trumbull devoted much of his career to painting events and people related to the American Revolution. He himself participated briefly in the war, at the Battle of Bunker Hill in June 1775, and later as an aide to both Washington and General Horatio Gates. Resigning from the army in 1777, he journeyed to London in 1780 to focus on art and study painting with Benjamin West. From him, Trumbull learned techniques of artistic rendition of historical events. In 1785, he wrote to his father, "The great object of my wishes . . . is to take up the History of Our Country, and paint the principal Events particularly of the late War" (quoted in Cooper 1982: 7).

For years, he dreamed of creating a series of paintings related to America's founding that he could reproduce in etchings to be sold by subscription. The series was to include thirteen events—the Battle of Bunker's Hill, the Battle of Quebec, the Declaration of Independence, the Battle of Trenton, the Battle of Princeton, the surrender of Burgoyne at Saratoga, the treaty with France, the siege of Yorktown, the signing of the Treaty of Peace in 1783, the evacuation of New York by the British in 1783, the resignation of General Washington in 1783, the president received by the ladies of Trenton and the Arch in 1789, and the inauguration of the president in 1789—but only four of these were ultimately painted for the Capitol. Four others he completed as individual paintings. The others were never realized.

Over the next three decades, while engaging in numerous other activities to support himself, Trumbull worked on the series, traveling and making numerous portraits of individuals whom he would later include in his large commemorative tableaus. He tried to generate support for creating and selling the entire series but failed to stimulate sufficient interest. Nonetheless, Trumbull distinguished himself from most of his artistic contemporaries with his interest in commemorating some aspects of the global dimensions of the war.

Following the War of 1812 and the burning of the original Capitol building in Washington, D.C., in 1814, public interest in commemorating the Revolution at last began to grow. In 1815, Trumbull, then fifty-nine, petitioned Congress for a commission to create historical paintings for the dome of the new Capitol. In 1817, he received his commission to create four canvases "commemorative of the most important events of the American Revolution" (Trumbull 1841: 262).

As required by the legislation authorizing funds for the paintings, he met with President James Madison, and the two decided on the four scenes.

Paintings by John Trumbull on display in the U.S. Capitol dome in Washington, D.C. Clockwise from top left: *The Declaration of Independence*, 1818; *The Surrender of General Burgoyne*, 1821; *The Surrender of Lord Cornwallis*, 1820; and *General George Washington Resigning His Commission*, 1824. All oil on canvas. (Architect of the Capitol)

Trumbull was particularly pleased that two of the paintings would show civil events—the signing of the Declaration of Independence and Washington's resignation—while the other two would show military events—the surrenders of British armies at Saratoga in 1777 and Yorktown in 1781. Creating and hanging the paintings took Trumbull until 1826.

Even Trumbull, who had great aspirations for his legacy, would likely be surprised by the continuing influence of these four works. They have been reproduced hundreds of thousands of times in articles, monographs, textbooks, exhibitions, programs, and—more recently—websites and blogs. When the U.S. Postal Service issued a series of commemorative stamps recognizing the bicentennial of the American Revolution in the mid-1970s, it included portions of two of Trumbull's paintings: *The Declaration of Independence* and *The Surrender of Lord Cornwallis*. Unlike most other stamps in this series, these two were printed as souvenirs and were designed more as keepsakes than as postage.

By highlighting the British surrender to American officers, Trumbull's paintings portrayed a distinctly American perspective of the victory. The French saw the outcome differently, as totally dependent on French support and leadership. King Louis XVI commissioned two paintings to commemorate his nation's successful intervention as America's ally. Created by the court artist Louis-Nicolas van Blarenberghe, these paintings, *The Siege of Yorktown* and *The Surrender at Yorktown* (both 1786), are still on display today at Versailles.

When planning them, van Blarenberghe used eyewitness accounts, maps, and sketches from the French engineers Louis-Alexandre Berthier and his brother, Charles-Louis-Berthier. Like the Trumbull paintings, they are more symbolic than literal, but they are more descriptive than Trumbull's works of the actual events. Jean-Baptiste Donatien de Vimeur, comte de Rochambeau, who commanded the French land forces at the siege of Yorktown, admired the paintings so much that the king had van Blarenberghe create a second copy for him. Together with a Charles Willson Peale portrait of George Washington (page 214), they hung in Rochambeau's home for the remainder of his life as souvenirs of his involvement in the French and American alliance. These three paintings are shown together for the first time in a major American museum in the Smithsonian exhibition related to this book.

Commemorative postal stamps showing details of John Trumbull's *The Declaration of Independence*, 1818 (top), and *The Surrender of Lord Cornwallis*, 1820 (bottom). Based on the original oil paintings displayed in the U.S. Capitol dome, the stamps were issued in 1976 to recognize the Bicentennial of the American Revolution. (U.S. Postal Service)

In *The Surrender of Lord Cornwallis*, Trumbull's selection of significant events in the Yorktown siege differs from van Blarenberghe's. Trumbull emphasizes the triumph of the victorious leaders. In his painting, the American leaders are set on the right, in a commanding position. Higher-ranking leaders are mounted on horseback; lower-level leaders are on foot. French dignitaries are placed on the left, in a supporting role.

Although Trumbull included Cornwallis's name in the painting's title and—choosing symbolism over fact—originally identified the lead British officer in his painting as Cornwallis himself, General Charles Cornwallis did not, in fact, attend the surrender ceremony. Instead, pleading illness, he sent his second in command, General Charles O'Hara. Before the canvas was hung, viewers troubled by the fiction of including Cornwallis strongly objected. Trumbull responded by saying that the British shown were "principal officers" and avoided naming any of them individually in the key to the painting (Jaffe 1975: 262). Nonetheless, the title of the image has remained the same.

In reality, when O'Hara appeared, he first tried to surrender to the French, perhaps in recognition of their role in the battle, or perhaps to slight the former colonists. The French refused to accept the surrender and directed him to the Americans. Washington, however, also refused to accept a surrender from a second-ranking officer and in turn directed O'Hara to his own second in command, General Benjamin Lincoln, who is seated on the white horse at the center of the painting. Washington is behind him, to the viewer's right, in front of the American flag. Eyewitnesses reported that Washington was actually several hundred yards away, but Trumbull placed him in a prominent location to symbolize his importance.

Trumbull's primary focus in this painting was on individual portraiture, and he spent considerable time determining both to whom to include and how to arrange the figures. Although his painting gives greatest prominence to the Americans, it also includes individual French leaders. (The U.S. Postal Service, with an even narrower nationalist focus than Trumbull, cropped the picture to eliminate the French entirely in its design of the 1976 stamp.)

Van Blarenberghe's two paintings illustrate strategic elements of the siege that are missing from the Trumbull depiction. Taken together, the van Blarenberghe paintings illustrate that this operation, by far the most complex of the war, represented the high point of the French and American alliance.

Louis-Nicolas van Blarenberghe, *The Siege of Yorktown*, 1786. Gouache on board. (Courtesy Nicholas Taubman)

Louis-Nicolas van Blarenberghe, *The Surrender at Yorktown*, 1786. Gouache on board. (Courtesy Nicholas Taubman)

Charles Willson Peale, *Washington at Yorktown*, ca. 1780–82. Oil on canvas. (Courtesy Nicholas Taubman)

Interpreting these two French paintings requires further background. In 1780, Louis XVI sent Rochambeau's expeditionary forces to North America and a naval fleet to the Caribbean. The king's goal was to reverse what he feared was becoming a losing cause. A year earlier, soon after the French-American alliance was concluded, a French force led by Admiral Jean-Baptiste Charles Henri Hector, comte d'Estaing, had failed in France's first joint operations with the Americans, including the attempt to besiege and recapture Savannah from the British in 1779. D'Estaing had then taken his demoralized forces back to France. In 1780, Washington's army, after years of inconclusive battles, irregular pay, and poor support from Congress, had dwindled to a few thousand men and was in desperate condition. As Alexander Hamilton wrote to John Laurens in June of that year, "If we are [to be] saved, France and Spain must save us" (Hamilton 1780). The French alliance had to provide a convincing victory soon if the war was to be won.

The allies now developed an audacious plan to attack Cornwallis's British forces in Virginia. Washington had initially opposed this strategy, as both he and Gilbert du Motier, the marquis de Lafayette, aspired to attack the larger British stronghold in New York. Rochambeau, older and more experienced than either of the other men, believed the British were too strong there and that such an attack would fail. In addition, he and the commander of the French naval forces in the Caribbean, Admiral François Joseph Paul de Grasse, recognized that the French navy was more likely to succeed in combating British naval forces in Chesapeake Bay than off the coast of New York. Furthermore, the Chesapeake was closer to the French navy's principal area of concern in the war, the Caribbean, whose sugar plantations yielded huge profits for France. Although Washington was the supreme commander of the joint operation and the final decision was nominally his, he also understood that he could initiate no major action without French support, so he eventually acceded to the French plan.

In August 1781, the allies learned that Cornwallis had given up his campaign in the Virginia countryside, where he had tried to reduce support for the rebellion and rally Loyalists. He now was concentrating his army at Yorktown, Virginia, near the mouth of the Chesapeake, where British ships from New York could evacuate them. This news made the allies' plan even more urgent. Rochambeau, located in Newport, Rhode Island, and Washington, then outside New York, quickly started their armies on the long march south to trap Cornwallis. By late September, they had surrounded Yorktown, blocking his escape by land. Several weeks earlier, while the land forces had been on the march, de Grasse had sailed up from the Caribbean, and in the pivotal Battle of the Chesapeake, he blocked a British fleet, under Admiral Thomas Graves, from rescuing Cornwallis by sea. Thus the British were entrapped.

In October, Rochambeau and Washington began their siege, orchestrated primarily by Rochambeau and his engineers, who had years of experience in conducting such operations. The French forces also had brought with them the necessary tools, siege guns, artillery, and ammunition, most of which the Americans lacked. Together, the two armies dug trenches and cut Yorktown off from supplies. Then, beginning on October 9, 1781, they pounded the British with thousands of artillery shells (around 1,700 per day), as they gradually

Louis-Nicolas van Blarenberghe, *The Siege of Yorktown* (detail), 1786. Gouache on board. (Courtesy Nicholas Taubman)

closed in. On October 17, Cornwallis signaled that he was ready to give up. The formal surrender, painted by van Blarenberghe, occurred on October 19, 1781.

The scale of the two French paintings gives a sense of the scope of the operations, which involved thousands of troops on both sides and stretched over miles. As would be expected, van Blarenberghe presents the operation and surrender from a French perspective. In *The Siege of Yorktown*, for example, the French forces are shown marching proudly into the field in well-ordered ranks from the left, while the American troops, to their right, are hardly visible. In the center, Rochambeau directs operations, while Washington studies a map. The view shows an effective collaboration, but one that is led by the French.

Even more noteworthy is the focus of the *Surrender* painting. Here the emphasis is not on commemorating the victorious leaders, as Trumbull sought to do, but on showing a large British army, arrayed in red, marching in humiliating surrender in front of the French army, in blue. With remarkable detail, the

Louis-Nicolas van Blarenberghe, *The Surrender at Yorktown* (detail), 1786. Gouache on board. (Courtesy Nicholas Taubman)

artist depicts each of the key French regiments in order, distinguished by their unit flags. Again, the American soldiers are present but not emphasized. They are in brown, to the right of the British troops, with their backs to the viewer.

The paintings of both van Blarenberghe and Trumbull are carefully constructed, full of intricate details and symbols meant to memorialize numerous aspects of a landmark victory. Both works are based on actual events, and both are slanted to suit nationalistic perspectives. Most important is that both these visual interpretations continue to be widely reproduced and to influence broad public audiences. They remain prominently displayed in Washington and Versailles.

As essays in this volume explain, neither perspective alone is sufficient to understand the importance and character of the French-American alliance that resulted in the victory at Yorktown. Thus, the ongoing use of these images in contemporary historic interpretations is problematic as a guide to understanding the Revolution. To echo John Adams's view, expressed in the epigraph to this essay, the American Revolution must be seen not only as a revolt of American colonists against their British masters, or even as the victory of an American partnership with French allies, but as a world war. It included engagements around the globe, at sea as well as on land. Indeed, the fight over control of the sea was as significant in determining the outcome of the war as the battle over control of land in North America. Moreover, the fighting began before the Declaration of Independence in 1776 and continued around the world after Yorktown.

As Alan Taylor notes in his essay in this book, the Revolution was a continuation of the Seven Years' War. It too was sparked in North America before spreading around the world. Many of the leaders who later fought one another in the American Revolution had gained knowledge and experience during the Seven Years' War, including Cornwallis, Rochambeau, de Grasse, and Washington. Because France and Spain lost land, power, and influence in the earlier war, they quickly began plotting revenge. A decade later, when they joined with the American colonies in their Revolution, they did so more to redress their own losses in the earlier war than because they supported the colonists' quest for independence and democracy.

Public history venues, such as historic sites and museums commemorating the American Revolution, tend to downplay or ignore the important background of the Seven Years' War; Fort Necessity National Battlefield in rural Pennsylvania, south of Pittsburgh, is the only national park site devoted to the conflict. This is where the war began and where clashes between British, French, and Native American forces initiated the fight for control of North America. It is also the site where George Washington first led troops into battle. The park offers helpful educational materials but draws many fewer visitors than Independence Hall, Valley Forge, or Yorktown. Fortunately, both the new Museum of the American Revolution in Philadelphia and the American Revolution Museum at Yorktown, along with the Smithsonian's National Museum of American History, are now providing further background on how the Seven Years' War created the context for the American Revolution.

Many Americans believe that the first major act of the American Revolution was the Declaration of Independence in 1776. This belief is reinforced by Trumbull's heroic image of the signing of this foundational document, the best-known and most widely disseminated of the four images in the Capitol. Yet the war was already under way when the Continental Congress wrote and published the Declaration; the battles at Lexington, Concord, Ticonderoga, and Bunker Hill, for example, had already occurred. Indeed, recent scholars contend that American leaders issued the Declaration less to promulgate the reasons that they were fighting for independence than to convince potential allies—especially France—that they would never renounce their struggle and reunify with Britain. This meant that allies could safely recognize the United States and join in its struggle.

France was not willing to be the sole supporter of the Americans. In 1778, soon after it had formally signed an alliance with the United States, France convinced Spain, then ruled by the Bourbon king Charles III (who refused to recognize the United States or ally directly with it) to join its war against Britain. Together the two Bourbon regimes planned a combined naval and land invasion of Britain. In the years since the Seven Years' War, they had been coordinating the modernization of their navies with just such a joint operation in mind. Their goals were to weaken Britain, force it to direct more of its power toward domestic defense, and build a stronger bargaining position for negotiating territorial concessions elsewhere.

In the summer of 1779, with British naval forces stretched thin by the war in North America, France and Spain determined that it was time to act. The combined fleet they amassed for the assault numbered 150 vessels—more than the 128 ships that had composed the Spanish Armada in 1588. The operation began in July, but a series of difficulties, including disease, poor communication, lack of effective coordination, and severe weather, ultimately led the Bourbon allies to suspend their invasion. Yet despite this failure, Britain recognized the growing threat not only to its homeland but also to all the areas of its empire where it contended with France and Spain.

A second important event occurred in the Caribbean. In September 1781, the French naval victory in the Battle of the Chesapeake had proved that British naval power could be challenged. Admiral de Grasse subsequently took his fleet south with the goals of allying with Spanish forces, reducing British sea control, and threatening Britain's lucrative sugar islands, including Jamaica.

At the time, Jamaica by itself was more lucrative for the British than its thirteen American colonies combined, and thus capturing it would have been as important as the victory at Yorktown. Indeed, conducting operations in the Caribbean, rather than supporting Rochambeau, had been the main reason that de Grasse's ships were sent to America in the first place.

In the Caribbean, however, the outcome was different. In April 1782, de Grasse was sailing with thirty-five warships (also called ships of the line) near Martinique on his way to meet his Spanish allies and assault Jamaica. He encountered a British fleet of thirty-six ships of the line under Admiral George Brydges Rodney. The two navies maneuvered for several days before fighting the Battle of the Saintes on April 12. The French were decisively defeated, and both de Grasse and his flagship, the *Ville de Paris*, were captured. France and Spain subsequently abandoned their plan to seize Jamaica and instead focused on protecting their own territories in the Caribbean. This reversal had a significant effect on peace negotiations to end the American Revolution, which were already well under way and would lead to an agreement by the end of the year. Few Americans today know of the Battle of the Saintes or have seen visual depictions of it, as compared to their mental images of the heroic Yorktown paintings.

A third critical event in the war outside North America was a contemporaneous European siege that was bigger, lasted longer, and ultimately was as critical to establishing peace as the Yorktown victory: the siege of Gibraltar. Spain had formally ceded the peninsula of Gibraltar, with its commanding position over the western entrance to the Mediterranean, to Britain in 1713. When Spain agreed to ally with France in 1779, regaining Gibraltar was among its major objectives. The siege began in June 1779, but England was able periodically to resupply its outpost, and its forces held on. Finally, in September 1782, a year after the successful siege of Yorktown, a combined French and Spanish force launched a great attack against Gibraltar. It included both more ships and more men than had been involved in the American engagement. Yet the attack failed, in large part because "floating batteries," essentially rafts loaded with cannon used by the allies in an effort to destroy the Gibraltar fortifications, proved ineffective. Within several weeks, a British fleet was able to replenish its Gibraltar forces with supplies, food, and ammunition. Finally, in February 1783, the siege was lifted. Gibraltar remained under British control.

Thomas Whitcombe, *Battle of the Saintes, 12 April 1782; Surrender of the* Ville de Paris, 1783. Oil on canvas. On the right is the flagship *Ville de Paris*, engaged in cannon fire against HMS *Barfleur*. The battle, fought from April 9 to April 12, 1782, in the Saintes Passage in the West Indies, ended as the British forced French and Dutch ships to abandon their planned invasion of Britain's principal sugar island, Jamaica. (© National Maritime Museum, Greenwich, London, BHC0446)

Ironically, John Trumbull himself created a commemorative image of this important battle, *The Sortie Made by the Garrison of Gibraltar* (1789; page 222), which depicts the British defeat of a Spanish land assault. At the time, Trumbull was courting British patrons for his paintings: while they had no interest in American victories in the Revolution, he realized that they might well be interested in a depiction of a British triumph. Although the painting indeed gained some recognition, Trumbull soon returned to focusing on American successes.

The British victories in Gibraltar and the Caribbean were followed by subsequent battles in India, a subject covered in an earlier essay in this volume (see page 92). These, not the siege of Yorktown, were the last engagements of the American Revolution. France had lost most of its trading outposts in India as a result of the Seven Years' War and had hoped to regain territory and influence there while the Revolution was distracting the British. However, in a series of battles in which the French supported local Indian forces against the British, they failed to attain their goal, and their influence in India continued to wane.

John Trumbull, *The Sortie Made by the Garrison of Gibraltar*, 1789. Oil on canvas. British forces repel a land assault on Gibraltar made by the Spanish on November 26, 1781. (Public domain, The Metropolitan Museum of Art, Purchase, Pauline V. Fullerton Bequest; Mr. and Mrs. James Walter Carter and Mr. and Mrs. Raymond J. Horowitz Gifts; Erving Wolf Foundation and Vain and Harry Fish Foundation Inc. Gifts; Gift of Hanson K. Corning, by exchange; and Maria DeWitt Jesup and Morris K. Jesup Funds, 1976)

The war did not end even with the Treaty of Paris between Britain and the United States in 1783. Instead, separate treaties were concluded among Britain and the three other European nations it had fought in the war: France, Spain, and the Dutch Republic. The last treaty was not signed until 1784. Surprisingly, Britain agreed to very generous terms with its former colonies in North America, not only granting them independence but also giving up British claim to all land east of the Mississippi River. It agreed to give the United States fishing rights in the Grand Banks off the coast of Newfoundland and the Gulf of St. Lawrence, and it did not insist that the United States compensate British Loyalists for their loss of property and rights. Why was Britain willing to agree to these generous terms? Although it had lost colonies in North America, it had held on to other territory in North America and Canada and its Caribbean islands, and it had defeated France and Spain elsewhere in the world. Moreover, Britain hoped the terms would foster an amicable relationship and future trade with the United States—at the expense of America's wartime allies. In large part because of the outcome of the battles fought after Yorktown, France and Spain did not achieve many of the gains they had sought when they joined the fledgling United States in its Revolution, and their failure would continue to provoke tensions around the world.

The ways we remember, commemorate, and envision the American Revolution continue to evolve—and need to do so. In 2026, the United States will celebrate the 250th anniversary of its birth as an independent nation. The years leading up to this important date will invite extensive review and reinterpretation of the American Revolution and what it means to the American public today. This will likely be the broadest reexamination of the significance of the Revolution undertaken since the Bicentennial in 1976. Scholarship and public exhibitions at museums and historic sites have already begun to explore new dimensions of the conflict, particularly the roles of African Americans, Native Americans, and women. More attention is also being given to the Loyalists who did not support the Revolution but instead sought to continue or renegotiate the colonies' relationship with England.

The essays in this book demonstrate that another area ripe for reexamination is the global dimension of the American Revolution: its background, its alliances, its battles around the world, and its legacies. If these reinterpretations and new insights are to become firmly established in the memories and imaginations of the American public, however, compelling new visualizations will be needed to accompany the new scholarship. The grand Trumbull tableaus in the Capitol dome will certainly remain American icons. But they should be supplemented with new public art and visual displays commissioned to serve as the 2026 analogs to the commemorative stamps and exhibitions of 1976. The American Revolution needs not only reinterpretation, but also reimagining.

REWRITING THE AMERICAN REVOLUTION

Larrie D. Ferreiro

Historical accounts of the American Revolution have varied in their coverage of the global dimensions of the war, in response to the intellectual and political trends of the era. As the nation approaches its 250th anniversary, reexamining the broader context of the conflict becomes increasingly important. — *Editors*

Americans who lived through the American Revolution understood that the war was being waged across the continent and around the world. News of the French-British Battle of Ouessant, fought off the coast of Brittany on July 7, 1778, reached attentive American ears shortly after the French admiral d'Estaing's failed assault on Newport at the end of August. Britain's capture of the Dutch Caribbean island of Sint Eustatius in early 1781 caused uproar among American merchants, but the fall of Pensacola in British Florida to Bernardo de Gálvez a few months later garnered warm congratulations from American leaders. And in 1782, the Pennsylvania State Navy gave a sloop of war the punning name *Hyder Ally* in recognition of the leader of the Kingdom of Mysore, Hyder Ali, in his fight against their common British enemy.

Americans who actually fought on the front lines could also see, hear, and feel the presence of the other nations involved in the conflict. The muskets they were issued were lighter than the traditional British "Brown Bess" they had used when they were still colonials, and the language of the metal stamping on their new guns revealed their origins. Guns from Liège bore the Latin motto *Pro Libertate* (For Liberty). Others came from France, Spain, and the Dutch Republic. American troops could hear the accents of the French and other European volunteers who fought side by side with them. Even the cloth of the American uniforms, from factories in Placencia, Spain, and Montpelier, France, felt different from the rough British weave to which they had been accustomed.

Given this international involvement, how did Americans come to rewrite the narrative of the Revolution in a way that leaves out the participation of these other nations, which—as the essays in this book have so clearly demonstrated—was crucial to the winning of independence? It was not the gradual amnesia of an aging nation; nor was it a sudden great forgetting of an undesirable past. History has always been the continuation of politics by other means, and the story of the American Revolution has been rewritten many times over the course of two and a half centuries to suit the political needs of each era. These retellings help us understand where the United States has been as a nation, what it is today, and what kind of nation it is to become.

Writing the American Revolution as a Work in Progress

Histories of the American Revolution were being written even as the early campaigns were being fought in the United States. Among them were several works by French writers who, soon after the 1778 Treaty of Paris had brought France into the war, rushed to interpret the unfolding drama not so much as an accurate description of events in America (the accounts were largely secondhand, from newspapers controlled by the monarchy) but as a canvas on which they could paint their own ideals of government.

For the playwright Pierre-Ulric Dubuisson, in *Summary of the American Revolution* (1778), and the philosophers Guillaume-Thomas Raynal and Denis Diderot in *American Revolution* (1781), the American war provided the perfect backdrop for showcasing their anticolonial views. Meanwhile, the lawyer Michel René Hilliard d'Auberteuil railed against the "excesses and decadence" of European governments in *Historical and Political Essays on the North American Revolution* (1781). American writers and politicians were outraged at what they saw as partisan screeds with a thin veneer of inaccurate history. Benjamin Franklin never acknowledged Dubuisson's work, despite many entreaties from the author; Thomas Paine objected to Raynal's statement that taxation was the cause of the Revolution; and Thomas Jefferson lamented, "If the histories of D'Auberteuil . . . can be read and believed by those who are contemporary with the events they pretend to relate, how may we expect future ages shall be better informed?" (Jefferson 1894: 439–40).

By contrast, Jefferson looked with favor on some later French works that provided a more realistic accounting of the war. Their authors—all noted historians and scholars—took great pains to show the global dimensions of the conflict. Pierre Charpentier de Longchamps's *Impartial History of the Military and Political Events of the Previous War in the Four Corners of the World* (1785), as the title implies, looks at the conflict in each of the theaters of war: in fact, almost the entire third volume is devoted to the post-Yorktown battles in the Mediterranean, South Africa, India, and the Caribbean. Odet-Julien Leboucher underlined the importance of the coalition facing Britain by titling his book *History of the Preceding War between Great Britain and the United States of America, France, Spain, and Holland* (1787). And François Soulès, with the help of Jefferson himself for primary-source material, produced a sweeping four-volume work, *History of the English-American Troubles* (1787), that enters into the halls of power in Philadelphia, London, Versailles, and Madrid and takes its readers to battles around the globe.

Contemporary historians in the United States, who had witnessed events at first hand, also wrote about the American Revolution as a world war, though without the sweep and grandeur of Soulès's account. William Gordon, who spent many weeks copying the personal files of George Washington, Nathanael Green, and others, produced the four-volume *History of the Rise, Progress, and Establishment of the Independence of the United States of America* (1788), whose final volume is largely given over to the events overseas that led to the final peace treaties, including a blow-by-blow account of the war in India. David Ramsay, who served in the South Carolina militia, notes the importance of the sieges of Pensacola and Gibraltar in the second volume of his *History of the American Revolution* (1789). The playwright Mercy Otis Warren, whose family fought in the war, produced the magisterial three-volume *History of the Rise, Progress, and Termination of the American Revolution* (1805), which gives proper weight to the combat overseas and its effect on the peace negotiations and was much favored by Jefferson. Two lesser-known writers also took pains to place these events in their appropriate context: Charles Stedman (a Loyalist officer in the war) in *History of the Origin, Progress, and Termination of the American War* (1794), and John Lendrum in *A Concise and Impartial History of the American Revolution* (1795).

The war may have been over, but at the end of the eighteenth century the Revolution was still a work in progress; as John Adams told Jefferson in 1815, the war "was only an effect and consequence" of the Revolution, and the final form of that Revolution was still being debated within communities and in the halls of government (Adams 1815). These historians were striving for accuracy based on their own experiences and observations, while still aiming to create an American culture and identity separate from their European origins. The tension between these two motivations would come to define the writing of the American Revolution in subsequent generations.

Writing the American Revolution as Living Memory

As the original participants in the Revolution began to disappear from the scene, accounts of the war began to shift away from historical accuracy and toward creating a patriotic narrative. The involvement of other nations in the conflict was largely erased from the historical record, with the exception of France's role, and even that was included primarily because of the marquis de Lafayette. His prominence was assured in part by his grand tour of the United States of 1824–25 and his death in 1834, which cemented his reputation as "the hero of two worlds," the focus of the French-American alliance, as is evident in the spike in references to him in English-language books. Spain, the Dutch Republic, and the Kingdom of Mysore were largely forgotten, as were any conflicts fought outside the thirteen colonies.

The marquis de La Fayette (as his name was then usually written) certainly played important roles during the war, first distinguishing himself at the Battle of Brandywine and then in independent command during the southern campaigns against General Charles Cornwallis. His exploits receive notice in the histories by Soulès, Gordon, Ramsay, and Warren in proportion to his activities. But so do the exploits of his fellow volunteer the Baron von Steuben and his countrymen Rochambeau and de Grasse, who actually receive more mentions in these earlier works than does Lafayette. By contrast, in Samuel Farmer Wilson's *A History of the American Revolution* (1834), Lafayette garners thirty-two mentions, compared with seven for

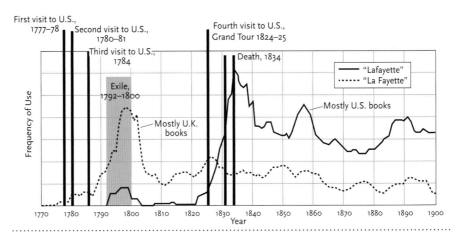

First visit to U.S., 1777–78

Second visit to U.S., 1780–81

Third visit to U.S., 1784

Fourth visit to U.S., Grand Tour 1824–25

Death, 1834

Exile, 1792–1800

Mostly U.K. books

Mostly U.S. books

"Lafayette"
"La Fayette"

Frequency of Use

1770 1780 1790 1800 1810 1820 1830 1840 1850 1860 1870 1880 1890 1900
Year

Mentions of La Fayette or Lafayette in English-language books published between 1770 and 1900. Lafayette's death was a great boost to his fame. (Graph by author; drawn by Bill Nelson)

Rochambeau and twelve for de Grasse, both of whom were far more important to the American victory than the young marquis.

This glorification of Lafayette began as early as 1824. Jedidiah Morse's *Annals of the American Revolution* appeared just as Lafayette was invited to visit the United States for its fiftieth anniversary. In a biographical appendix, Morse devotes nine pages to Lafayette's story, more than twice as much space as he devotes to George Washington. Gálvez's assault on Pensacola is captured in one sentence, and the campaigns at Minorca, Gibraltar, and in India are left out entirely. In Samuel Wilson's book, Gálvez and Pensacola are left out completely, while Gibraltar merits just two lines, one of which refers to "the memorable defence by [British] General Eliot," which was then promptly forgotten (Wilson 1834: 315). Even well-regarded authors such as Noah Webster (*History of the United States*, 1832) and John Frost (*The History of the United States of North America*, 1838) give scant attention to the role of foreign forces.

But the greatest injury by far to the understanding of the American Revolution as a world war came from the way children were taught. Two very popular works intended as school textbooks, Salma Hale's *History of the United*

States of America (1820) and Samuel Williams's *A History of the American Revolution* (1824), were published as potted histories of the American republic and reprinted many times during the subsequent decades. They manage to economize the presence of foreign volunteers on American soil and the global nature of the war almost to the point of invisibility. Schoolchildren in the nineteenth century and into the twentieth would grow up learning that Lafayette was "among the chief actors" of the Revolution, but they could be forgiven if they were unaware of the presence of either Rochambeau or de Grasse, and they might never have known that places such as Pensacola and Gibraltar even existed.

Writing the American Revolution as Manifest Destiny
The tightening of the historical focus of the American Revolution to the events within the thirteen colonies, excluding the wider global context and the substantial presence of foreign volunteers in the Continental Army, accorded perfectly with the emerging ethos of American exceptionalism. As the United States expanded westward and began exerting its influence over the American hemisphere, narratives of the American Revolution, whether aimed at a scholarly audience or at schoolchildren, embraced the notion of manifest destiny. This ideology was nowhere more pronounced than in George Bancroft's highly influential ten-volume *History of the United States of America* (1834–78), which served as the archetype for American history for generations to come.

Bancroft was a polymath who served as ambassador, secretary of the navy, and founder of the U.S. Naval Academy even as he was serially publishing and continually revising his history of the United States, which begins with the voyages of Leif Eriksson and ends with the peace negotiations of 1782. Although a consummate historian—he consulted hundreds of primary-source documents from European archives for his research—Bancroft was also an unabashed partisan of American exceptionalism: the notion that the progress toward a democratic republic was a uniquely American undertaking that derived not from soil or ancestry but from the nation's distinctive ideologies of republicanism and liberalism, which were inimical to the older, corrupt monarchies of Europe. America was destined to become independent, so Bancroft's million-word narrative explains, in order to leave

John Gast, *American Progress*, 1872. Oil on canvas. Gast's painting has become a widely recognized symbol for the idea of the United States' manifest destiny. Here, personified as a woman in white, Manifest Destiny leads American pioneers westward toward the Pacific. (Library of Congress, Prints and Photographs Division, LC-DIG-ppmsca-09855)

those decaying roots behind. The obvious implication is that America was also manifestly destined to expand westward to the Pacific Ocean, spreading those values of liberty and equality.

Bancroft was also quite partisan when it came to the overseas aspects of the Revolutionary War. Throughout volumes 7–10, devoted to the war, Bancroft admires French assistance to the United States, from the early materiel aid of Beaumarchais to the combined campaign at Yorktown. He describes the French foreign minister, the comte de Vergennes, as "wise," "able," and "honorable," and even notes the bravery of the French engineer François-Louis de Fleury at the battles of Brandywine and Stony Point. He especially fawns over Lafayette—whose portrait graces the frontispiece of volume 9—and mentions him more often than Rochambeau and de Grasse combined. The Dutch Republic gets several nods, and Hyder Ali a single line.

But he reserves his particular enmity for the Spanish. Bancroft, a diplomat, was writing his *History* at a difficult period in Spanish-American relations. Each side had good reason to mistrust the other. Spain's loss of much of its American empire, combined with the Monroe Doctrine, which extended American influence over the hemisphere, meant that the two nations were continually elbowing each other over such matters as Cuban independence, influence in Santo Domingo, and intervention in Mexico. America's distrust of Spain as a threat to its manifest destiny is reflected in Bancroft's historical narrative: he heaps venom on Spanish actions and motives at every opportunity. Don José Moñino y Redondo, the Count of Floridablanca, in charge of Spain's foreign affairs and effectively Vergennes's counterpart, receives the brunt of Bancroft's attacks; he is "devoured by ambition," "irritable," full of "intrigues"; he "dissimulates," "cavils," and hates the idea of American independence (Bancroft 1834–78: 10: 189). More than any other factor, Bancroft's dismissal of the Spanish involvement in the Revolutionary War is why Americans came to forget how critical it was to victory.

Other contemporary histories were shaped in the same mold. Richard Hildreth, who professed accuracy and abjured the kinds of "sermons and Fourth-of-July orations" (Hildreth 1849–52: 1: iii) that Bancroft was accused of, nevertheless glorifies Lafayette and gives the Spanish short shrift in his six-volume *History of the United States of America* (1849–52). John Ludlow's *War of American Independence* (1876) labels Lafayette the "foremost of French heroes" but notes only that Pensacola "capitulated" to the Spanish, without ever identifying the Spanish heroes of that important battle. Children's textbooks also repeated this pattern; Jacob Abbott's *American History* (8 vols., 1860–65) states that of all the French naval and military officers, Lafayette offered the most valuable services; the Spanish do not even rate a mention.

Writing the American Revolution as a Rising Power

"By the end of the nineteenth century," notes Ray Raphael in *Founding Myths* (2004), "romantic stories of the nation's founding had been fine-tuned and firmly implanted in the mainstream of American culture." The post–Civil War nation was finally entering the throes of industrialization that had already transformed Britain from a nation of shopkeepers into the workshop of the

General John J. Pershing and staff at Lafayette's tomb, Picpus Cemetery, Paris, July 4, 1917. (Library of Congress, Prints and Photographs Division, LC-B2-4281-1L)

world. America was beginning to flex its diplomatic and military muscles, and the historical narrative of American exceptionalism perfectly suited this age. Among its proponents was John Fiske, described as the "Bancroft of his generation" (Raphael 2004: 294). In 1889, he wrote *The War of Independence,* a short (250-page) introductory text that was intended for students but came to wield substantial influence on the American psyche. Fiske, like Bancroft, completely ignores the Spanish and does even more to pare down the presence of foreign troops, mentioning only those of Lafayette; Rochambeau, in Fiske's telling, was not even at Yorktown. And the subsequent battles at Gibraltar and Cuddalore never happened. This was in keeping with the received narrative, for, as Raphael points out, "Popular historians . . . simply decreed that their histories ended at Yorktown. There, the Americans won and the British lost. The Americans celebrated, while the British, following Lord North, declared, 'Oh, God! It is all over.' End of story" (Raphael 2004: 258). This narrative certainly contributed to the famous account of America's arrival in France during the First World War, marked by General John J. Pershing's chief of staff, Charles Stanton, declaring, "Lafayette, we are here!," as if the sole reason America went to war with Germany was to repay its debt to the marquis.

As the increasingly self-confident nation, which could send the Great White Fleet of naval ships around the world, passed its century mark,

The Great White Fleet under way off Hampton Roads, Virginia, 1907–09. This round-the-globe voyage by a U.S. naval battle fleet demonstrated to other nations that the United States was now a rising power in world affairs. (Naval Historical Center, photo no. NH 100349)

less one-sided accounts appeared. Edward Channing, whose last volume of the epic six-volume *History of the United States* (1905–25) garnered a Pulitzer Prize for history, is a bit more generous in his treatment of Spain and reinstates Rochambeau at Yorktown. He also makes the point that by 1782, the fact that British military strength was "dissipated" around the world was a factor in Britain's coming to the peace table. Historians also began drawing attention to hitherto-ignored aspects of the international scope of the war. Edwin Stone's *Our French Allies* (1884), Thomas Balch's *The French in America during the War of Independence* (1891), and Joachim Merlant's *Soldiers and Sailors of France in the American War for Independence* (1920) describe French and American operations from Newport to Yorktown, while biographies of individual French participants also began to appear. Friedrich Edler's *The Dutch Republic and the American Revolution*, published in 1911, remains the only full-length treatment of the subject. And for the first time, a proper accounting of Spanish operations in the South was given in John Caughey's *Bernardo de Gálvez in Louisiana* (1934).

Writing the American Revolution as a Superpower

For most of the twentieth century after World War II, America was the dominant global power, but it was in constant conflict with the other great power, the Soviet Union. The experience of World War II, the possibility of war with the Soviet Union, and actual fighting against its proxies in Korea and Vietnam led to the wholesale rethinking of the American armed forces. With the increasing professionalization of men and women in uniform, there was greater emphasis on using history to teach critical thinking. America's expanded military role around the world meant that "lessons learned" from current and previous conflicts took on new significance in both the uniformed services and in academia. Histories of the American Revolution now took a sharp turn toward its military and strategic aspects. There was certainly much to learn from that war: how to fight in an asymmetric conflict, the need for popular support, the importance of a navy, and the value of alliances and coalitions.

One of the first postwar historians to take this military and strategic perspective was Howard Peckham, in *The War for Independence: A Military History* (1950). Among several achievements in this short (220-page) volume is the recognition of the strategic importance of Gálvez's campaign: it "undermined the British western scheme" and prompted General Henry Clinton to abandon Newport. In 1964, the British historian Piers Mackesy, although focusing on the strategic and political issues behind Britain's stumbling efforts to retain an empire, brought a much-needed global perspective to his *War for America, 1775–1783*. Its breadth of vision makes this one of the most important histories of the war even today. In a similar vein, John Alden's *History of the American Revolution* (1969) balances the military, diplomatic, and political aspects of the war and takes note of the strategic importance that France and Spain placed on invading Britain and besieging Gibraltar. Perhaps the best treatment of the American Revolution as a world war was undertaken by the team of Richard Ernest Dupuy, Gay Hammerman, and Grace P. Hayes in *The American Revolution: A Global War* (1977), which brought a renewed emphasis on the naval battles around the world: the section on the campaigns in India and Ceylon alone is worth the price of the book.

It was also during the later twentieth century that comprehensive histories of the coalition nations began to appear. *The American Revolution and the French Alliance,* by William Stinchcombe (1969), explains how the two sides came to develop a cautious cooperation, despite having been on opposite sides of the Seven Years' War not long before. Jonathan Dull's *The French Navy and American Independence* (1975) not only stresses the war's naval battles and strategies but also reveals the diplomatic maneuverings of the French and Spanish courts that had been, until recently, unknown to Americans. And Barbara Tuchman's *The First Salute* (1988), while not a comprehensive history per se of the Dutch Republic's involvement, nevertheless places front and center its fight with the British as a crucial part of the war.

Writing the American Revolution in the Age of Globalization

The fall of the Berlin Wall, in 1989, left the United States as the world's only superpower, attempting to manage a chaotic, newly interconnected world. Americans began to reflect on what the United States represents as a nation and what it means to be an American today. Many of the recent histories of the American Revolution have undertaken more introspective analyses of the era, questioning received wisdom as to the causes, actions, and consequences of the war. Gordon Wood's *The Radicalism of the American Revolution* (1991) and *The American Revolution: A History* (2002) are leading examples of this inward focus, stressing the consequences of the Revolution for the lives of slaves, women, and the common laborer, while leaving aside the larger global context.

Other histories have been more international in their outlook, showing that the networks of alliances and coalitions back then have echoes today. In 2002, Thomas E. Chávez published the first comprehensive examination of Spanish participation in the war, *Spain and the Independence of the United States: An Intrinsic Gift.* John Ferling's *Almost a Miracle: The American Victory in the War of Independence* (2007) pays particular attention to the French alliance and the Anglo-Dutch wars, less to Spanish involvement. And Richard Middleton's *The War of American Independence* (2012) not only stresses the importance of the French alliance but also gives over entire chapters and subchapters to Spanish and Dutch motives and actions.

Writing the American Revolution on the 250th Anniversary of the Nation

The American Revolution began as a civil war between English colonists and their British rulers, confined to a small strip of coastline in North America. It soon pulled in American Indian nations, free and enslaved people of color, and Spanish and French inhabitants in the South on the Gulf Coast and along the Mississippi River. By its end, the American Revolution had turned into a global war involving six separate nation-states fighting across five continents and two vast oceans. As the authors in this volume have so clearly shown, both in their essays here and in their numerous published works elsewhere, the American Revolution was "the History of Mankind for the whole Epocha of it," as John Adams so astutely noted (Adams 1783). The global nature of the Revolution was, in fact, a reflection of what the American nation was at its inception and is today—the centerpiece of international efforts for a common good.

The United States is approaching its 250th anniversary in 2026 in a world that is increasingly coming to resemble that of 1776. America's position as the single preeminent superpower is giving way to a multipolar world in which regional spheres of influence are dominated by other powers—not just Russia and China but also blocs of nations in Europe and South Asia. Global politics is marked increasingly by the struggle for a balance of power among the United States and these nations, much as the American Revolution was really part of the balance-of-power struggle among Britain, France, and Spain. The fabric of the nation is today as diverse as it was then, especially with the growing number of citizens of Hispanic and Latino origin. And the influence of immigration, international travel, and trade is now greater than at almost any time in U.S. history.

History is not only the continuation of politics by other means: it is also the means by which we come to understand who we are and who we will become. The study of the American Revolution will continue to offer fresh interpretations of our nation's origins and its relationship with the world to help guide the way we create our future.

Former allies and enemies who are now an international coalition securing the peace: Dutch, Spanish, British, American, and French warships operating together in Combined Task Force 150, Gulf of Oman, May 6, 2004. (U.S. Navy 040506 N7586B 141)

References

Introduction

Buffinton, Arthur H. 1929. *The Second Hundred Years' War, 1689–1815*. New York: Henry Holt and Co.

Crouzet, François. 1996. "The Second Hundred Years War: Some Reflections." *French History* 10: 432–50.

Ferreiro, Larrie D. 2016. *Brothers at Arms: American Independence and the Men of France and Spain Who Saved It*. New York: Alfred A. Knopf.

Seeley, John Robert. 1883. *The Expansion of England*. London: Macmillan.

Global Revolutions

Anderson, Fred. 2000. *Crucible of War: The Seven Years' War and the Fate of Empire in British North America, 1754–1766*. New York: Alfred A. Knopf.

Anderson, Fred, and Andrew Cayton. 2005. *The Dominion of War: Empire and Liberty in North America, 1500–2000*. New York: Penguin.

Brewer, John. 1989. *The Sinews of Power: War, Money, and the English State, 1688–1783*. New York: Alfred A. Knopf.

Calloway, Colin G. 2006. *The Scratch of a Pen: 1763 and the Transformation of North America*. New York: Oxford University Press.

Chávez, Thomas E. 2002. *Spain and the Independence of the United States: An Intrinsic Gift*. Albuquerque: University of New Mexico Press.

Conway, Stephen. 2006. *War, State, and Society in Mid-Eighteenth-Century Britain and Ireland*. New York: Oxford University Press.

Draper, Theodore. 1996. *A Struggle for Power: The American Revolution*. New York: Random House.

Dull, Jonathan R. 1985. *A Diplomatic History of the American Revolution*. New Haven, CT: Yale University Press.

DuVal, Kathleen. 2015. *Independence Lost: Lives on the Edge of the American Revolution*. New York: Random House.

Franklin, Benjamin. 1760. Letter to Lord Kames. January 3. Founders Online, National Archives, Washington, DC. www.franklinpapers.org/franklin/framedVolumes.jsp?vol=9&page=005a.

Gould, Eliga H. 2005. "Fears of War, Fantasies of Peace: British Politics and the Coming of the American Revolution." In *Empire and Nation: The American Revolution in the Atlantic World*, edited by Eliga H. Gould and Peter S. Onuf, 19–34. Baltimore: Johns Hopkins University Press.

Gould, Eliga H. 2012. *Among the Powers of the Earth: The American Revolution and the Making of a New World Empire*. Cambridge, MA: Harvard University Press.

Higginbotham, Don. 1983. *The War of American Independence: Military Attitudes, Policies, and Practice, 1763–1789*. Boston: Northeastern University Press.

Marshall, Peter J. 2003. "The Case for Coercing America." In *"A Free though Conquering People": Eighteenth-Century Britain and Its Empire*, edited by Peter J. Marshall, sec. 7, 9–22. Burlington, VT: Ashgate Publishing.

O'Shaughnessy, Andrew Jackson. 2000. *An Empire Divided: The American Revolution and the British Caribbean*. Philadelphia: University of Pennsylvania Press.

O'Shaughnessy, Andrew Jackson. 2013. *The Men Who Lost America: British Leadership, the American Revolution, and the Fate of the Empire.* New Haven, CT: Yale University Press.

Sadosky, Leonard J. 2009. *Revolutionary Negotiations: Indians, Empires, and Diplomats in the Founding of America.* Charlottesville: University of Virginia Press.

Shy, John. 1990. *A People Numerous and Armed: Reflections on the Military Struggle for American Independence.* Ann Arbor: University of Michigan Press.

Stinchcombe, William C. 1969. *The American Revolution and the French Alliance.* Syracuse, NY: Syracuse University Press.

Thomas, Peter D. G. 1991. *Tea Party to Independence: The Third Phase of the American Revolution, 1773–1776.* Oxford: Clarendon Press.

Weber, David J. 1992. *The Spanish Frontier in North America.* New Haven, CT: Yale University Press.

The British Grand Strategy

Conway, Stephen. 1995. *The War of American Independence, 1775–1783.* London: Longman.

Edelson, S. Max. 2017. *The New Map of Empire: How Britain Imagined America before Independence.* Cambridge, MA: Harvard University Press.

Mackesy, Piers. 1965. *The War for America, 1775–1783.* London: Longman.

Madariaga, Isabel de. 1962. *Britain, Russia, and the Armed Neutrality of 1780.* London: Hollis & Carter.

Richmond, Herbert. W. 1931. *The Navy in India, 1763–83.* London: Ernest Benn.

Russett, Alan. 2001. *Dominic Serres, R.A., 1719–1793.* Woodbridge, UK: Antique Collector's Club. (One-third of this

study is devoted to the battle art of the American War.)

Starkey, David. J. 1990. *British Privateering Enterprise in the Eighteenth Century.* Exeter: University of Exeter Press.

French Naval Operations

Antier, Jean-Jacques. 1965. *Admiral de Grasse, Hero of the American Independence.* Paris: Plon.

Barbée, Maurice Lynier de la. 1972. *The Chevalier de Ternay: Life of Charles-Henry Louis d'Arsac de Ternay, Rear Admiral of the French Navy.* Grenoble: Éditions des 4 Seigneurs.

Bonnichon, Philippe. 1987. "Grenada, Savannah (1779), Saint Kitts (1782): Three Examples of the Role of the Navy in Amphibious and Troop Support Operations during the War of American Independence." In *Wars and Peace: Proceedings of Conference on French-English Naval History, Rochefort, 1986,* 261–73. Vincennes: Service Historique de la Marine.

Caron, François. 1989. *The Stolen Victory: Battle of the Chesapeake.* Vincennes: Service Historique de la Marine.

Caron, François. 1996. *The Misunderstood War, or Suffren's Myth.* Vincennes: Service Historique de la Marine.

Chaline, Olivier. 2013. "Franco-British Naval Rivalry and the Crisis of the Monarchy, 1759–1789." In *The Crisis of the Absolute Monarchy: France from Old Regime to Revolution,* edited by Julian Swann and Joël Félix, 205–21. Oxford: Oxford University Press.

Chaline, Olivier. 2016. "A New Historical Approach to Naval Operations and History of Command: The Example of the Fleet of Admiral de Grasse,

1781–1783." In *The Maritimization of the World, from Prehistory to the Present Day,* edited by GIS d'Histoire Maritime, 611–22. Paris: PUPS.

Chaline, Olivier. 2017. "Admiral Louis Guillouet, Comte d'Orvilliers (1710–92): A Style of Command in the Age of the American War." In *Naval Leadership in the Atlantic World: The Age of Reform and Revolution, 1700–1850,* edited by Richard Harding and Agustín Guimerá Ravina, 73–84. London: University of Westminster Press.

Chaline, Olivier, Philippe Bonnichon, and Charles-Philippe de Vergennes, eds. 2008. *France and American Independence.* Paris: PUPS.

Chaline, Olivier, Philippe Bonnichon, and Charles-Philippe de Vergennes, eds. 2013, 2018. *Navies and the War of American Independence, 1763–1783.* 2 vols. Paris: PUPS.

Chevalier, Louis Édouard. 1877. *History of the French Navy during the War of American Independence.* Paris: Hachette.

Dull, Jonathan. 1975. *The French Navy and American Independence: A Study of Arms and Diplomacy, 1774–1787.* Princeton, NJ: Princeton University Press.

Fontainieu, Emmanuel de. 1992. *The Hermione, from Rochefort to American Glory.* Paris: De Monza.

Girault de Coursac, Paul, and Pierrette Girault de Coursac. 1991. *The War of America and Freedom of the Seas, 1778–1783.* Paris: F. X. de Guibert.

Hattendorf, John B. 2005. *Newport, the French Navy, and American Independence.* Newport, RI: Redwood Press.

Jonquière, Christian de La. 1996. *French Sailors under Louis XVI: The War of American Independence.* Issy-les-Moulineaux, France: Muller.

Lacour-Gayet, Georges. 1905. *The French Navy under the Reign of Louis XVI.* Paris: Honoré Champion.

Meyer, Jean. 1999. "From 1763 to 1780: The Establishment of a New Balance of Power." In *The French and British Navies Confronting the United States (1776–1865),* edited by Jean-Charles Lefebvre, 5–43. Vincennes: Service Historique de la Marine.

Michel, Jacques. 1976. *The Adventurous and Memorable Life of Charles-Henri, Comte d'Estaing.* Paris: J. Michel.

Monaque, Rémi. 2009. *Suffren: An Unfulfilled Destiny.* Paris: Tallandier.

Perugia, Paul del. 1939. *The French Attempt to Invade Britain, 1779.* Paris: Alcan-PUF.

Trentinian, Jacques de. 2016. *France to the Aid of America: Analysis of the Expédition Particulière of the Comte de Rochambeau and the Chevalier du Ternay, March to December 1780.* Paris: SPM.

Vergé-Franceschi, Michel. 1996. *The French Navy in the Eighteenth Century: Wars, Administration, Exploration.* Paris: SEDES.

Villiers, Patrick. 1985. *Louis XVI's Navy: From Choiseul to Sartine.* Grenoble: J. P. Debbane.

Pierre-Augustin Caron de Beaumarchais

Ferreiro, Larrie. 2016. *Brothers at Arms: American Independence and the Men of France and Spain Who Saved It.* New York: Alfred A. Knopf.

Spanish Naval Operations

Alsina Torrente, Juan. 2006. *A Romantic War, 1778–1783: Spain, France, and*

England at Sea: The Naval Background of the Independence of the United States. Madrid: Ministerio de Defensa.

Beerman, Eric. 1984. "The Last Battle of the War of Independence Was Not Yorktown: The Spanish–North American Expedition to the Bahamas in 1782." *Journal of Naval History* 5: 89–102.

Beerman, Eric. 1991. *Spain and the Independence of the United States.* Madrid: Fundación Mapfre.

Beerman, Eric. 2014. "José Solano, Marquis of Socorro, and the Spanish Navy in the Battle of Pensacola in 1781." *General Naval Journal* 204: 903–10.

Blanco Nuñez, José María. 2004. *The Spanish Navy in the Second Half of the Eighteenth Century.* Bazán, Spain: Izar Construcciones Navales SA.

Calleja Leal, Guillermo, and Gregorio Calleja Leal. 2016. *Gálvez and Spain in the American Revolution.* Valencia: Albatros.

Fernández Duro, Cesáreo. 1973. *The Spanish Navy since the Union of the Kingdoms of Castille and Aragon.* Vol. 7. Facsimile ed. Madrid: Museo Naval de Madrid.

Garrigues, Eduardo. 2016. *He Who Has the Courage, Follow Me: Living with Bernardo Gálvez.* Madrid: La Esfera de los Libros.

Guimerá Ravina, Agustín. 2016. "A Shared Leadership: The Conquest of Pensacola, 1781." In "270th Anniversary of Bernardo de Gálvez: Bernardo de Gálvez and His Times," special issue, *Journal of Military History* 1: 141–66.

Mazarredo, Jose de. 1781. "General Idea How the Combined Fleet Should Maneuver to Attack the Enemy Forces." August. Archivo del Museo Naval, Madrid, Colección Vargas y Ponce, vol. 3, tome 2, doc. 152.

Medina Rojas, Francisco de Borja. 1980. *José de Ezpeleta, Governor of Mobile, 1780–1781.* Seville: EEHA-CSIC y Diputación Foral de Navarra.

Ministerio de Defensa. 2015. *Bernardo de Gálvez: The Spanish Presence in Mexico and the United States.* Exhib. cat. Madrid: Ministerio de Defensa.

Quintero Saravia, Gonzalo M. 2015. "Bernardo de Gálvez and America at the End of the Eighteenth Century." PhD diss., Universidad Complutense de Madrid.

Reparaz, Carmen. 1986. *I Am Alone: Bernardo de Gálvez and the Conquest of Pensacola.* Madrid: Instituto de Cooperación Hispanoamericana.

Ruigómez de Hernández, María del Pilar. 1978. *The Spanish Government of the Enlightenment Faces the Independence of the United States.* Madrid: Ministerio de Asuntos Exteriores.

Ruiz de Oña Domínguez, Alberto. 2017. "Another Forgotten Hero on His 300th Anniversary: Matías de Gálvez y Gallardo, 1717–1784." *Bicentennial Notebooks* 30 (August): 5–47.

Santaló Rodríguez de Viguri, José Luis. 1973. *José Solano y Bote, First Marquis of Socorro, Admiral of the Spanish Navy.* Madrid: Instituto Histórico de la Marina.

Uniforms, Supplies, and Money from Spain

Correspondence between Diego de Gardoqui and John Jay. 1780. Archivo Histórico Nacional, Estado legajo 3884. Madrid, Spain.

Correspondence from Robert Morris to George Washington and from *the comte de Grasse to the comte de Rochambeau, August 30, 1781.* Rochambeau Papers, Yale University, Beinecke Library, box 3, folder 143.

Correspondence from Francisco Rendón to José de Gálvez, Philadelphia, April 27, 1781. Archivo General de Indias, Santo Domingo, 2597. Seville, Spain.

Correspondence from Friedrich Wilhelm von Steuben to George Washington, May 23, 1781; from Lewis Nicola to Washington, August 17, 1781; and from John Moylan to Washington, December 27, 1781. George Washington Papers, Founders Online, National Archives, Washington, DC. https://founders.archives.gov.

British Global Ambitions and Indian Identity

Bryant, G. J. 2013. *The Emergence of British Power in India, 1600–1784: A Grand Strategic Interpretation.* Woodbridge, UK: Boydell Press.

Burke, Edmund. 1981. *The Writings and Speeches of Edmund Burke,* vol. 2: *Party, Parliament and the American Crisis.* Edited by Paul Langford. Oxford: Clarendon Press.

Dalrymple, William. 2015. "The East India Company: The Original Corporate Raiders." *Guardian,* March 4, 2015. www.theguardian.com/world/2015/mar/04/east-india-company-original-corporate-raiders.

Dickinson, John. 1895. *The Writings of John Dickinson,* vol. 1: *Political Writings, 1764–1774.* Edited by Paul Leicester Ford. Philadelphia: Historical Society of Philadelphia.

Embree, Ainslie Thomas, and Robin Jeanne Lewis. 1988. *Encyclopedia of Asian History,* vol. 4. New York: Macmillan Publishing.

Fay, Eliza. (1817) 2010. *Original Letters from India.* Edited by E. M. Forster. New York: New York Review of Books.

Fortescue, J., ed. 1928. *Correspondence of King George III, 1760–1783.* London: Macmillan and Co.

Kaushik, Roy. 2011. *War, Culture, and Society in Early Modern South Asia.* New York: Routledge.

Kausir, Kabir. 1980. *Secret Correspondence of Tipu Sultan.* New Delhi: Light and Life Publishers.

Keay, John. 2000. *India: A History.* New York: Grove Press.

Mahan, Alfred Thayer. (1890) 1918. *The Influence of Sea Power upon History, 1660–1783.* Boston: Little, Brown, and Company.

Marshall, P. J. 2005. *The Making and Unmaking of Empires: Britain, India, and America c. 1750–1783.* New York: Oxford University Press.

Robins, Nick. 2006. *The Corporation That Changed the World: How the East India Company Shaped the Modern Multinational.* Ann Arbor, MI: Pluto Press.

Revolution in America and the Dutch Republic

Attema, Ypie. 1976. *Sint Eustatius: A Short History of the Island and Its Monuments.* Zutphen, Netherlands: Walburg Pers.

Bartstra, J. S. 1952. *Fleet Restoration and Army Augmentation, 1770–1780.* Assen, Netherlands: Van Gorkum.

Dorreboom, M. L. 2000. "'As He Is Condemned Provided That . . .': Military Criminal Justice of the Land Forces, 1700–1795." PhD diss., Amsterdam University, Netherlands.

Ferreiro, Larrie D. 2016. *Brothers at Arms: American Independence and the Men of France and Spain Who Saved It*. New York: Alfred A. Knopf.

Hartog, J. 1976. *History of Sint Eustatius*. Aruba: De Wit Stores.

Huibrechts, Marion M. A. 2009. "Swampin' Guns and Stabbing Irons: The Austrian Netherlands, Liège Arms, and the American Revolution (1770–1783)." PhD diss., Catholic University of Leuven.

Klein, S. R. E. 1995. *Patriotic Republicanism: Political Culture in the Netherlands (1766–1787)*. Amsterdam: Amsterdam University Press.

Mott, William H. IV. 1999. *Military Assistance: An Operational Perspective*. Westport, CT: Greenwood Press.

O'Shaughnessy, Andrew Jackson. 2013. *The Men Who Lost America: British Leadership, the American Revolution, and the Fate of the Empire*. New Haven, CT: Yale University Press.

Rodger, N. A. M. 1999. "The British View of the Functioning of the Anglo-Dutch Alliance, 1688–1795." In *Navies and Armies: The Anglo-Dutch Relationship in War and Peace, 1688–1988*, edited by G. J. A. Raven and N. A. M. Rodger, 12–32. Edinburgh, Scotland: John Donald Publishers.

Rodger, N. A. M. 2004. *The Command of the Ocean: A Naval History of Britain, 1649–1815*. London: Allen Lane.

Schama, Simon. 1977. *Patriots and Liberators: Revolution in the Netherlands, 1780–1813*. New York: Knopf.

Schulte Nordholt, J. W. 1979. *Example at a Distance: The Influence of the American Revolution in the Netherlands*. Baarn, Netherlands: In den Toren.

Tuchman, Barbara. 1988. *The First Salute: A View of the American Revolution*. New York: Ballantine Books.

Van der Capellen tot den Pol, Joan Derk. 1775. *Advice of Squire—On the Request of His Majesty the King of Great Britain, Touching the Loan of the Scots Brigade, Spoken on 16 December 1775, at the Council Meeting of Overijssel*. Pamphlet.

Van der Capellen tot den Pol, Joan Derk. 1781. *Address to the People of the Netherlands*. September 25. Pamphlet. (Although Van der Capellen tot den Pol was suspected at the time of being the anonymous pamphlet's author, this was ascertained only in 1871.)

Van Zijverden, J. 1997. "The Risky Alternative: Dutch Privateering during the Fourth Anglo-Dutch War, 1780–1783." In *Pirates and Privateers: New Perspectives on the War on Trade in the Eighteenth and Nineteenth Centuries*, edited by D. J. Starkey, E. S. van Eyck van Heslinga, and J. A. de Moor, 186–205. Exeter: University of Exeter Press.

Zwitzer, H. L. 1987. "The Military Dimension of the Patriot Movement." In *For Homeland and Freedom: The Revolution of the Patriots*, edited by F. Grijzenhout, W. W. Mijnhardt, and N. C. F. van Sas, 27–52. Amsterdam: De Bataafsche Leeuw.

Zwitzer, H. L. 2012. *The Army of the Dutch Republic, 1568–1795*. Vol. 9. Amsterdam: De Bataafsche Leeuw.

The International War on the Gulf Coast

Carleton, Guy, first Baron Dorchester. Papers. British National Archives, Kew. Microfilm. University of North Carolina Libraries, Chapel Hill. 23 reels.

Cegielski, Wendy, and Brad R. Lieb. 2011. *"Hina' Falaa*, 'The Long Path': An Analysis of Chickasaw Settlement Using GIS in Northeast Mississippi, 1650–1840." *Native South* 4: 24–54.

Documents of the American Revolution, 1770–1783. 1972–81. 21 vols. Colonial Office Series. Edited by K. G. Davies. Shannon, Ireland: Irish University Press.

DuVal, Kathleen. 2015. *Independence Lost: Lives on the Edge of the American Revolution*. New York: Random House.

Ferreiro, Larrie D. 2016. *Brothers at Arms: American Independence and the Men of France and Spain Who Saved It*. New York: Alfred A. Knopf.

Gálvez, Bernardo de, to Josef de Gálvez. 1777–81. Correspondence. Transcripts from Archivo Nacional de la República de Cuba. 3 vols. Ayer Collection, Newberry Library, Chicago.

Hodson, Christopher. 2012. *The Acadian Diaspora: An Eighteenth-Century History*. New York: Oxford University Press.

Mississippi Provincial Archives: English Dominion. 1911. Edited by Dunbar Rowland. Nashville, TN: Brandon Printing Co.

O'Shaughnessy, Andrew Jackson. 2000. *An Empire Divided: The American Revolution and the British Caribbean*. Philadelphia: University of Pennsylvania Press.

Papeles Procedentes de Cuba. Microfilm. P. K. Yonge Library, University of Florida, Gainesville.

Papers of the Continental Congress. 1774–89. National Archives and Records Service, Washington, DC. No. M247. Microfilm. University of North Carolina Libraries, Chapel Hill. 204 reels.

Piecuch, Jim. 2008. *Three Peoples, One King: Loyalists, Indians, and Slaves in the Revolutionary South, 1775–1782*.

Columbia: University of South Carolina Press.

Records of the British Colonial Office, class 5. Microfilm. Library of Congress, Washington, DC. 53 reels.

Starr, J. Barton. 1976. *Tories, Dons, and Rebels: The American Revolution in British West Florida, 1763–1783*. Gainesville: University Press of Florida.

Lafayette

Chatel de Brancion, Laurence, and Patrick Villiers. 2013. *La Fayette: Dreams of Glory*. Paris: Monelle Hayot.

Lafayette, Gilbert du Motier, marquis de. 1837–38. *Memoirs, Correspondence, and Manuscripts of General Lafayette*. 6 vols. Paris: H. Fournier.

Lafayette, Gilbert du Motier, marquis de, to George Washington, February 5, 1783. Founders Early Access, http://rotunda.upress.virginia.edu/founders/default.xqy?keys=FOEA-print-01-02-02-4575.

Larquier-Rochefort, Bernard de. 1987. *La Fayette, Usurper of the Vessel* La Victoire. Surgères, France: B. de Larquier.

Pottier, Serge Le. 2011. *Duportail, or George Washington's Engineering Genius*. Paris: Economica.

Taillemite, Étienne. 1989. *La Fayette*. Paris: Fayard.

Villiers, Patrick, and Jean-Claude Lemineur. 2016. *The* Hermione, *La Fayette, and Latouche-Tréville: Two Men and a Frigate Serving American Independence*. Nice: ANCRE.

War Supplies from the Low Countries

Ferreiro, Larrie D. 2016. *Brothers at Arms: American Independence and the Men of France and Spain Who Saved It*. New York: Alfred A. Knopf.

Gaier, Claude. 1996. *Five Centuries of Liège Gunmaking*. Alleur, Belgium: Éditions du Perron.

Huibrechts, Marion M. A. 2009. "Swampin' Guns and Stabbing Irons: The Austrian Netherlands, Liège Arms, and the American Revolution (1770–1783)." PhD diss., Catholic University of Leuven.

Hessian Savages, Frog-Eating Frenchmen, and Virtuous Americans

Acomb, Evelyn, ed. 1958. *The Revolutionary Journal of Baron Ludwig von Closen, 1780–1783*. Chapel Hill: University of North Carolina Press.

Atwood, Rodney. 1980. *The Hessians: Mercenaries from Hessen-Kassel in the American Revolution*. New York: Cambridge University Press.

Burgoyne, Bruce E. 2012. "Diary of Private Johannes Reuber, Grenadier, Regiment Rall/von Wöllwarth/von Trümbach/d'Angelelli, 1776–1783, Part 1: 1776–1777." *Hessians: Journal of the Johannes Schwalm Historical Association* 15: 16–29.

"Cato" (William Smith). 1776. "To the People of Pennsylvania. Letter V." *Pennsylvania Packet*, April 1.

Dupont d'Aubevoye, Louis François Bertrand, comte de Lauberdière. 1780–83. *Journal of the Army under the Orders of Monsieur le Comte de Rochambeau during the Campaigns of 1780, 1781, 1782, 1783 in North America*. 4 vols. Paris: Bibliothèque Nationale.

Ewald, Johann von. 1976. *Diary of the American War*. Translated and edited by Joseph P. Tustin. Princeton, NJ: Princeton University Press.

"Extract of a Letter from an Officer in General Frazier's Battalion, dated September 3, 1776." In Peter Force, *Peter Force's American Archives*, 5th ser., vol. 1, 1259. Washington, DC: M. St. Clair Clarke and Peter Force, 1848.

Fersen, Axel de. 1879. "Letters of Axel de Fersen, Aide-de-Camp to Rochambeau: Written to His Father in Sweden, 1780–1782." *Magazine of American History* 3, no. 6 (June): 369–76.

Fitch, Asa. n.d. *Notes for a History of Washington County, N.Y.* 7 vols. New York: New York Public Library, mss. NYGB 18065.

Flohr, Georg Daniel. 1784. *Description of Travels in America by the Distinguished Regiment of Zweybrücken, on both Water and Land, from the Years 1780 to 1784*. Fonds Patrimoniaux MS 15. Strasbourg, France: Bibliothèque Municipale. Unpaginated.

Franklin, Benjamin. 1755. *Observations Concerning the Increasing of Mankind, Peopling of Countries, &c.* Boston: S. Kneeland.

Idzerda, Stanley, Roger E. Smith, Linda J. Pike, and Mary Ann Quinn, eds. 1979. *Lafayette in the Age of the American Revolution: Selected Letters and Papers, 1776–1700*. 5 vols. Ithaca, NY: Cornell University Press.

"Johannes in Eremo" (John Cleaveland). 1776. "To the Publick." January 1. In Peter Force, *American Archives*, 4th ser, vol. 4, col. 529. Washington, DC: M. St. Clair Clarke and Peter Force, 1843.

Kipping, Ernst. 1971. *The Hessian View of America, 1776–1783*. Monmouth Beach, NJ: Philip Freneau Press.

Massoni, Gérard-Antoine. 1996. *Interesting Details of Events in the American War, Winter 1781–1782: Hampton, Charlotte, and After; Manuscript by Claude Hugau,*

Lieutenant Colonel of the Legion of Foreign Volunteers of Lauzun. Besançon: Université de Franche-Comté.

Monbron, Louis Charles Fougeret de. 1757. *Prophylactic against Anglomania.* Minorca: M. DeCombreux.

Neimeyer, Charles. 1996. *America Goes to War.* New York: New York University Press.

The Parliamentary History of England from the Earliest Period to the Year 1777. 1813. 36 vols. London: T. C. Hansard.

The Parliamentary History of England from the Earliest Period to the Year 1803. 1814. 36 vols. *Comprising the Period from the Twenty-Ninth of January 1777, to the Fourth of December 1778.* London: T. C. Hansard.

Popp, Stephan. 1953. *A Hessian Soldier in the American Revolution: The Diary of Stephan Popp.* Translated and edited by Reinhard J. Pope. Privately printed.

"Recollections of the Revolution in Long Island." 1869. *Memoirs of the Long Island Historical Society,* 503–07.

Rice, Howard C. Jr., and Anne S. K. Brown, eds. 1972. *The American Campaigns of Rochambeau's Army, 1780, 1781, 1782, 1783.* 2 vols. Princeton, NJ: Princeton University Press.

Scott, Samuel F. 1983. "Strains in the Franco-American Alliance: The French Army in Virginia, 1781–82." In *Virginia in the American Revolution: A Collection of Essays,* ed. Richard A. Rutyna and Peter C. Stewart, vol. 2, 80–100. Norfolk, VA: Old Dominion University.

Scott, Samuel F. 1984. "Foreign Mercenaries, Revolutionary War, and Citizen Soldiers in the Late Eighteenth Century." *War and Society* 2 (September): 42–58.

Scudder, H. E. 1877. *Recollections of Samuel Breck with Passages from His Note-Books*

(1771–1862). Philadelphia: Porter & Coates.

Smith, Paul H., Gerard W. Gawalt, Rosemary Fry Plakas, and Eugene R. Sheridan. 1963. *Letters of Members of the Continental Congress.* 26 vols. Washington, DC: Library of Congress.

Wasmus, J. F. 1990. *An Eyewitness Account of the American Revolution and New England Life: The Journal of J. F. Wasmus, German Company Surgeon, 1776–1783.* Translated by Helga Doblin. Edited by Mary C. Lynn. Westport, CT: Greenwood Press.

Wiederhold, Andreas (?). 2010. *Krieg in Amerika und Aufklärung in Hessen: Die Privatbriefe (1772–1784) an Georg Ernst von und zu Gilsa.* Edited by Holger Th. Gräf, Lena Haunert, Christoph Kampmann, and Patrick Sturm. Marburg: Hessisches Landesamt für geschichtliche Landeskunde.

Saint-Domingue's Free Men of Color

Affiches américaines. 1779–80. Cap Français. (Newspaper.)

ANOM (Archives Nationales d'Outre-Mer, France) Series D. N.d. Naval troops and civil employees, registers, and reviews: $D^{2c}41$, "Regiment of the Chasseurs Volontaires de St Domingue."

ANOM Series E. N.d. Colonial personnel files. E251, dossier "De Lamorlière du Tillet (Louis-Antoine)"; E278, dossier "Lenoir de Rouvray"; E310, dossier "Mesnier."

ANOM Series F. 1779. Collection Moreau de Saint-Méry. F^3188, "History of Saint-Domingue: Letters, Memoirs, and Notes, Originals and Copies, 1778–1779"; F^3189, "History of Saint-Domingue: Letters, Memoirs, and Notes, Originals and Copies, 1779–1780."

Garrigus, John D. 2011. "Vincent Ogé Jeune (1757–91): Social Class and Free Colored Mobilization on the Eve of the Haitian Revolution." *Americas* 68, no. 1 (July): 33–62.

Lawrence, Alexander. 1951. *Storm over Savannah: The Story of Count d'Estaing and the Siege of the Town in 1779*. Athens: University of Georgia Press.

Moreau de Saint-Méry, Médéric-Louis-Élie. 1786. *Loix et constitutions des colonies française de l'Amérique sous le vent*. 6 vols. Paris: Chez l'auteur.

Moreau de Saint-Méry, Médéric-Louis-Élie. 1797. *Description topographique, physique . . . de la partie française de l'isle de Saint-Domingue*. 3 vols. Repr., 1959, Paris: Société de l'Histoire des Colonies Françaises.

Saint-Rémy, Joseph. 1854–57 [1956]. *Pétion et Haïti: Étude monographique et historique*. Edited by François Dalencour. Paris: Berger-Levrault.

Thésée, Françoise. 1982. "Les assemblées paroissiales des Cayes à St. Domingue (1774–1793)." *Revue de la société haitienne d'histoire et de géographie* 40, no. 137 (December): 5–179.

Voelz, Peter. 1993. *Slave and Soldier: The Military Impact of Blacks in the Colonial Americas*. New York: Garland Publishing, Inc.

Crafting the Peace

Bancroft, George. 1876. *History of the Joint Action of France and America for the Independence of the United States*. 3 vols. Paris: F. Vieweg.

Bemis, Samuel. 1935. *The Diplomacy of the American Revolution*. New York: Appleton-Century.

Boswell, James. 1826. *The Life of Samuel Johnson, L.L.D.* Oxford: Talboys & Wheeler.

Bowood Archives, Bowood, UK.

Hancock, David. 1995. *Citizens of the World: London Merchants and the Integration of the British Atlantic Community, 1735–1785*. New York: Cambridge University Press.

Hancock, David. Forthcoming. *The Man of Twists and Turns: William Fitzmaurice, 2nd Earl of Shelburne and the End of Enlightenment*.

Harlow, Vincent T. 1952–64. *The Founding of the Second British Empire, 1763–1793*. 2 vols. London: Longmans, Green & Co.

Knox, William. 1902. Memoranda (ca. April 1783). In *"Curious Political Anecdotes" of William Knox (Manuscripts of Capt. H. V. Knox)*. Historical Manuscript Commission, *Report on Manuscripts in Various Collections*. Dublin.

Morris, Richard B. 1965. *The Peacemakers: The Great Powers and American Independence*. New York: Harper & Row.

Robinson, Fritz. Letter to his brother Thomas Robinson, second Baron Grantham, February 9, 1779, L 30/14/333/177. Grantham Manuscripts, Bedfordshire and Luton Archives, England.

Rose, George. 1860. *The Diaries and Correspondence of the Right Hon. George Rose*. Edited by Leveson Venables-Vernon-Harcourt. 2 vols. London: R. Bentley.

Stockley, Andrew. 2001. *Britain and France at the Birth of America: The European Powers and the Peace Negotiations of 1782–1783*. Exeter: University of Exeter Press.

Reimagining the American Revolution

Adams, John. 1783. Letter to the abbé de Mably, Paris. January 15. Adams Papers. Founders Online, National Archives, Washington, DC. https://founders.archives.gov/documents/

Adams/06-14-02-0111-0004#ADMS-06-14-02-0111-0004-fn-0001.

Cooper, Helen A. 1982. *John Trumbull: The Hand and Spirit of a Painter.* New Haven, CT: Yale University Art Gallery.

Hamilton, Alexander. 1780. Letter to Lieutenant Colonel John Laurens. June 30. Founders Online, National Archives, Washington, DC. https://founders.archives.gov/documents/Hamilton/01-02-02-0742.

Jaffe, Irma B. 1975. *John Trumbull: Patriot Artist of the American Revolution.* Boston: New York Graphic Society.

Trumbull, John. 1841. *Autobiography, Reminiscences and Letters of John Trumbull, from 1756 to 1841.* New York: Wiley and Putnam. https://books.google.com/books/about/Autobiography_Reminiscences_and_Letters.html?id=jPI1AAAAMAAJ.

Rewriting the American Revolution

Abbott, Jacob. 1860–65. *American History.* 8 vols. New York: Sheldon & Co.

Adams, John. 1783. Letter to the abbé de Mably, Paris. January 15. Adams Papers. Founders Online, National Archives, Washington, DC. https://founders.archives.gov/documents/Adams/06-14-02-0111-0004#ADMS-06-14-02-0111-0004-fn-0001.

Adams, John. 1815. Letter to Thomas Jefferson. August 24. Jefferson Papers. Founders Online, National Archives, Washington, DC. http://founders.archives.gov/documents/Jefferson/03-08-02-0560.

Alden, John. 1969. *A History of the American Revolution.* New York: Knopf.

Balch, Thomas. 1891. *The French in America during the War of Independence.* Philadelphia: Porter & Coates.

Bancroft, George. 1834–78. *History of the United States of America.* 10 vols. Boston: Little, Brown.

Caughey, John. 1934. *Bernardo de Gálvez in Louisiana.* Berkeley: University of California Press.

Channing, Edward. 1905–25. *A History of the United States.* 6 vols. New York: Macmillan.

Chávez, Thomas E. 2002. *Spain and the Independence of the United States: An Intrinsic Gift.* Albuquerque: University of New Mexico Press.

d'Auberteuil, Michel René Hilliard. 1781. *Historical and Political Essays on the North American Revolution.* Brussels: n.p.

Dubuisson, Pierre-Ulric. 1778. *Summary of the American Revolution.* Paris: Cellot & Jombert.

Dull, Jonathan. 1975. *The French Navy and American Independence: A Study of Arms and Diplomacy, 1774–1787.* Princeton, NJ: Princeton University Press.

Dupuy, Richard Ernest, Gay Hammerman, and Grace P. Hayes. 1977. *The American Revolution: A Global War.* New York: McKay.

Edler, Friedrich. 1911. *The Dutch Republic and the American Revolution.* Baltimore: Johns Hopkins University Press.

Ferling, John. 2007. *Almost a Miracle: The American Victory in the War of Independence.* Oxford: Oxford University Press.

Fiske, John. 1889. *The War of Independence.* Boston: Houghton Mifflin.

Frost, John. 1838. *The History of the United States of North America.* London: C. Tilt.

Gordon, William. 1788. *History of the Rise, Progress, and Establishment of the*

Independence of the United States of America. 4 vols. London: Charles Dilly.

Hale, Salma. 1820. *History of the United States of America.* New York: H. Wallis.

Hildreth, Richard. 1849–52. *History of the United States of America.* 6 vols. New York: Harper & Bros.

Jefferson, Thomas. 1894. *The Writings of Thomas Jefferson,* vol. 4, *1784–1787.* Edited by Paul Leicester Ford. New York: G. Putnam's Sons.

Leboucher, Odet-Julien. 1787. *History of the Preceding War between Great Britain and the United States of America, France, Spain, and Holland.* Paris: Brocas.

Lendrum, John. 1795. *A Concise and Impartial History of the American Revolution.* Boston: I. Thomas and E. T. Andrews.

Longchamps, Pierre Charpentier de. 1785. *Impartial History of the Military and Political Events of the Previous War in the Four Corners of the World.* Paris: Veuve Duchesnel.

Ludlow, John. 1876. *The War of American Independence.* Boston: Estes and Lauriat.

Mackesy, Piers. 1964. *The War for America, 1775–1783.* Cambridge, MA: Harvard University Press.

Merlant, Joachim. 1920. *Soldiers and Sailors of France in the American War for Independence.* New York: C. Scribner's Sons.

Middleton, Richard. 2012. *The War of American Independence.* New York: Routledge.

Morse, Jedidiah. 1824. *Annals of the American Revolution.* Hartford, CT: n.p.

Peckham, Howard. 1950. *The War for Independence: A Military History.* Chicago: University of Chicago Press.

Ramsay, David. 1789. *The History of the American Revolution.* Philadelphia: R. Aitken.

Raphael, Ray. 2004. *Founding Myths: Stories That Hide Our Patriotic Past.* New York: New Press.

Raynal, Guillaume-Thomas. 1781. *American Revolution.* London: Lockyer Davis.

Soulès, François. 1787. *History of the English-American Troubles.* 4 vols. Paris: Buisson.

Stedman, Charles. 1794. *History of the Origin, Progress, and Termination of the American War.* London: J. Murray.

Stinchcombe, William C. 1969. *The American Revolution and the French Alliance.* Syracuse, NY: Syracuse University Press.

Stone, Edwin. 1884. *Our French Allies: 1778–1881.* Providence, RI: Providence Press Co.

Tuchman, Barbara. 1988. *The First Salute: A View of the American Revolution.* New York: Knopf.

Warren, Mercy Otis. 1805. *History of the Rise, Progress, and Termination of the American Revolution.* 3 vols. Boston: E. Larkin.

Webster, Noah. 1832. *History of the United States.* New Haven, CT: Durrie & Peck.

Williams, Samuel. 1824. *A History of the American Revolution.* New Haven, CT: W. Storer.

Wilson, Samuel Farmer. 1834. *A History of the American Revolution.* Baltimore: Cushing & Sons.

Wood, Gordon. 1991. *The Radicalism of the American Revolution.* New York: Knopf.

Wood, Gordon. 2002. *The American Revolution: A History.* New York: Modern Library.

Contributors

David K. Allison is Senior Scholar and former Associate Director for Curatorial Affairs, Smithsonian National Museum of American History. He has served on the Smithsonian curatorial staff since 1986. His major exhibitions include *American Enterprise* (2015); *The Price of Freedom: Americans at War* (2004); *September 11, 2001: Bearing Witness to History* (2002); and *Information Age: People, Information, and Technology* (1990). He is the coauthor of *American Enterprise: A History of Business in America* (2015), a contributor to *Smithsonian Civil War: Inside the National Collection*, coauthor of *The Price of Freedom: Americans at War* (2004), and author of *New Eye for the Navy: The Origin of Radar at the Naval Research Laboratory* (1981).

Larrie D. Ferreiro was a finalist for the 2017 Pulitzer Prize in History for his book *Brothers at Arms: American Independence and the Men of France and Spain Who Saved It* (2016). He received his PhD in the history of science and technology from Imperial College London. He teaches history and engineering at George Mason University in Virginia; at Georgetown University in Washington, D.C.; and at the Stevens Institute of Technology in New Jersey. He has served for almost forty years in the U.S. Navy and U.S. Coast Guard and at the Department of Defense and was an exchange engineer in the French navy. He lives with his wife and their sons in Virginia.

José María Blanco Núñez, captain (ret.) in the Spanish navy and a member of both the Real Academia de la Historia (Spain) and the Academia de Marinha (Portugal), studies the Spanish navy in early modern history. His main books are *The Strategic Diversion of Toulon* (1983; with Indalecio Núñez Iglesias), *The Spanish Navy in the First Half of the 18th Century* (2001), *The Spanish Navy in the Second Half of the 18th Century* (2004), and *The Ships in the Naval Engineering School* (2009). He is coeditor of *XXXI International Congress of Military History* (2006) and *Naval War in the Age of Revolution and Empire: Blockades and Amphibious Operations, 1793–1815* (2008).

Olivier Chaline is professor of early modern history at Sorbonne Université, where he leads the Federation of Naval History & Archeology (FED 4124). He is the head of the History Commission of the French Society of Cincinnati and works with the French Naval Academy on the study of Admiral de Grasse's fleet. He published, with Philippe Bonnichon and Charles-Philippe de Vergennes, *La France et l'indépendance américaine* (2008); and *Les marines de la guerre d'indépendance américaine (1763–1783)*, vol. 1, *L'instrument naval* (2013), and vol. 2, *L'opérationnel naval* (2018).

Kathleen DuVal is Bowman and Gordon Gray Professor in the History Department at the University of North Carolina, Chapel Hill. She earned her PhD in history at the University of California, Davis, and held a postdoctoral fellowship at the University of Pennsylvania before joining the faculty at UNC. She is the author of *Independence Lost: Lives on the Edge of the American Revolution* (2015) and *The Native Ground: Indians and Colonists in the Heart of the Continent* (2006), and she was coeditor of *Interpreting a Continent: Voices from Colonial America* (2009). She regularly reviews books for the *Wall Street Journal*.

John D. Garrigus is professor of history at the University of Texas at Arlington. He is the author of *Before Haiti: Race and Citizenship in Saint-Domingue* (2006), which won the Gilbert Chinard Prize of the Society for French Historical Studies. He coedited, with Laurent Dubois, a collection of primary sources on the Haitian Revolution titled *Slave Revolution in the Caribbean* (2006), now in its second edition (2017). He also coedited, with Christopher Morris, *Assumed Identities: The Meanings of Race in the Atlantic World* (2010). With Trevor Burnard, he wrote *The Plantation Machine: Atlantic Capitalism in French Saint-Domingue and British Jamaica* (2016).

José M. Guerrero Acosta is a colonel (reserve) in the Spanish army. He holds a degree in advanced studies in history from the Universidad Nacional de Educación a Distancia (UNED) and a specialist diploma in the direction and management of military museums. For seventeen years, he has been a member of the Instituto de Historia y Cultura Militar.

Agustín Guimerá Ravina is a maritime historian and research fellow of the Institute of History, Spanish National Research Council (CSIC), and member of the Real Academia de la Historia (Spain). He has written several studies of naval history in the eighteenth century, focusing mainly on strategy, leadership, finance, administration, battles, and amphibious operations. He is coeditor of *Trafalgar and the Atlantic World* (2004); *The Equilibrium of Empires: From Utrecht to Trafalgar* (2005); *Naval War in the Age of Revolution and Empire: Blockades and Amphibious Operations, 1793–1815* (2008); and *Naval Leadership in the Atlantic World: The Age of Revolution and Reform, 1700–1850* (2017).

David J. Hancock is professor of history at the University of Michigan and director of its Atlantic Studies Initiative. He teaches and researches on early America, the Atlantic world, and Britain as well as business. A specialist on the long eighteenth century, he is the author of *Citizens of the World: London Merchants and the Integration of the British Atlantic Community, 1735–1785* (1995) and *Oceans of Wine: Madeira and the Emergence of American Trade and Taste* (2009). He is completing a biography of William Fitzmaurice, second Earl of Shelburne. He received his AB in history from the College of William and Mary, an AM in musicology from Yale University in 1983, and an AM and PhD in history from Harvard University in 1990.

Marion Huibrechts is research fellow and coordinator of the University of Leuven American Studies Center in Antwerp, Belgium. After earning a master's degree in history in 1983, she started a career as a government employee, combining her full-time job with academic research. In 2009, she earned a doctoral degree at the University of Leuven; her dissertation was "Swampin' Guns and Stabbing Irons: The Austrian Netherlands, Liège Arms, and the American Revolution (1770–1783)," which she plans to publish. Huibrechts has participated in international conferences in Belgium, the Netherlands, Lisbon, Milan, and London.

Jean-Marie Kowalski is associate professor of ancient history at Sorbonne Université and head of humanities at the French Naval Academy. He has conducted research on ancient navigation techniques and modern naval operations, and he has been involved for several years in a major research program about the American War of Independence led by Olivier Chaline. This program is based on a thorough examination of both British and French sources. He has authored several papers and delivered several lectures about these naval operations.

Andrew Lambert is Laughton Professor of Naval History at King's College London. His work focuses on the development of British strategy, the evolution of naval historical writing, and the integration of technology. His books include *The Crimean War: British Grand Strategy against Russia, 1853–1856* (2011); *The Foundations of Naval History: Sir John Laughton, the Royal Navy and the Historical Profession* (1998); *Nelson: Britannia's God of War* (2005); *The Gates of Hell: Sir John Franklin's Tragic Quest for the Northwest Passage* (2009); *The Challenge:*

Britain against America in the Naval War of 1812 (2013); and *Crusoe's Island: A Rich and Curious History of Pirates, Castaways and Madness* (2016).

Alan Lemmers directed the cataloguing project of the Dutch Navy Model Collection (1700–1885) at the Rijksmuseum, Amsterdam, from 1985 to 1995. This project resulted in both the first digital catalogue of a museum collection in the Netherlands (CD-ROM 1995) and his PhD dissertation (1996). In 1997, he joined the Royal Netherlands Navy as a naval historian and became a researcher at the Netherlands Institute of Military History in the Hague. He has published and curated exhibitions on a wide variety of naval topics, including shipbuilding, scale models, the Dutch submarine service, the Dutch marine corps, hydrography, piracy, naval bases, and Dutch-Japanese relations.

Richard Sambasivam is a public policy professional who has conducted independent research on India (where his parents were born) and the American Revolution. He has served as an adviser to the U.S. executive director at the European Bank for Reconstruction and Development and as a research assistant at the Board of Governors of the Federal Reserve. He has a master's degree in public affairs from Princeton University's Woodrow Wilson School of Public and International Affairs.

Robert A. Selig holds a PhD in German history from the Universität Würzburg, Germany. A specialist in the role of French forces under the comte de Rochambeau in the American War of Independence, he serves as project historian to the U.S. National Park Service for the nine-state Washington-Rochambeau National Historic Trail. His site surveys and resource inventories are available at https://w3r-us.org/. He has worked as a historian for American Battlefield Protection Program projects, including the battles of Princeton, Bennington, Hubbardton, and Brandywine, and he has published in American and German scholarly and popular history magazines such as *William and Mary Quarterly*, *American Heritage*, *Colonial Williamsburg*, *Damals*, and the *Journal of the Johannes Schwalm Historical Association*.

Alan Taylor, holder of the Thomas Jefferson Foundation Chair at the University of Virginia, received his doctorate from Brandeis University in 1986. His publications include *William Cooper's Town: Power and Persuasion on the Early American Frontier* (1995) and *The Internal Enemy: Slavery and War in Virginia, 1772–1832* (2013), both of which won the Pulitzer Prize for American History. Most recently, he published *American Revolutions: A Continental History, 1750–1804* (2016).

Patrick Villiers is professor emeritus of modern, military, and naval history at the Université du Littoral–Côte d'Opale, France. He is the author of several volumes on these subjects, including *Le commerce colonial Atlantique français pendant la guerre d'indépendance américaine* (1976); *Traite des noirs et navires négriers au XVIIIe siècle* (1982); *La marine de Louis XVI* (1985); *Marine royale, corsaires et trafic dans l'Atlantique de Louis XIV à Louis XVI* (1992); *The Hermione, Lafayette, and Latouche-Tréville: Two Men and a Frigate Serving American Independence* (2015); and *La France sur mer 1610–1815* (2015). He is laureate of the Marine Academy of France, vice president of the French Society of Maritime History, and an honorary member of the Sons of the American Revolution (France).

Acknowledgments

This book began as a supplement to an exhibition of the same name on view at the Smithsonian National Museum of American History from June 2018 through July 2019. To develop it, Dr. David K. Allison, project director and chief curator of the exhibition, enlisted the support of Dr. Larrie D. Ferreiro, an award-winning historian of the American Revolution, as coeditor. Together we planned a book that was broader than the scope of the exhibition. We reasoned that readers interested in exploring the international dimensions of the Revolution would benefit greatly from the scholarship and perspective of authors who came from other nations that had been involved in the war, as well as Americans who were highly knowledgeable about that broader story. Museum director John L. Gray supported our pursuit of this ambitious objective. The staff at Smithsonian Books agreed to work closely with us to implement it on an aggressive schedule. We particularly thank Carolyn Gleason, Laura Harger, and Erika Bǔky for their tireless efforts on our behalf.

The book that resulted depended greatly on the cooperation and goodwill of all the authors whose writing it presents. The group never met face to face, but everyone adhered faithfully to tight deadlines for producing their essays and identifying the images that appear on the preceding pages. Their essays complement one another to an even greater degree than we had hoped. We give them all our heartfelt thanks.

We were ably assisted by numerous staff at the National Museum of American History. We owe an enormous debt of gratitude to Lauren Safranek, our lead photography researcher, who identified and procured the historic images that came from numerous repositories in both the United States and Europe. Others worked on the research, planning, and design of the companion exhibition: Tanya Garner, Stevan Fisher, Howard Morrison, Katharine Klein, Geoff Moore, and Margaret Grandine. Finally, we thank Smithsonian photographers Jaclyn Nash, Hugh Talman, and Richard Strauss for their excellent original photographs in the book.

Neither the exhibition nor the book would have been possible without the generous financial support of board members and friends of the National Museum of American History: Ambassador Nicholas F. Taubman and Mrs. Eugenia L. Taubman, Jeff and Mary Lynn Garrett, Susan and Elihu Rose, Laneta Dorflinger and Mark Graham, Brian and Barbara Hendelson, and Bill and Mary Kim. We deeply appreciate their confidence that this book would illuminate important dimensions of the creation of the United States that are little understood by most Americans today.

Index

Page ii: Louis-Nicolas van Blarenberghe, *Siege of Yorktown* (detail), 1786. Gouache on board. (Courtesy Nicholas Taubman)

Page iv: Phillips Melville, *Continental Brig Andrew Doria Receiving a Salute from the Dutch Fort at Sint Eustatius, West Indies, 16 November 1776* (detail), 1977. This was the first official salute made to a U.S.-flagged warship in a foreign port (Sint Eustatius, in the Caribbean, was then a colony of the Dutch Republic) and thus the first international acknowledgment of U.S. independence. (U.S. Naval History & Heritage Command, NH92866-KN)

This book may be purchased for educational, business, or sales promotional use. For information, please write: Special Markets Department, Smithsonian Books, P.O. Box 37012, MRC 513, Washington, DC 20013

Published by Smithsonian Books
Director: Carolyn Gleason
Creative Director: Jody Billert
Managing Editor: Christina Wiginton
Editor: Laura Harger
Editorial Assistant: Jaime Schwender
Edited by Erika Büky
Designed by Wilcox Design
Typeset by Amy Storm

Library of Congress Cataloging-in-Publication Data
Names: Allison, David K., 1950– editor of compilation. | Ferreiro, Larrie D., editor of compilation.
Title: The American Revolution : a world war / edited by David K. Allison and Larrie D. Ferreiro.
Other titles: American Revolution, a world war
Description: Washington, DC : Smithsonian Books, [2018] | Includes bibliographical references and index.
Identifiers: LCCN 2018009738 | ISBN 9781588346339 (hardcover)
Subjects: LCSH: United States—History—Revolution, 1775–1783—Participation, Foreign. | United States—History—Revolution, 1775–1783—Influence. | United States—Foreign relations—1775–1783. | United States—Foreign relations—Europe. | Europe—Foreign relations—United States.
Classification: LCC E269.F67 A48 2018 | DDC 973.3—dc23
LC record available at https://lccn.loc.gov/2018009738

Manufactured in China, not at government expense
22 21 20 19 18   5 4 3 2 1

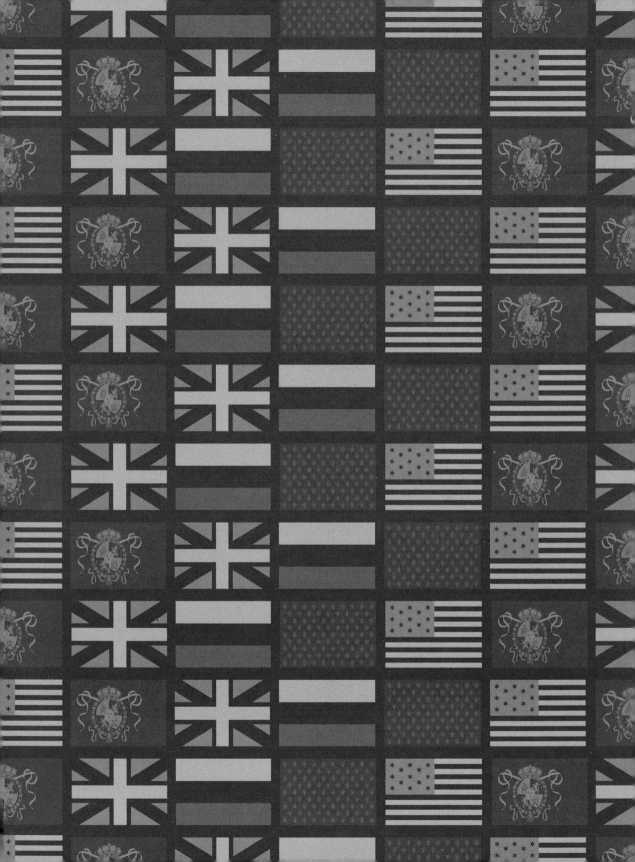